## Nominated for 3 EISNER AWARDS including
## Best New Series and Best Ongoing Series

"THE UNWRITTEN makes a leap from being just a promising new Vertigo title to being on-track to become the best ongoing Vertigo book since SANDMAN. And given that Vertigo has delivered the likes of 100 BULLETS, Y: THE LAST MAN, and FABLES since SANDMAN ended, that's saying something... A-"

**—THE A.V. CLUB**

"Casually literate and intelligent, engrossing from the first page, THE UNWRITTEN is a gem of a conspiracy story with enough metafictional layers to launch a thesis or two."

**— SCRIPPS HOWARD NEWS SERVICE**

"Fascinating. . . . With casual yet deeply informed writing from Mike Carey and accessible art from Peter Gross, THE UNWRITTEN sucks you in as a witty satire of heroic boy wizards . . . then blows your mind in the strange netherworld between truth and fiction."

**—WIRED/Underwire**

"One of the more intriguing comics on the horizon is THE UNWRITTEN, a fantasy series that starts off as a dark, smirking riff on the Harry Potter publishing phenomenon, that blends some of the bitterness of Christopher Robin Milne's life (the real-life model for the "Winnie the Pooh" character chafed under the weight of the literary legacy) and finally soars off into its own unexpected directions. . . . There's a lot of promise in its pages."

**— LA TIMES/HERO COMPLEX**

"A wish-I'd-thought-of-it premise, beautifully executed. Highly recommended for anyone who thinks that fantasy can do more than just help you escape the real world."

**— Brian K. Vaughan**
**(Eisner-winning writer of Y: The Last Man)**

"A tremendous story about stories, need, and the emptiness of the world. This could be Mike Carey's masterpiece."

**— Paul Cornell**
**(Hugo-nominated writer for BBC's Doctor Who)**

"About ten times as smart as anything else in comics right now, THE UNWRITTEN has deft story-telling grace, abruptly eerie imagining and quiet razor sharp wit. Outstanding!"

**— Richard Morgan**
**(Philip K. Dick Award-winning sci-fi novelist)**

"By the first page of the first issue of THE UNWRITTEN I was intrigued. By page 3 I knew I'd be finishing the issue. Two pages later and I knew I'd be a fan and loyal reader of this new series for its entire run. It's obvious that the adult adventures of (possible) child star Tommy Taylor were written specifically for my enjoyment, but I suppose they won't mind if you read along as well. No bull. This is a wonderful story. I want more."

**— Bill Willingham**
**(Eisner-winning writer of FABLES)**

"An analysis of the power of fiction that diagrams the life of a writer's son who's solely identified as a story book character. Expect post-modern twists galore."

**— PASTE Magazine**

"Carey and Gross perfectly capture the zeitgeist of our Harry Potter-obsessed-chaotic-apocalyptic-times with a depth and whimsy that makes me jealous, and I can't wait to read more of THE UNWRITTEN."

**— Ed Brubaker**
**(Eisner-winning writer of Captain America)**

the
## unwritten
### LEVIATHAN

FLATHEAD COUNTY LIBRARY
KALISPELL, MONTANA

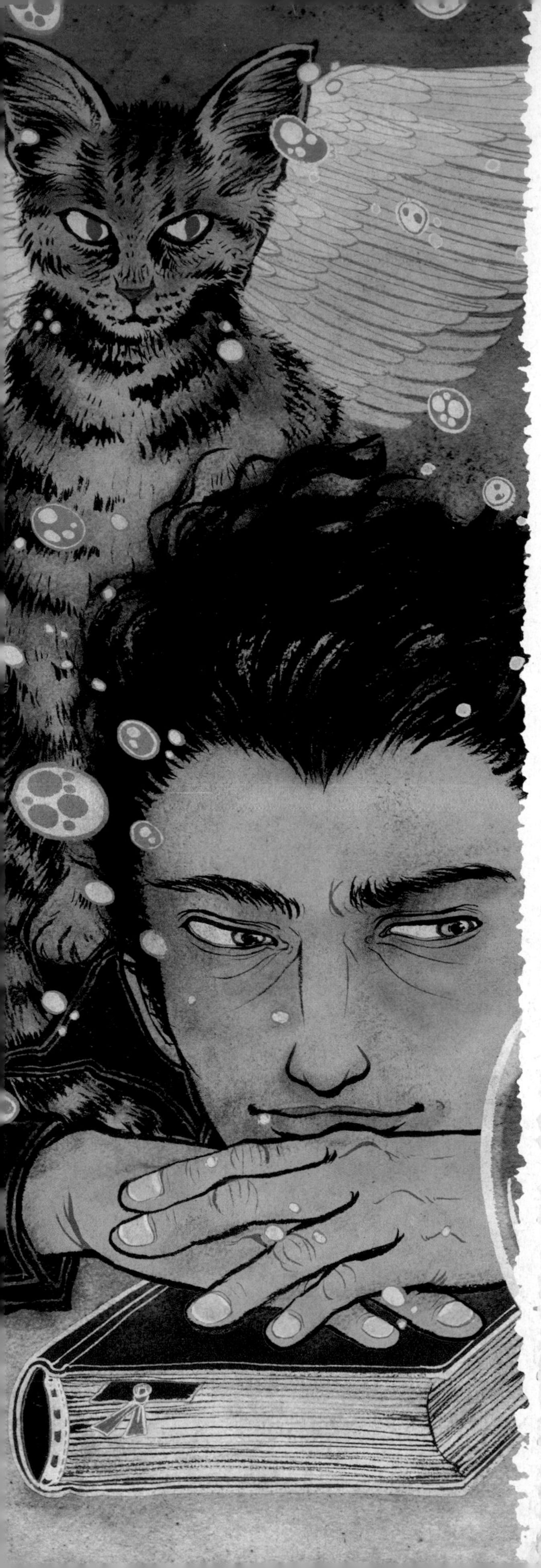

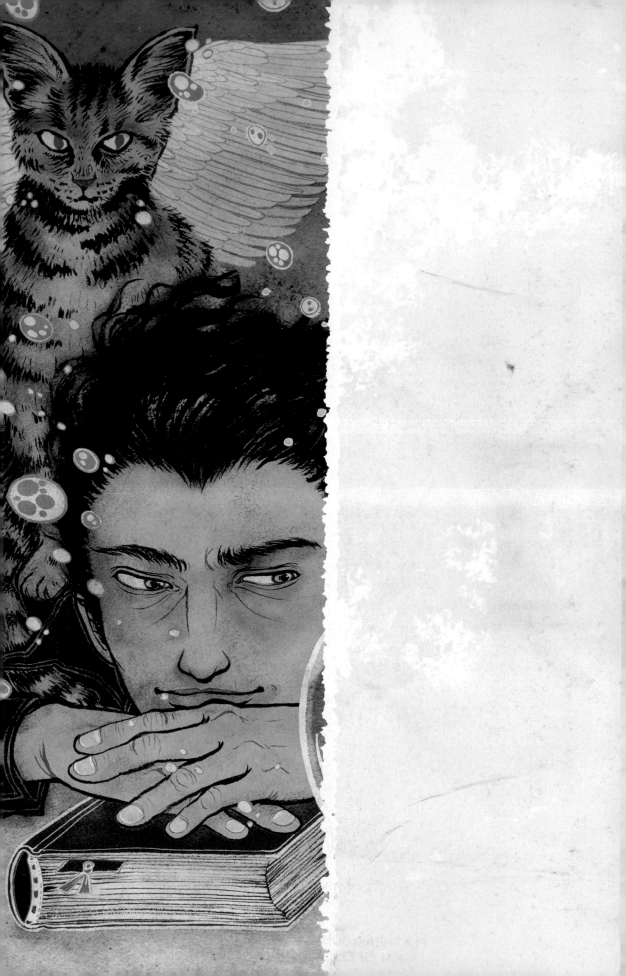

# the Unwritten

## LEVIATHAN

**Mike Carey & Peter Gross** Script – Story – Art
**Vince Locke** Finishes – Moby Dick sequences, The Stairway, Dumuzi and Enkimdu
**Al Davison** Finishes – Stairway to Heaven
**Chris Chuckry** Colorist
**Todd Klein** Letterer **Yuko Shimizu** Cover Artist
**THE UNWRITTEN** created by **Gross and Carey**

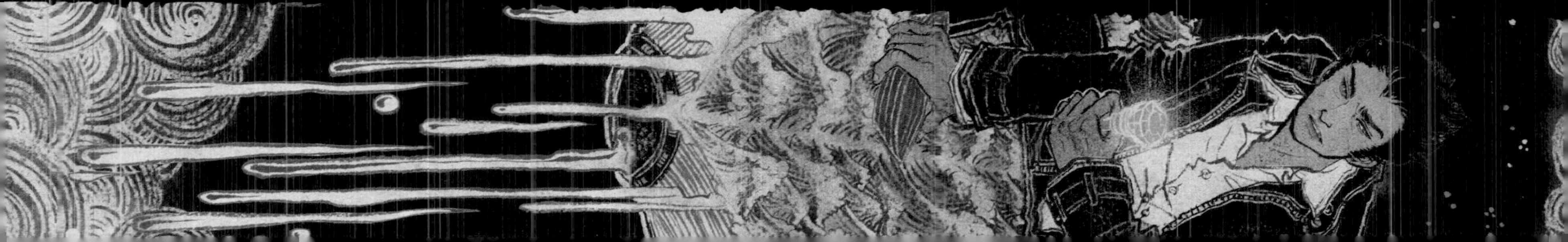

Pornsak Pichetshote Editor – Original Series
Joe Hughes Assistant Editor – Original Series
Ian Sattler Director Editorial, Special Projects and Archival Editions
Robbin Brosterman Design Director – Books
Louis Prandi Publication Design

Karen Berger Senior VP – Executive Editor, Vertigo
Bob Harras VP – Editor in Chief

Diane Nelson President
Dan DiDio and Jim Lee Co-Publishers
Geoff Johns Chief Creative Officer
John Rood Executive VP – Sales, Marketing and Business Development
Amy Genkins Senior VP – Business and Legal Affairs
Nairi Gardiner Senior VP – Finance
Jeff Boison VP – Publishing Operations
Mark Chiarello VP – Art Direction and Design
John Cunningham VP – Marketing
Terri Cunningham VP – Talent Relations and Services
Alison Gill Senior VP – Manufacturing and Operations
David Hyde VP – Publicity
Hank Kanalz Senior VP – Digital
Jay Kogan VP – Business and Legal Affairs, Publishing
Jack Mahan VP – Business Affairs, Talent
Nick Napolitano VP – Manufacturing Administration
Sue Pohja VP – Book Sales
Courtney Simmons Senior VP – Publicity
Bob Wayne Senior VP – Sales

THE UNWRITTEN: LEVIATHAN

Published by DC Comics. Cover and compilation
Copyright © 2011 Mike Carey and Peter Gross. All Rights
Reserved. Originally published in single magazine form as
THE UNWRITTEN 19-24 Copyright © 2011 Mike Carey and
Peter Gross. All Rights Reserved. The characters, their distinctive
likenesses and related elements featured in this publication are
trademarks of DC Comics. The stories, characters and incidents
mentioned in this publication are entirely fictional. DC Comics
does not read or accept unsolicited submissions of stories, ideas
or artwork. DC Comics, 1700 Broadway, New York, NY 10019.
A Warner Bros. Entertainment Company. Printed in the USA.
9/16/11. First Printing. ISBN: 978-1-4012-3292-4

SUSTAINABLE
FORESTRY
INITIATIVE
Certified Chain of Custody
Promoting Sustainable
Forest Management
www.sfiprogram.org
Fiber used in this product line meets the
sourcing requirements of the SFI program.
www.sfiprogram.org SGS-SFI/COC-US10/81072

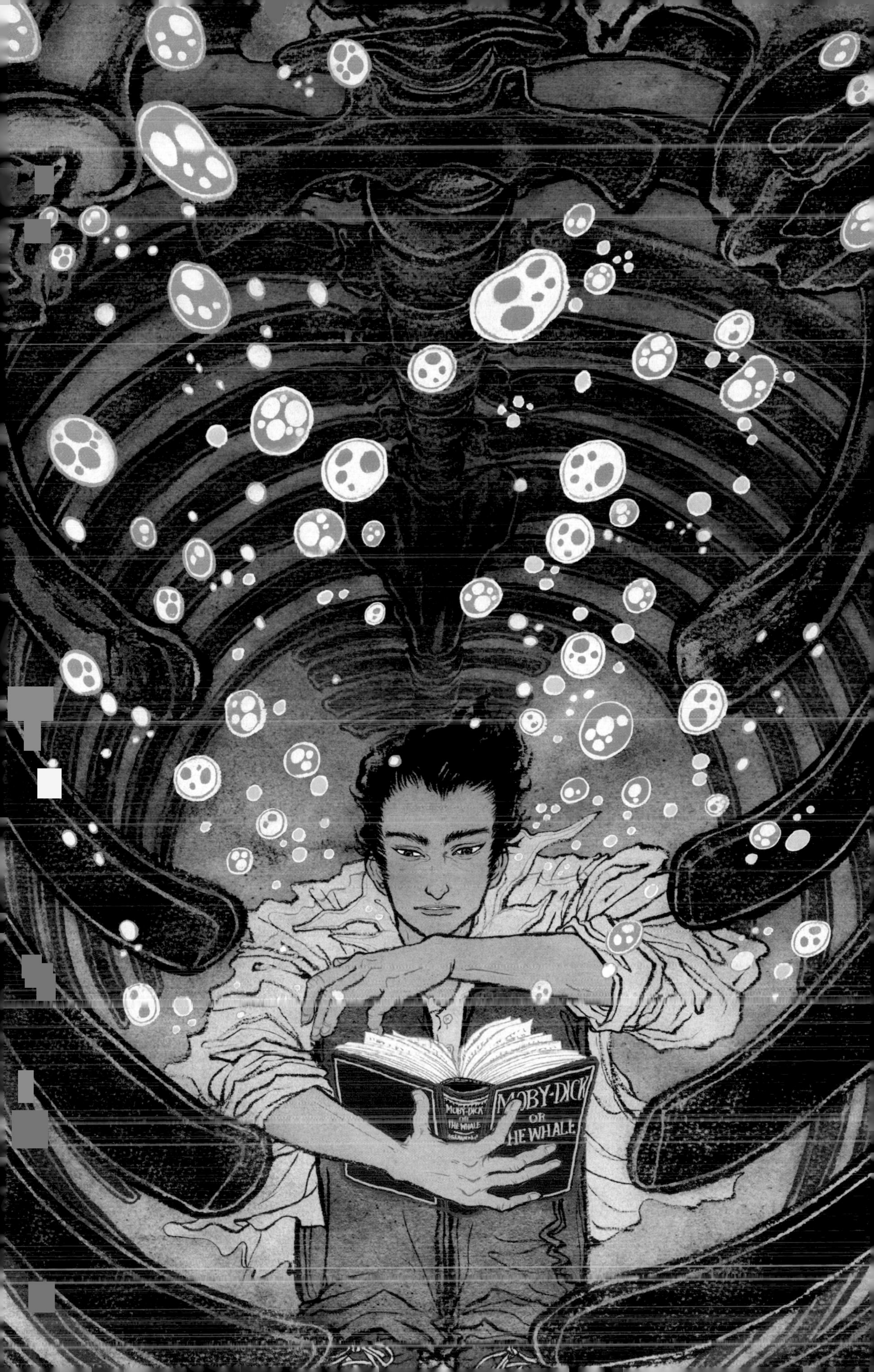
MOBY-DICK
OR
THE WHALE
MOBY-DICK
OR
THE WHALE

# The Stairway

TWENTY YEARS AGO.

IT ALL JUST... CAME *RIGHT* FOR YOU, SOMEHOW, DIDN'T IT?

Publishers Quarterly
Wilson Taylor

VERITY
Tommy Taylor Film R...

HOLLY SCOOP
Who will Direct Tomm...

THE REST OF US SWEAT *BLOOD* JUST TO GET BY, AND YOU BECOME THE KING OF THE *WORLD*.

SO YOU THOUGHT YOU'D CHANGE YOUR MIND.

WHY NOT?

AND GET A PIECE OF THE *ACTION*.

IT'S NOT ABOUT THE *MONEY*, WILSON. I WANT TO BE PART OF TOM'S LIFE.

SINCE I LET YOU *STRONG-ARM* ME INTO--

SHIT. I *HATE* HOW YOU DO THIS TO ME.

MAKE ME WHINE AND COMPLAIN, AS THOUGH I'M *WEAKER* THAN YOU.

SINCE I WALKED *AWAY* FROM TOM, NOTHING IN MY LIFE HAS FELT RIGHT.

IT WAS A *MISTAKE*. AND I HAVE TO PUT IT RIGHT.

IT'S NOT THAT EASY, *SUE*. YOU SIGNED A *CONTRACT*.

UP TO MY EYEBALLS IN POST-NATAL *DEPRESSION*. IT WON'T STAND UP.

OH, BELIEVE ME, MY *LAWYERS* WILL MAKE IT STAND UP, ROLL OVER AND BEG FOR BISCUITS.

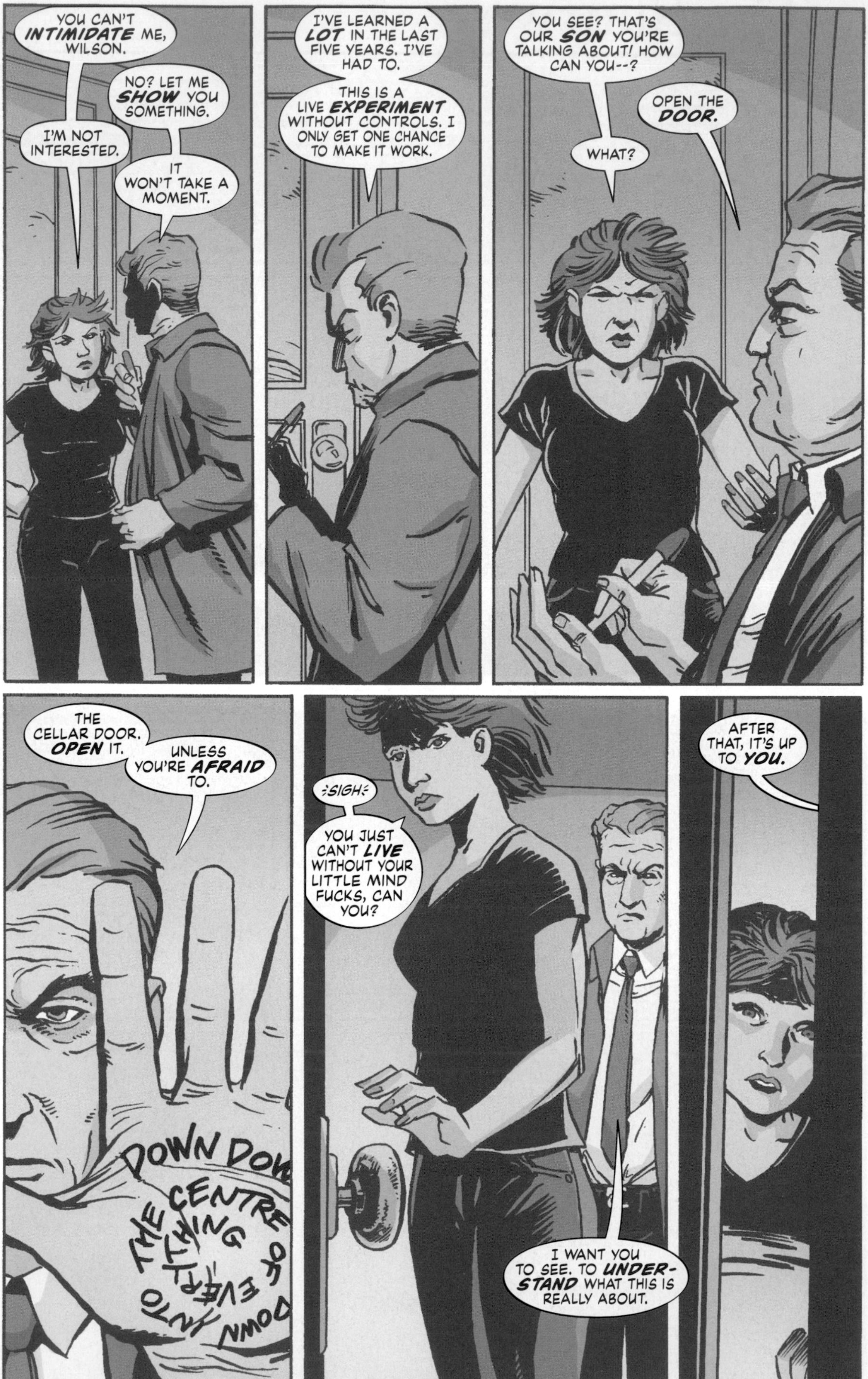

YOU CAN'T ***INTIMIDATE*** ME, WILSON.
NO? LET ME ***SHOW*** YOU SOMETHING.
I'M NOT INTERESTED.
IT WON'T TAKE A MOMENT.
I'VE LEARNED A ***LOT*** IN THE LAST FIVE YEARS. I'VE HAD TO.
THIS IS A LIVE ***EXPERIMENT*** WITHOUT CONTROLS. I ONLY GET ONE CHANCE TO MAKE IT WORK.
YOU SEE? THAT'S OUR ***SON*** YOU'RE TALKING ABOUT! HOW CAN YOU--?
OPEN THE ***DOOR.***
WHAT?
THE CELLAR DOOR. ***OPEN*** IT.
UNLESS YOU'RE ***AFRAID*** TO.
DOWN DOW
THE CENTRE OF EVERYTHING
DOWN INTO
*SIGH*
YOU JUST CAN'T ***LIVE*** WITHOUT YOUR LITTLE MIND FUCKS, CAN YOU?
I WANT YOU TO SEE. TO ***UNDER-STAND*** WHAT THIS IS REALLY ABOUT.
AFTER THAT, IT'S UP TO ***YOU.***

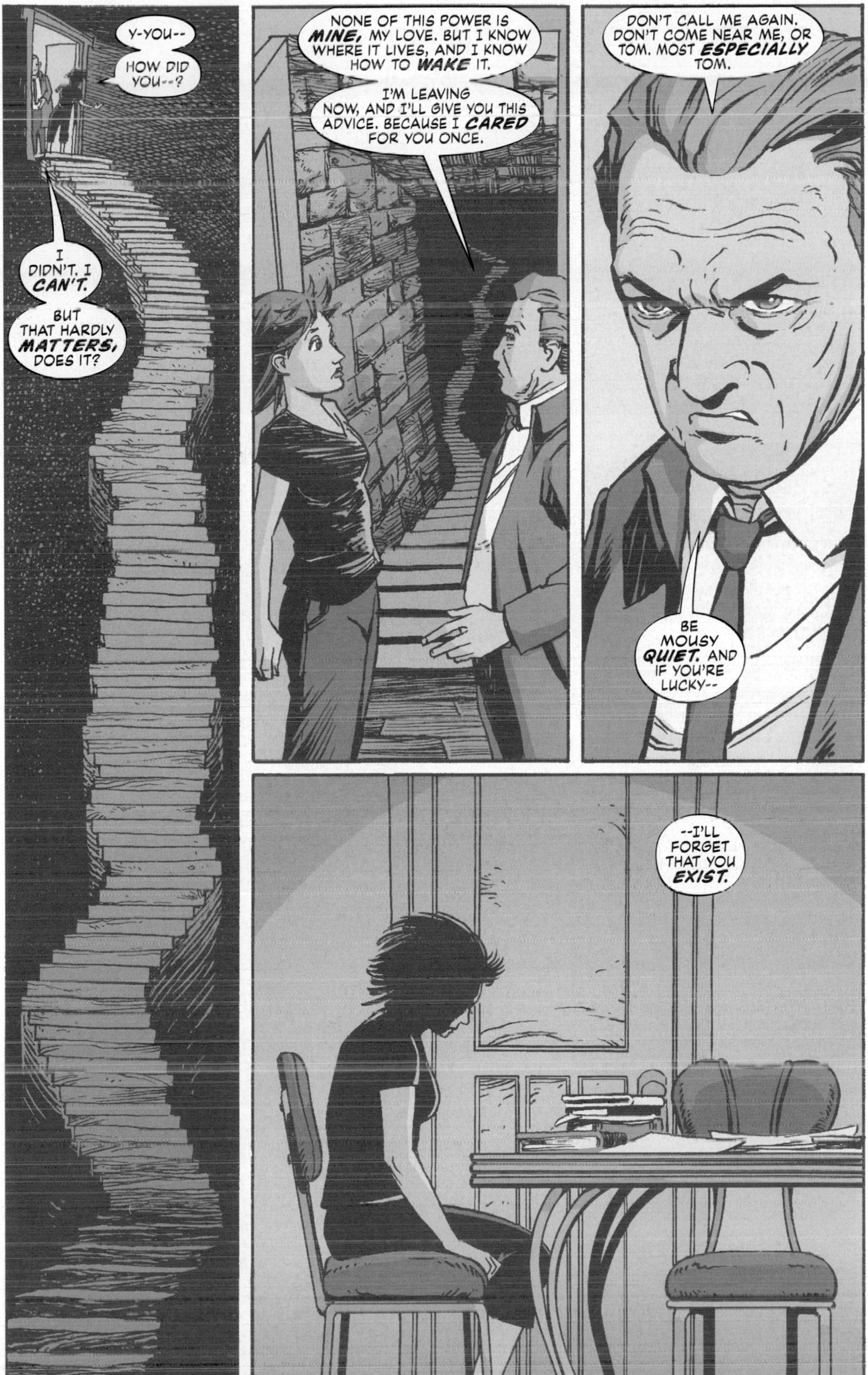
Y-YOU--
HOW DID YOU--?
I DIDN'T. I CAN'T.
BUT THAT HARDLY MATTERS, DOES IT?
NONE OF THIS POWER IS MINE, MY LOVE. BUT I KNOW WHERE IT LIVES, AND I KNOW HOW TO WAKE IT.
I'M LEAVING NOW, AND I'LL GIVE YOU THIS ADVICE. BECAUSE I CARED FOR YOU ONCE.
DON'T CALL ME AGAIN. DON'T COME NEAR ME, OR TOM. MOST ESPECIALLY TOM.
BE MOUSY QUIET. AND IF YOU'RE LUCKY--
--I'LL FORGET THAT YOU EXIST.

# An Unwritten Life

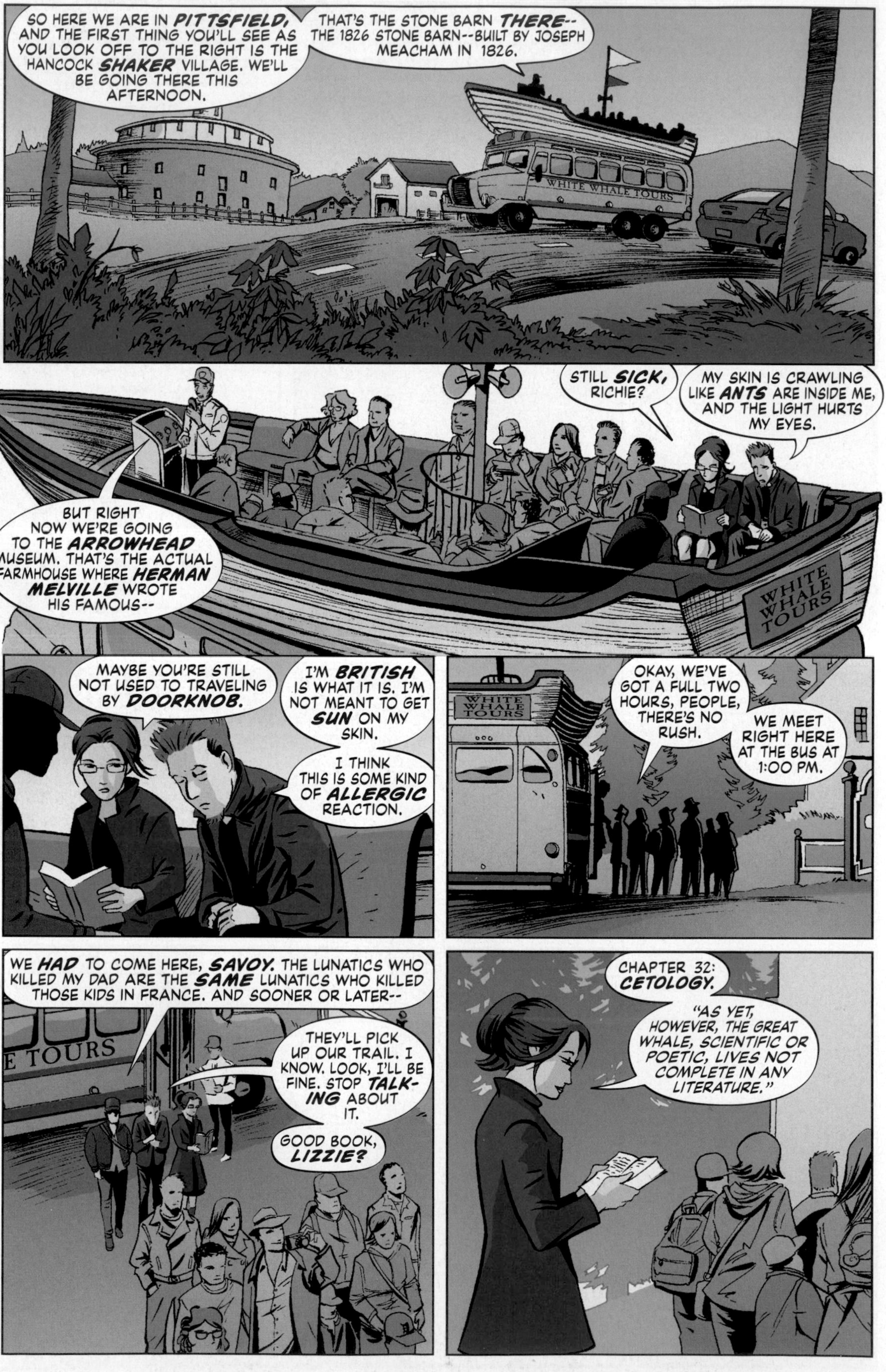
SO HERE WE ARE IN PITTSFIELD, AND THE FIRST THING YOU'LL SEE AS YOU LOOK OFF TO THE RIGHT IS THE HANCOCK SHAKER VILLAGE. WE'LL BE GOING THERE THIS AFTERNOON.
THAT'S THE STONE BARN THERE-- THE 1826 STONE BARN--BUILT BY JOSEPH MEACHAM IN 1826.
WHITE WHALE TOURS
BUT RIGHT NOW WE'RE GOING TO THE ARROWHEAD MUSEUM. THAT'S THE ACTUAL FARMHOUSE WHERE HERMAN MELVILLE WROTE HIS FAMOUS--
STILL SICK, RICHIE?
MY SKIN IS CRAWLING LIKE ANTS ARE INSIDE ME, AND THE LIGHT HURTS MY EYES.
WHITE WHALE TOURS
MAYBE YOU'RE STILL NOT USED TO TRAVELING BY DOORKNOB.
I'M BRITISH IS WHAT IT IS. I'M NOT MEANT TO GET SUN ON MY SKIN.
I THINK THIS IS SOME KIND OF ALLERGIC REACTION.
WHITE WHALE TOURS
OKAY, WE'VE GOT A FULL TWO HOURS, PEOPLE, THERE'S NO RUSH.
WE MEET RIGHT HERE AT THE BUS AT 1:00 PM.
WE HAD TO COME HERE, SAVOY. THE LUNATICS WHO KILLED MY DAD ARE THE SAME LUNATICS WHO KILLED THOSE KIDS IN FRANCE. AND SOONER OR LATER--
THEY'LL PICK UP OUR TRAIL. I KNOW. LOOK, I'LL BE FINE. STOP TALKING ABOUT IT.
GOOD BOOK, LIZZIE?
E TOURS
CHAPTER 32: CETOLOGY.
"AS YET, HOWEVER, THE GREAT WHALE, SCIENTIFIC OR POETIC, LIVES NOT COMPLETE IN ANY LITERATURE."

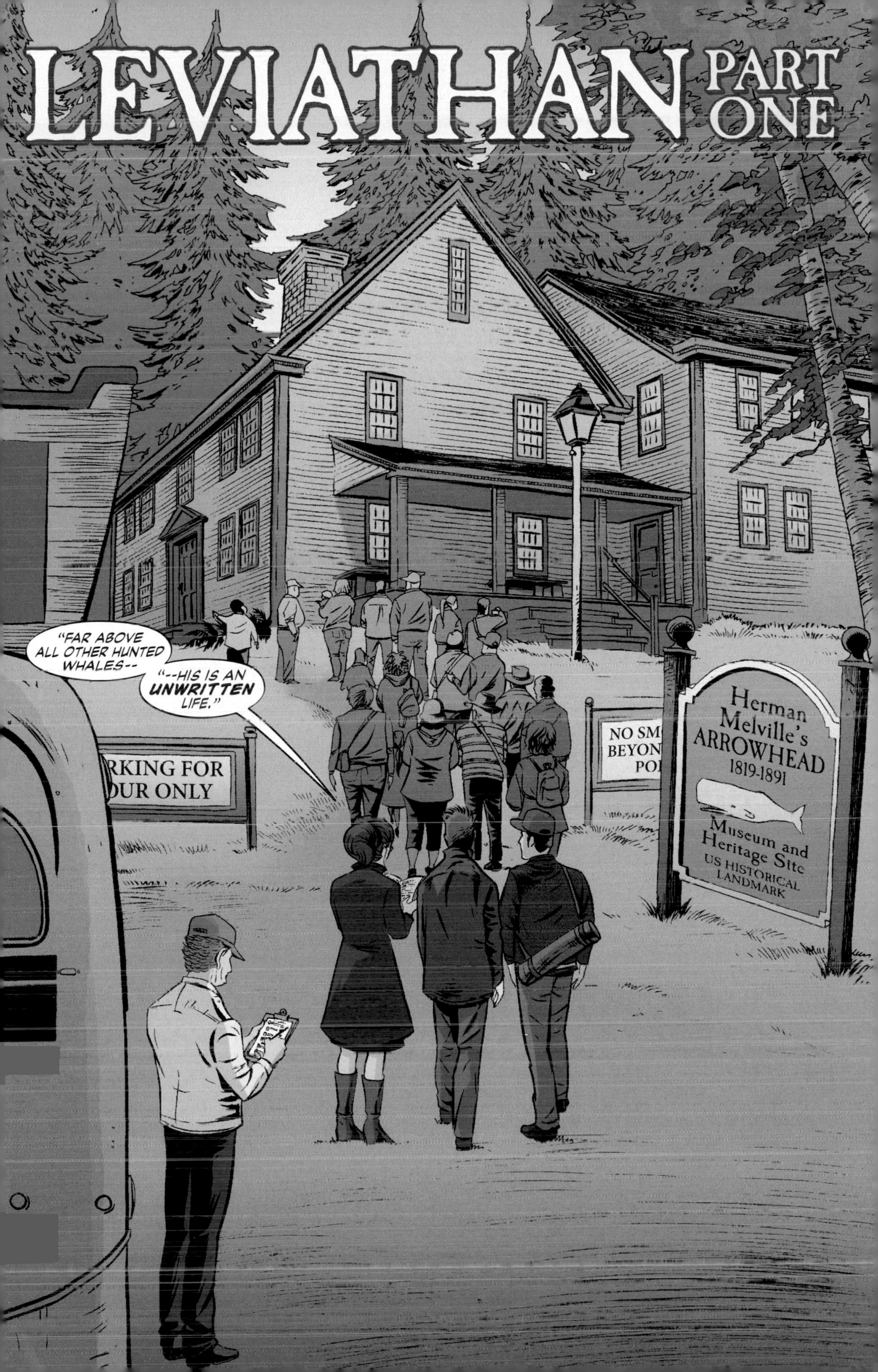
LEVIATHAN PART ONE
"FAR ABOVE ALL OTHER HUNTED WHALES--
"--HIS IS AN UNWRITTEN LIFE."
RKING FOR
OUR ONLY
NO SM
BEYON
PO
Herman Melville's ARROWHEAD 1819-1891
Museum and Heritage Site
US HISTORICAL LANDMARK

# The Toymaker

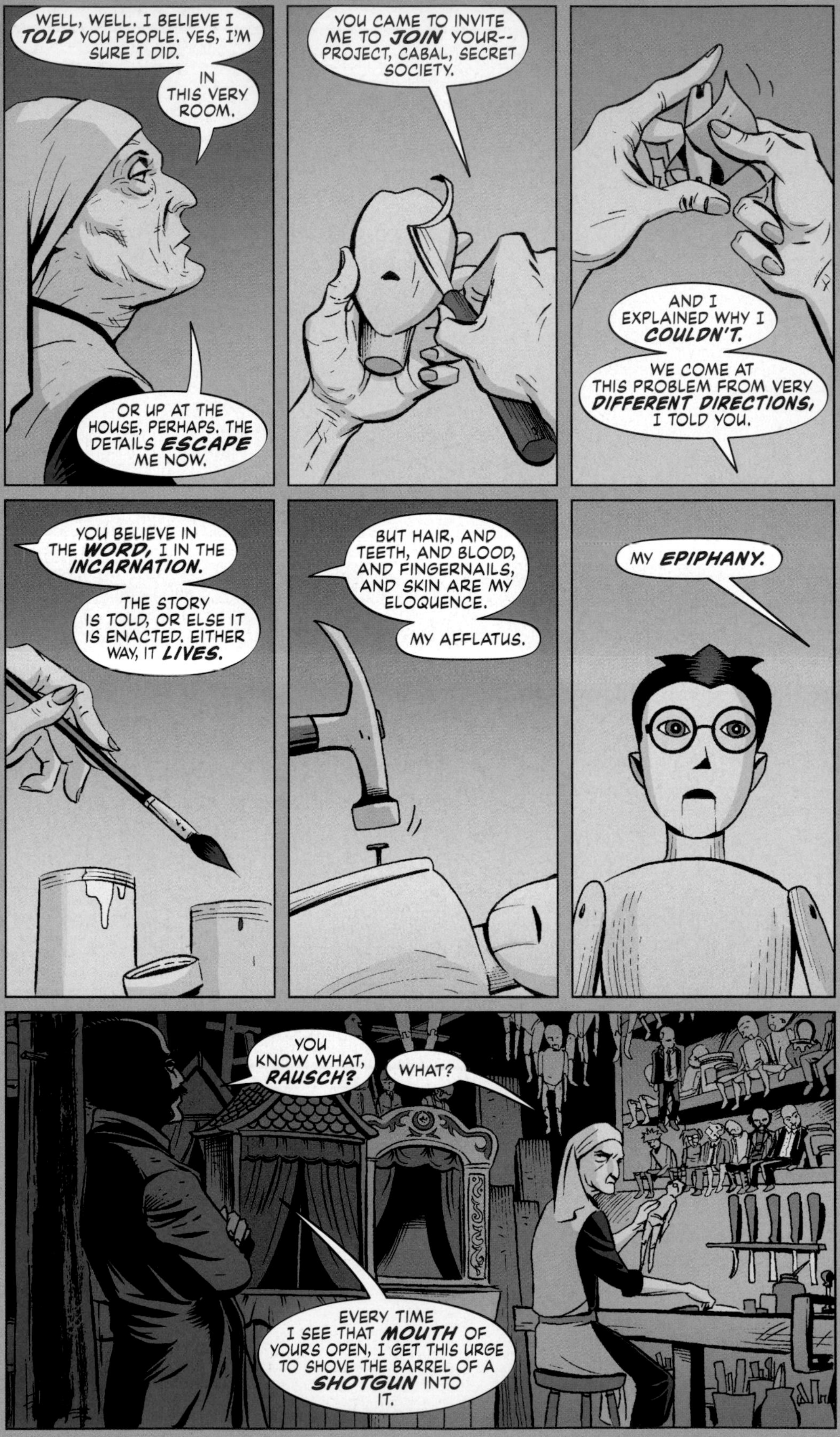

WELL, WELL. I BELIEVE I TOLD YOU PEOPLE. YES, I'M SURE I DID.
IN THIS VERY ROOM.
OR UP AT THE HOUSE, PERHAPS. THE DETAILS ESCAPE ME NOW.
YOU CAME TO INVITE ME TO JOIN YOUR-- PROJECT, CABAL, SECRET SOCIETY.
AND I EXPLAINED WHY I COULDN'T.
WE COME AT THIS PROBLEM FROM VERY DIFFERENT DIRECTIONS, I TOLD YOU.
YOU BELIEVE IN THE WORD, I IN THE INCARNATION.
THE STORY IS TOLD, OR ELSE IT IS ENACTED. EITHER WAY, IT LIVES.
BUT HAIR, AND TEETH, AND BLOOD, AND FINGERNAILS, AND SKIN ARE MY ELOQUENCE.
MY AFFLATUS.
MY EPIPHANY.
YOU KNOW WHAT, RAUSCH?
WHAT?
EVERY TIME I SEE THAT MOUTH OF YOURS OPEN, I GET THIS URGE TO SHOVE THE BARREL OF A SHOTGUN INTO IT.

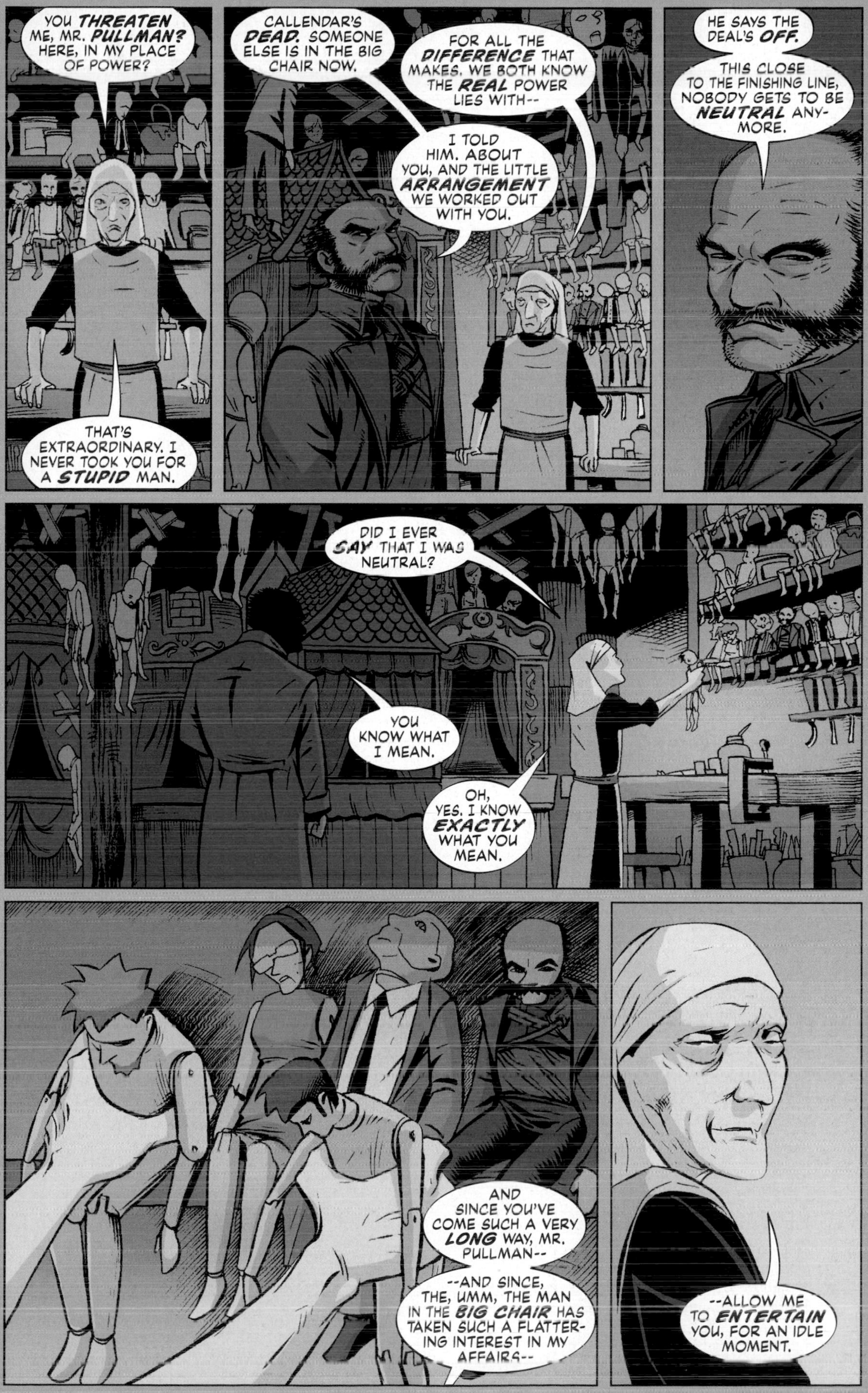
YOU THREATEN ME, MR. PULLMAN? HERE, IN MY PLACE OF POWER?
THAT'S EXTRAORDINARY. I NEVER TOOK YOU FOR A STUPID MAN.
CALLENDAR'S DEAD. SOMEONE ELSE IS IN THE BIG CHAIR NOW.
FOR ALL THE DIFFERENCE THAT MAKES. WE BOTH KNOW THE REAL POWER LIES WITH--
I TOLD HIM. ABOUT YOU, AND THE LITTLE ARRANGEMENT WE WORKED OUT WITH YOU.
HE SAYS THE DEAL'S OFF.
THIS CLOSE TO THE FINISHING LINE, NOBODY GETS TO BE NEUTRAL ANY-MORE.
DID I EVER SAY THAT I WAS NEUTRAL?
YOU KNOW WHAT I MEAN.
OH, YES. I KNOW EXACTLY WHAT YOU MEAN.
AND SINCE YOU'VE COME SUCH A VERY LONG WAY, MR. PULLMAN--
--AND SINCE, THE, UMM, THE MAN IN THE BIG CHAIR HAS TAKEN SUCH A FLATTER-ING INTEREST IN MY AFFAIRS--
--ALLOW ME TO ENTERTAIN YOU, FOR AN IDLE MOMENT.

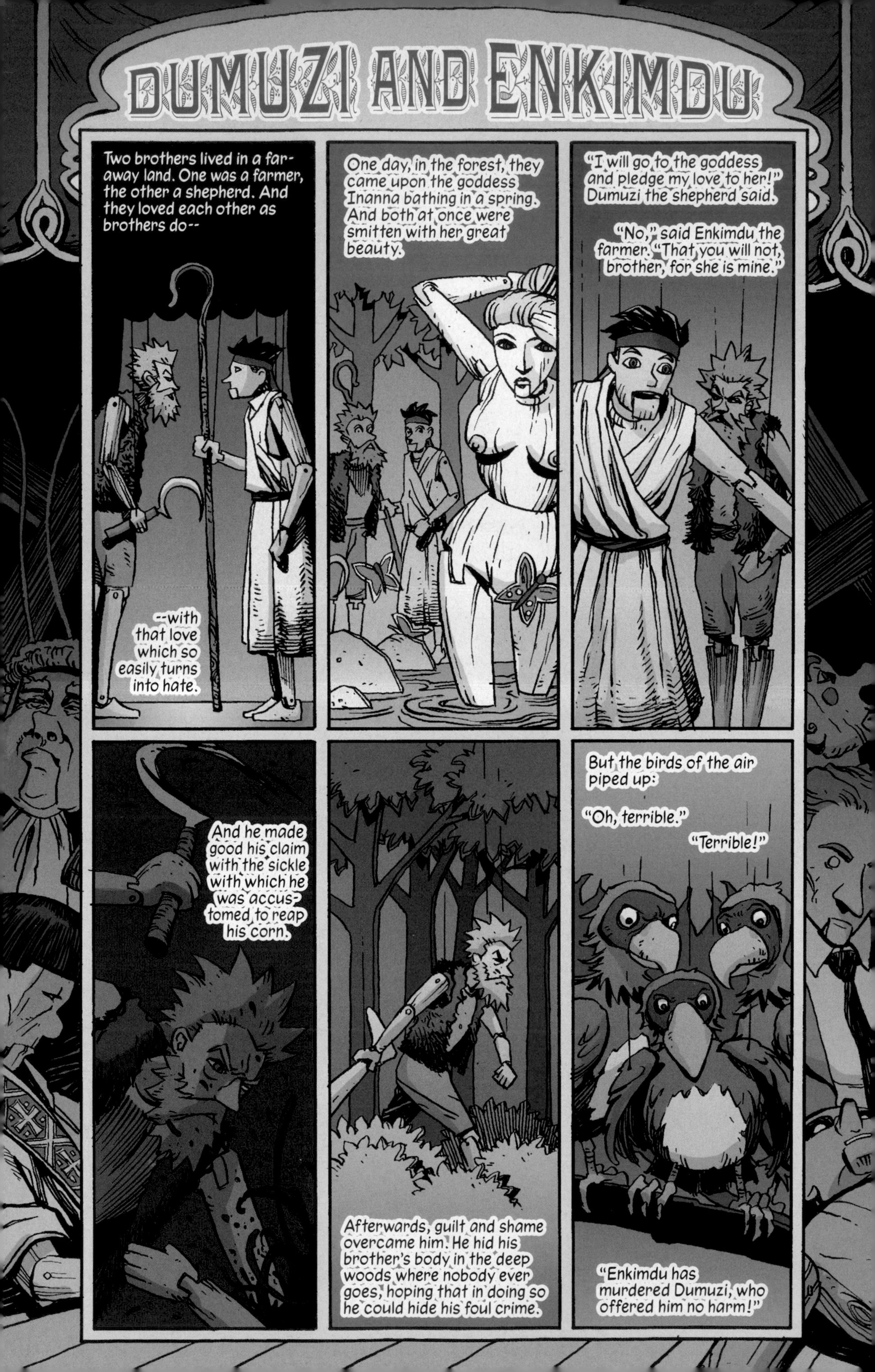
DUMUZI AND ENKIMDU
Two brothers lived in a far-away land. One was a farmer, the other a shepherd. And they loved each other as brothers do--
--with that love which so easily turns into hate.
One day, in the forest, they came upon the goddess Inanna bathing in a spring. And both at once were smitten with her great beauty.
"I will go to the goddess and pledge my love to her!" Dumuzi the shepherd said.
"No," said Enkimdu the farmer. "That you will not, brother, for she is mine."
And he made good his claim with the sickle with which he was accus-tomed to reap his corn.
Afterwards, guilt and shame overcame him. He hid his brother's body in the deep woods where nobody ever goes, hoping that in doing so he could hide his foul crime.
But the birds of the air piped up:
"Oh, terrible."
"Terrible!"
"Enkimdu has murdered Dumuzi, who offered him no harm!"

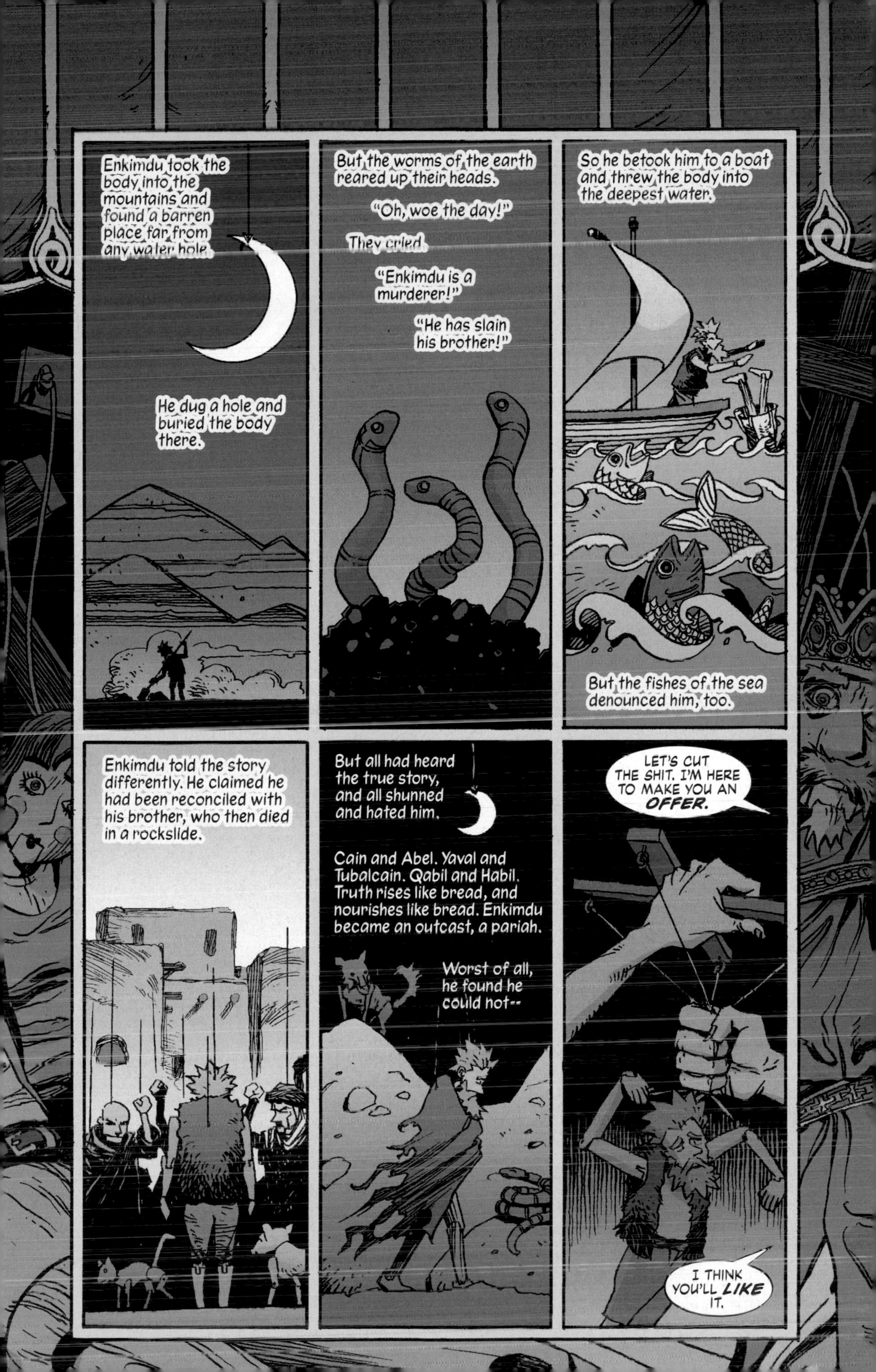
Enkimdu took the body into the mountains and found a barren place far from any water hole.
He dug a hole and buried the body there.
But the worms of the earth reared up their heads.
"Oh, woe the day!"
They cried.
"Enkimdu is a murderer!"
"He has slain his brother!"
So he betook him to a boat and threw the body into the deepest water.
But the fishes of the sea denounced him, too.
Enkimdu told the story differently. He claimed he had been reconciled with his brother, who then died in a rockslide.
But all had heard the true story, and all shunned and hated him.
Cain and Abel. Yaval and Tubalcain. Qabil and Habil. Truth rises like bread, and nourishes like bread. Enkimdu became an outcast, a pariah.
Worst of all, he found he could not--
LET'S CUT THE SHIT. I'M HERE TO MAKE YOU AN OFFER.
I THINK YOU'LL LIKE IT.

# Arrowhead

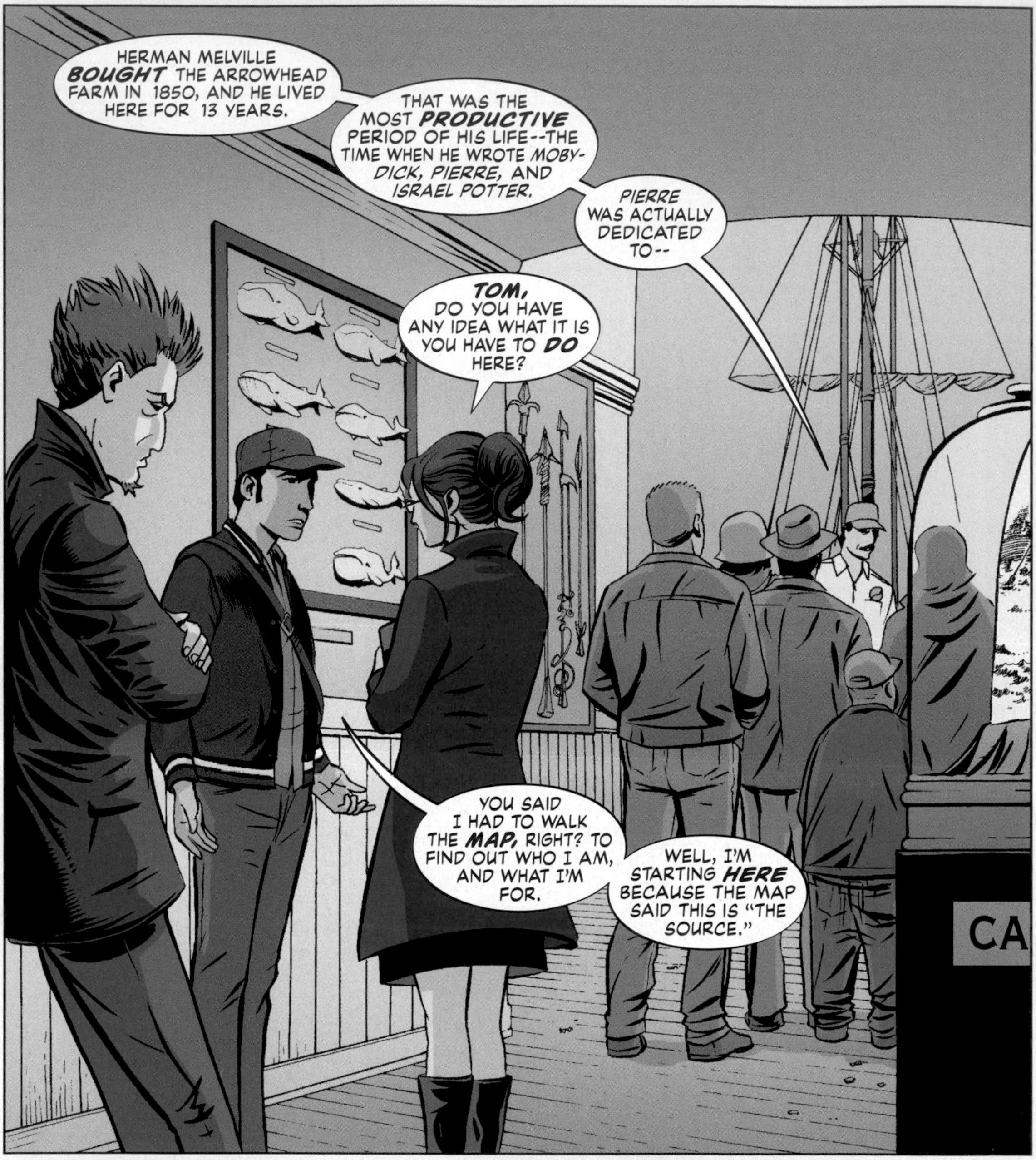
HERMAN MELVILLE BOUGHT THE ARROWHEAD FARM IN 1850, AND HE LIVED HERE FOR 13 YEARS.
THAT WAS THE MOST PRODUCTIVE PERIOD OF HIS LIFE--THE TIME WHEN HE WROTE MOBY-DICK, PIERRE, AND ISRAEL POTTER.
PIERRE WAS ACTUALLY DEDICATED TO--
TOM, DO YOU HAVE ANY IDEA WHAT IT IS YOU HAVE TO DO HERE?
YOU SAID I HAD TO WALK THE MAP, RIGHT? TO FIND OUT WHO I AM, AND WHAT I'M FOR.
WELL, I'M STARTING HERE BECAUSE THE MAP SAID THIS IS "THE SOURCE."
CA

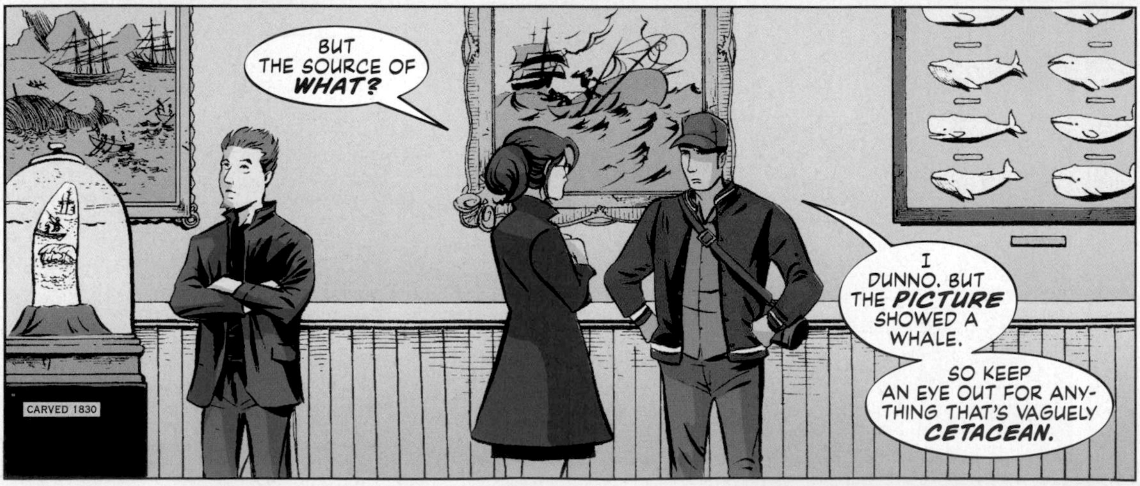
BUT THE SOURCE OF WHAT?
CARVED 1830
I DUNNO. BUT THE PICTURE SHOWED A WHALE.
SO KEEP AN EYE OUT FOR ANYTHING THAT'S VAGUELY CETACEAN.

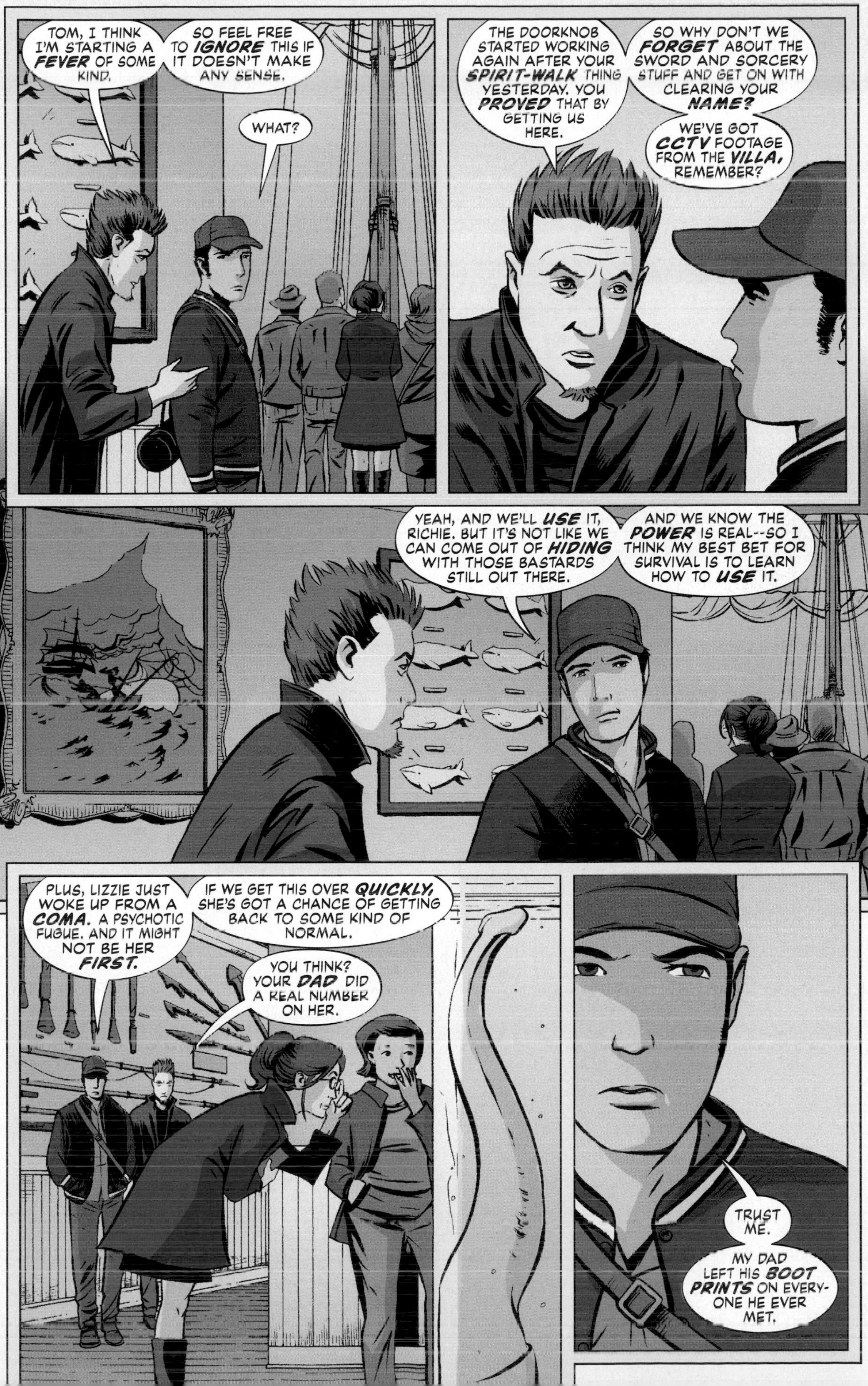

TOM, I THINK I'M STARTING A FEVER OF SOME KIND.
SO FEEL FREE TO IGNORE THIS IF IT DOESN'T MAKE ANY SENSE.
WHAT?
THE DOORKNOB STARTED WORKING AGAIN AFTER YOUR SPIRIT-WALK THING YESTERDAY. YOU PROVED THAT BY GETTING US HERE.
SO WHY DON'T WE FORGET ABOUT THE SWORD AND SORCERY STUFF AND GET ON WITH CLEARING YOUR NAME?
WE'VE GOT CCTV FOOTAGE FROM THE VILLA, REMEMBER?
YEAH, AND WE'LL USE IT, RICHIE. BUT IT'S NOT LIKE WE CAN COME OUT OF HIDING WITH THOSE BASTARDS STILL OUT THERE.
AND WE KNOW THE POWER IS REAL--SO I THINK MY BEST BET FOR SURVIVAL IS TO LEARN HOW TO USE IT.
PLUS, LIZZIE JUST WOKE UP FROM A COMA. A PSYCHOTIC FUGUE. AND IT MIGHT NOT BE HER FIRST.
IF WE GET THIS OVER QUICKLY, SHE'S GOT A CHANCE OF GETTING BACK TO SOME KIND OF NORMAL.
YOU THINK? YOUR DAD DID A REAL NUMBER ON HER.
TRUST ME.
MY DAD LEFT HIS BOOT PRINTS ON EVERY-ONE HE EVER MET.

# Wet Ink

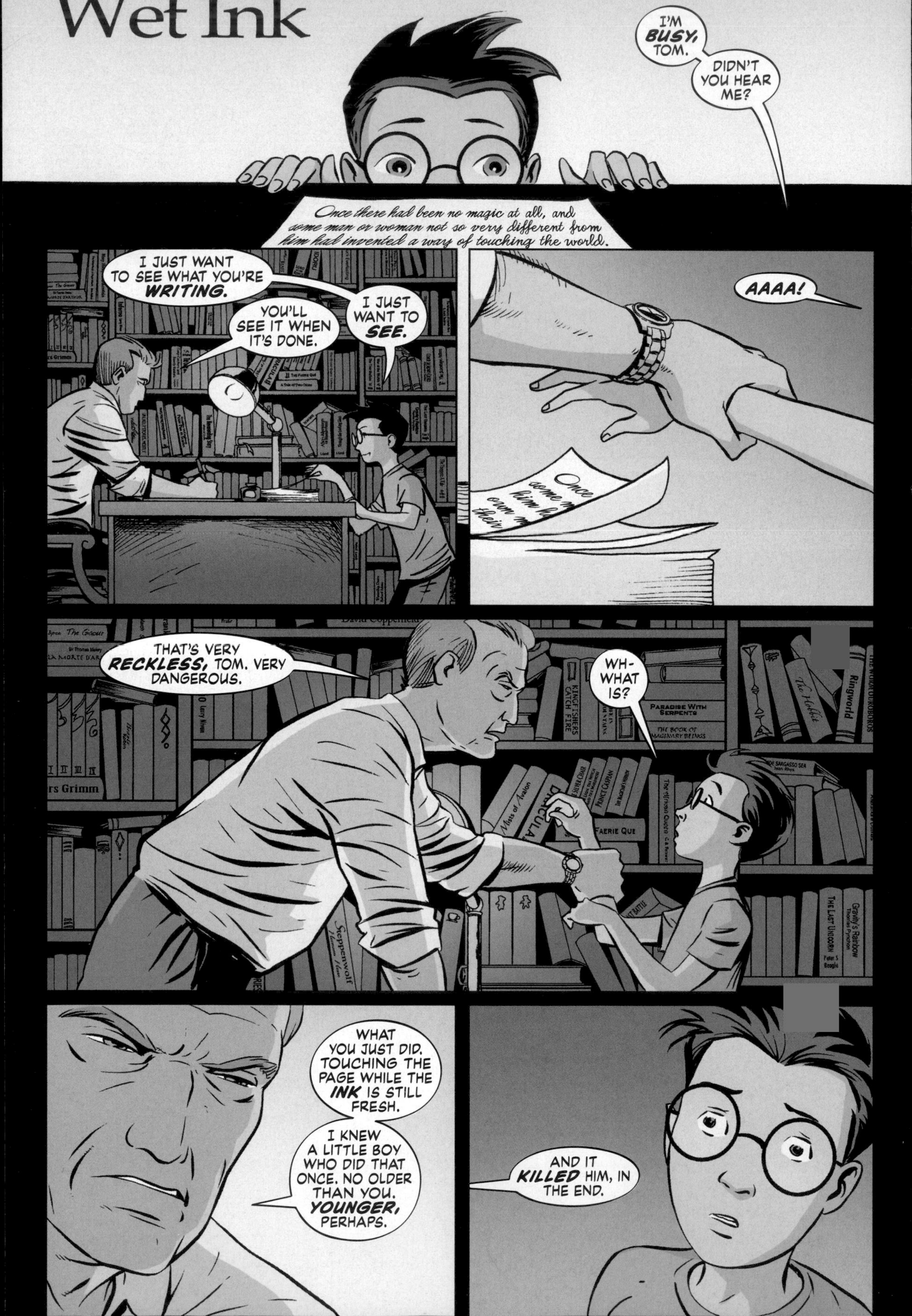
I'M BUSY, TOM.
DIDN'T YOU HEAR ME?
Once there had been no magic at all, and some man or woman not so very different from him had invented a way of touching the world.
I JUST WANT TO SEE WHAT YOU'RE WRITING.
YOU'LL SEE IT WHEN IT'S DONE.
I JUST WANT TO SEE.
AAAA!
THAT'S VERY RECKLESS, TOM. VERY DANGEROUS.
WH-WHAT IS?
WHAT YOU JUST DID. TOUCHING THE PAGE WHILE THE INK IS STILL FRESH.
I KNEW A LITTLE BOY WHO DID THAT ONCE. NO OLDER THAN YOU. YOUNGER, PERHAPS.
AND IT KILLED HIM, IN THE END.

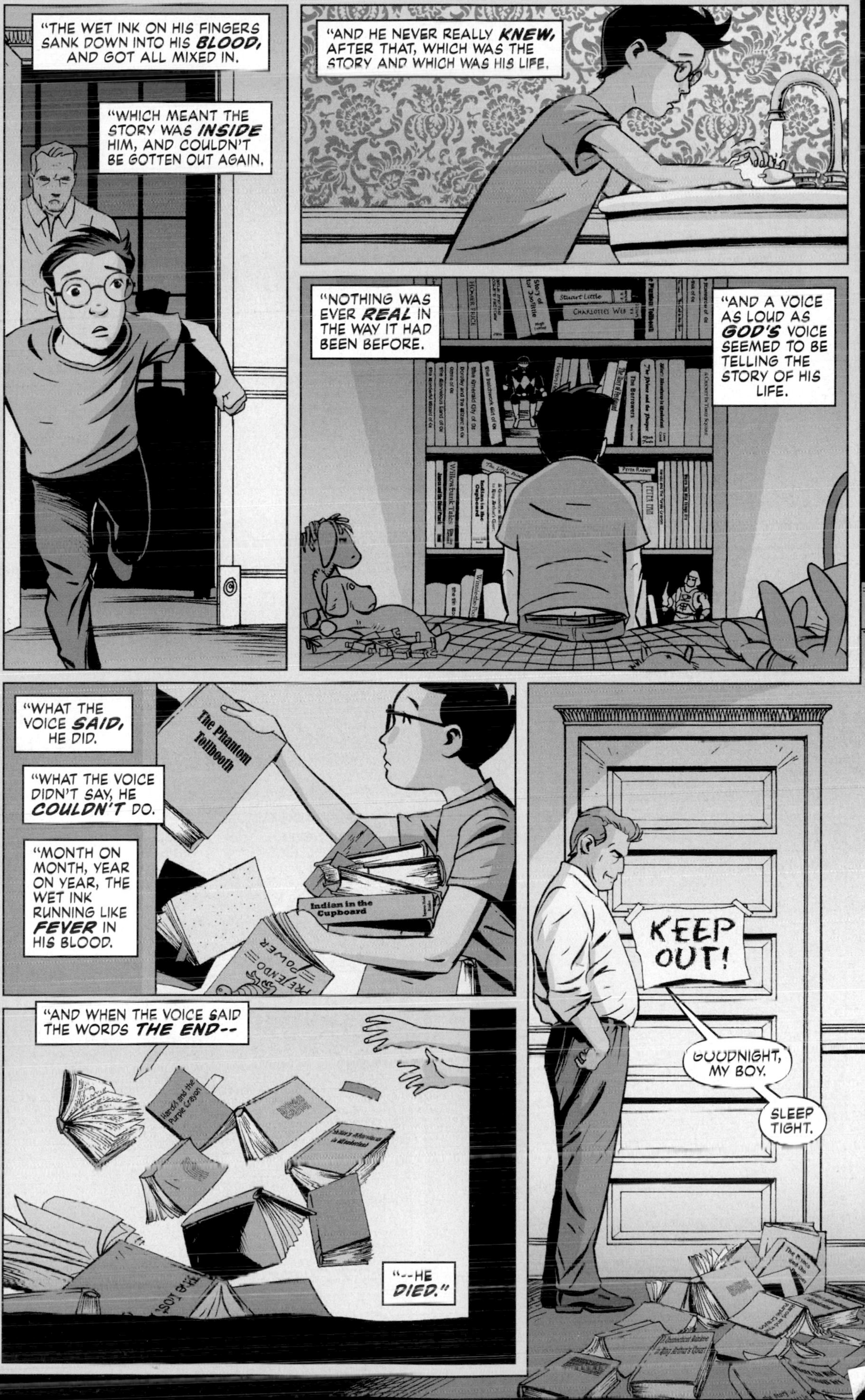
"THE WET INK ON HIS FINGERS SANK DOWN INTO HIS BLOOD, AND GOT ALL MIXED IN.
"WHICH MEANT THE STORY WAS INSIDE HIM, AND COULDN'T BE GOTTEN OUT AGAIN.
"AND HE NEVER REALLY KNEW, AFTER THAT, WHICH WAS THE STORY AND WHICH WAS HIS LIFE.
"NOTHING WAS EVER REAL IN THE WAY IT HAD BEEN BEFORE.
"AND A VOICE AS LOUD AS GOD'S VOICE SEEMED TO BE TELLING THE STORY OF HIS LIFE.
"WHAT THE VOICE SAID, HE DID.
"WHAT THE VOICE DIDN'T SAY, HE COULDN'T DO.
"MONTH ON MONTH, YEAR ON YEAR, THE WET INK RUNNING LIKE FEVER IN HIS BLOOD.
The Phantom Tollbooth
Indian in the Cupboard
"AND WHEN THE VOICE SAID THE WORDS THE END--
Harold and the Purple Crayon
"--HE DIED."
KEEP OUT!
GOODNIGHT, MY BOY.
SLEEP TIGHT.

# The Spouter

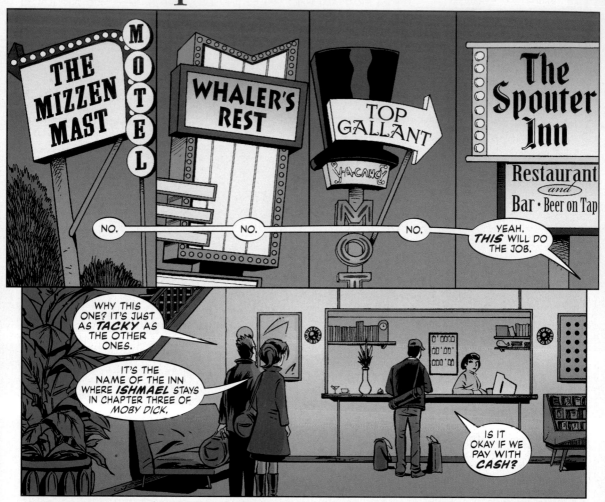

THE MIZZEN MAST **M·O·T·E·L**

WHALER'S REST

TOP GALLANT

**VA-CANCY**

The **Spouter Inn**

Restaurant *and* Bar · Beer on Tap

NO.

NO.

NO.

YEAH, *THIS* WILL DO THE JOB.

WHY THIS ONE? IT'S JUST AS *TACKY* AS THE OTHER ONES.

IT'S THE NAME OF THE INN WHERE *ISHMAEL* STAYS IN CHAPTER THREE OF MOBY DICK.

IS IT OKAY IF WE PAY WITH *CASH?*

GET ME A *SMOKING* ROOM.

I'VE NEVER *SEEN* YOU SMOKE, RICHIE.

I *QUIT* A WHILE BACK.

THEN HOW COME--?

I LIKE TO BE REMINDED *WHY* I QUIT.

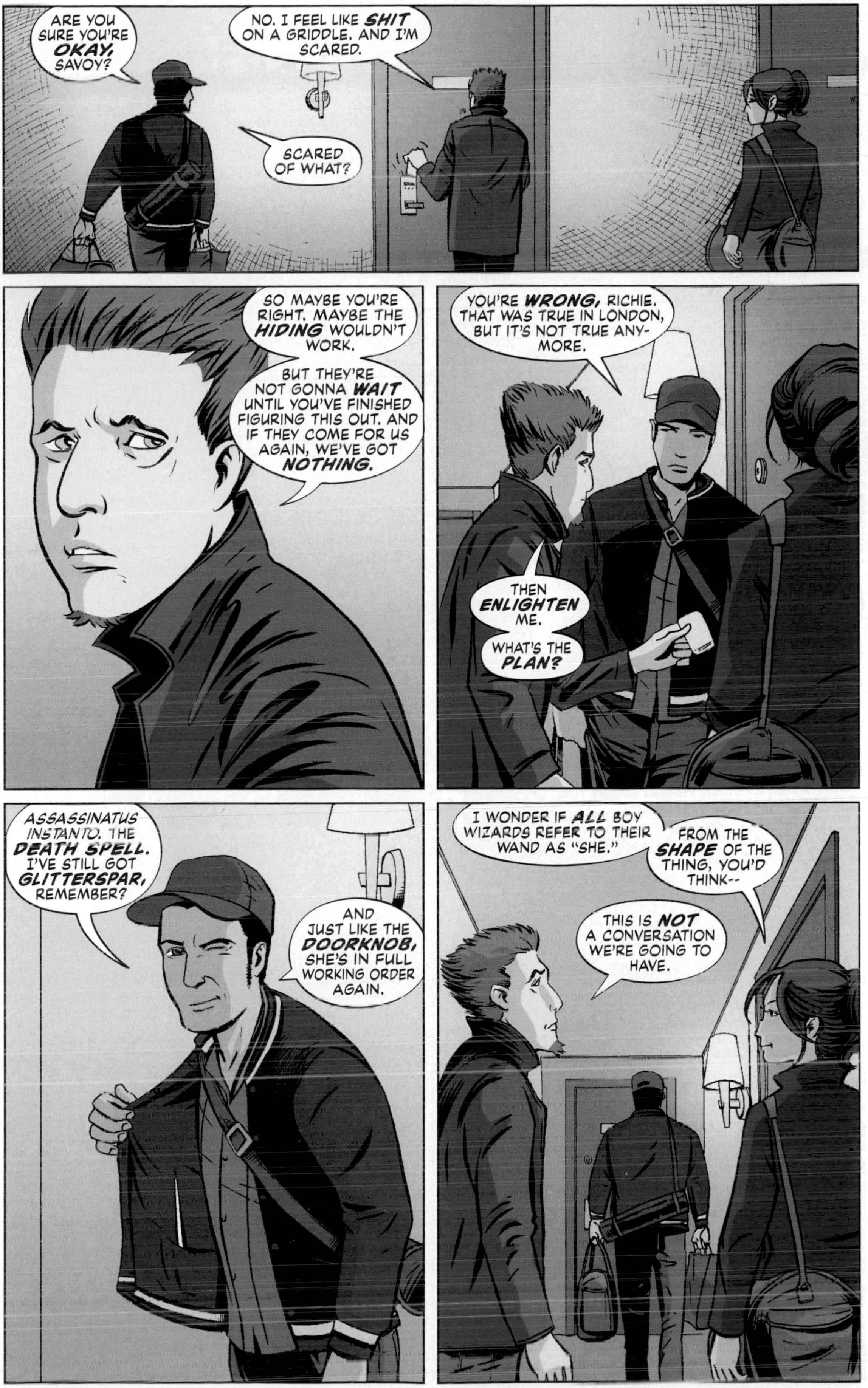
ARE YOU SURE YOU'RE OKAY, SAVOY?
NO. I FEEL LIKE SHIT ON A GRIDDLE. AND I'M SCARED.
SCARED OF WHAT?
SO MAYBE YOU'RE RIGHT. MAYBE THE HIDING WOULDN'T WORK.
BUT THEY'RE NOT GONNA WAIT UNTIL YOU'VE FINISHED FIGURING THIS OUT. AND IF THEY COME FOR US AGAIN, WE'VE GOT NOTHING.
YOU'RE WRONG, RICHIE. THAT WAS TRUE IN LONDON, BUT IT'S NOT TRUE ANYMORE.
THEN ENLIGHTEN ME.
WHAT'S THE PLAN?
ASSASSINATUS INSTANTO. THE DEATH SPELL. I'VE STILL GOT GLITTERSPAR, REMEMBER?
AND JUST LIKE THE DOORKNOB, SHE'S IN FULL WORKING ORDER AGAIN.
I WONDER IF ALL BOY WIZARDS REFER TO THEIR WAND AS "SHE."
FROM THE SHAPE OF THE THING, YOU'D THINK--
THIS IS NOT A CONVERSATION WE'RE GOING TO HAVE.

# The Commission

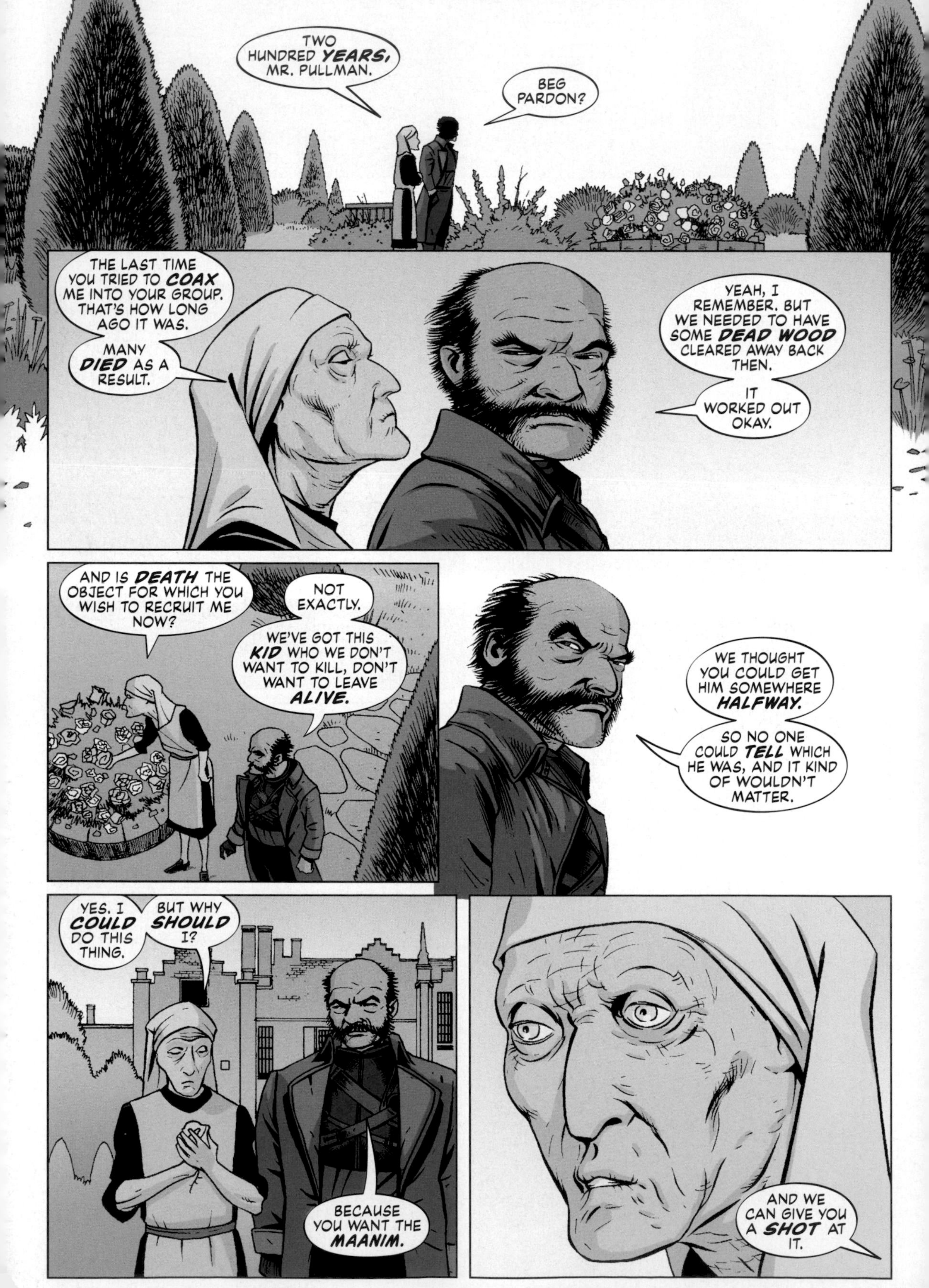
TWO HUNDRED YEARS, MR. PULLMAN.
BEG PARDON?
THE LAST TIME YOU TRIED TO COAX ME INTO YOUR GROUP. THAT'S HOW LONG AGO IT WAS.
MANY DIED AS A RESULT.
YEAH, I REMEMBER. BUT WE NEEDED TO HAVE SOME DEAD WOOD CLEARED AWAY BACK THEN.
IT WORKED OUT OKAY.
AND IS DEATH THE OBJECT FOR WHICH YOU WISH TO RECRUIT ME NOW?
NOT EXACTLY.
WE'VE GOT THIS KID WHO WE DON'T WANT TO KILL, DON'T WANT TO LEAVE ALIVE.
WE THOUGHT YOU COULD GET HIM SOMEWHERE HALFWAY.
SO NO ONE COULD TELL WHICH HE WAS, AND IT KIND OF WOULDN'T MATTER.
YES. I COULD DO THIS THING.
BUT WHY SHOULD I?
BECAUSE YOU WANT THE MAANIM.
AND WE CAN GIVE YOU A SHOT AT IT.

# The Mirror

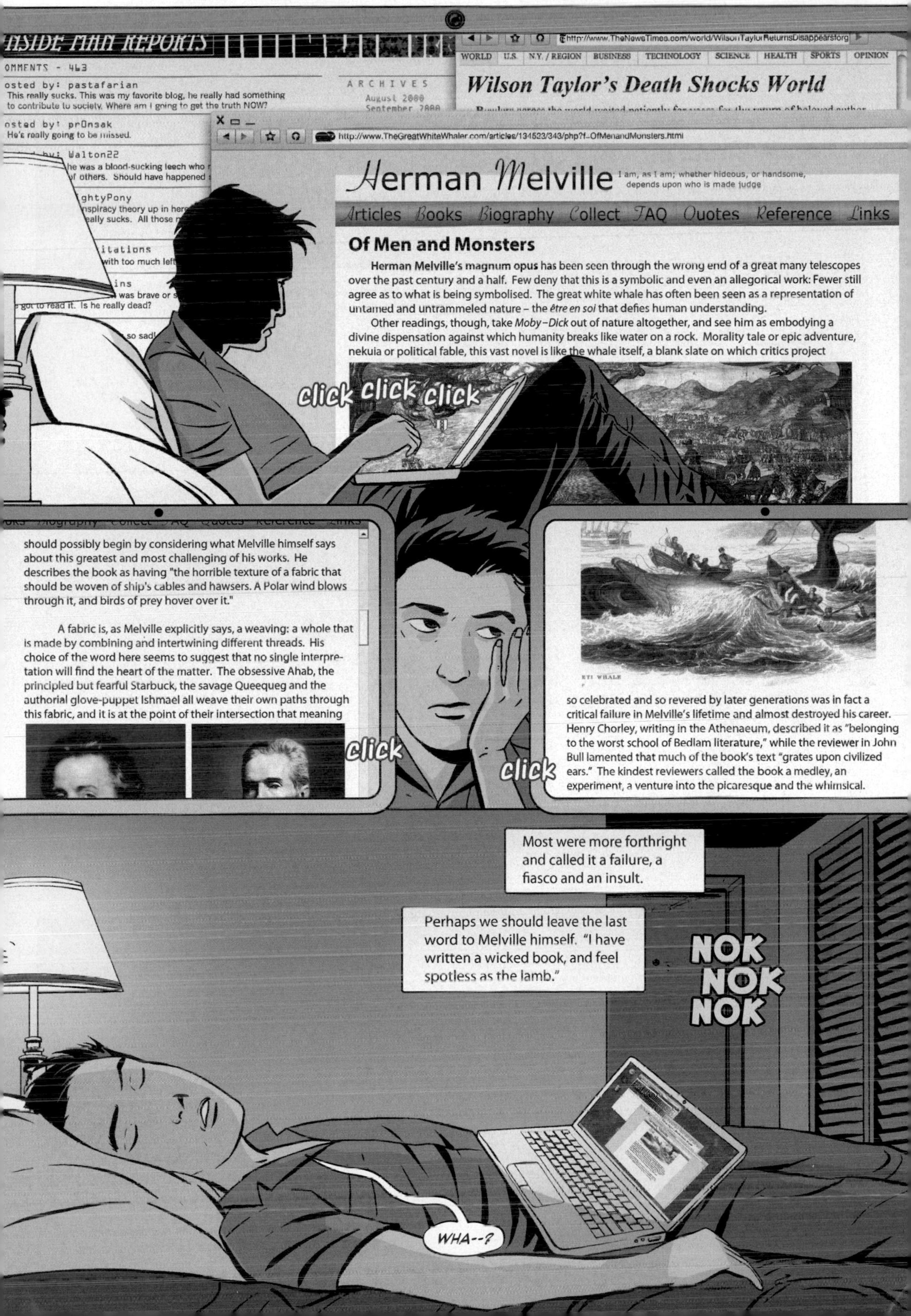

OMMENTS - 463
osted by: pastafarian
This really sucks. This was my favorite blog, he really had something to contribute to society. Where am I going to get the truth NOW?
ARCHIVES
August 2000
osted by: pr0nsak
He's really going to be missed.
he was a blood-sucking leech who
of others. Should have happened
ghtyPony
nspiracy theory up in here
ally sucks. All those
itations
with too much left
ins
was brave or
got to read it. Is he really dead?
so sad!
http://www.TheNewsTimes.com/world/WilsonTaylorReturnsDisappearsforg
WORLD U.S. N.Y. / REGION BUSINESS TECHNOLOGY SCIENCE HEALTH SPORTS OPINION
Wilson Taylor's Death Shocks World
http://www.TheGreatWhiteWhaler.com/articles/134523/343/php?f=OfMenandMonsters.html
Herman Melville
I am, as I am; whether hideous, or handsome, depends upon who is made judge
Articles Books Biography Collect FAQ Quotes Reference Links
Of Men and Monsters
Herman Melville's magnum opus has been seen through the wrong end of a great many telescopes over the past century and a half. Few deny that this is a symbolic and even an allegorical work: Fewer still agree as to what is being symbolised. The great white whale has often been seen as a representation of untamed and untrammeled nature – the être en soi that defies human understanding.
Other readings, though, take Moby-Dick out of nature altogether, and see him as embodying a divine dispensation against which humanity breaks like water on a rock. Morality tale or epic adventure, nekuia or political fable, this vast novel is like the whale itself, a blank slate on which critics project
click click click
should possibly begin by considering what Melville himself says about this greatest and most challenging of his works. He describes the book as having "the horrible texture of a fabric that should be woven of ship's cables and hawsers. A Polar wind blows through it, and birds of prey hover over it."
A fabric is, as Melville explicitly says, a weaving: a whole that is made by combining and intertwining different threads. His choice of the word here seems to suggest that no single interpretation will find the heart of the matter. The obsessive Ahab, the principled but fearful Starbuck, the savage Queequeg and the authorial glove-puppet Ishmael all weave their own paths through this fabric, and it is at the point of their intersection that meaning
click
click
so celebrated and so revered by later generations was in fact a critical failure in Melville's lifetime and almost destroyed his career. Henry Chorley, writing in the Athenaeum, described it as "belonging to the worst school of Bedlam literature," while the reviewer in John Bull lamented that much of the book's text "grates upon civilized ears." The kindest reviewers called the book a medley, an experiment, a venture into the picaresque and the whimsical.
Most were more forthright and called it a failure, a fiasco and an insult.
Perhaps we should leave the last word to Melville himself. "I have written a wicked book, and feel spotless as the lamb."
NOK NOK NOK
WHA--?

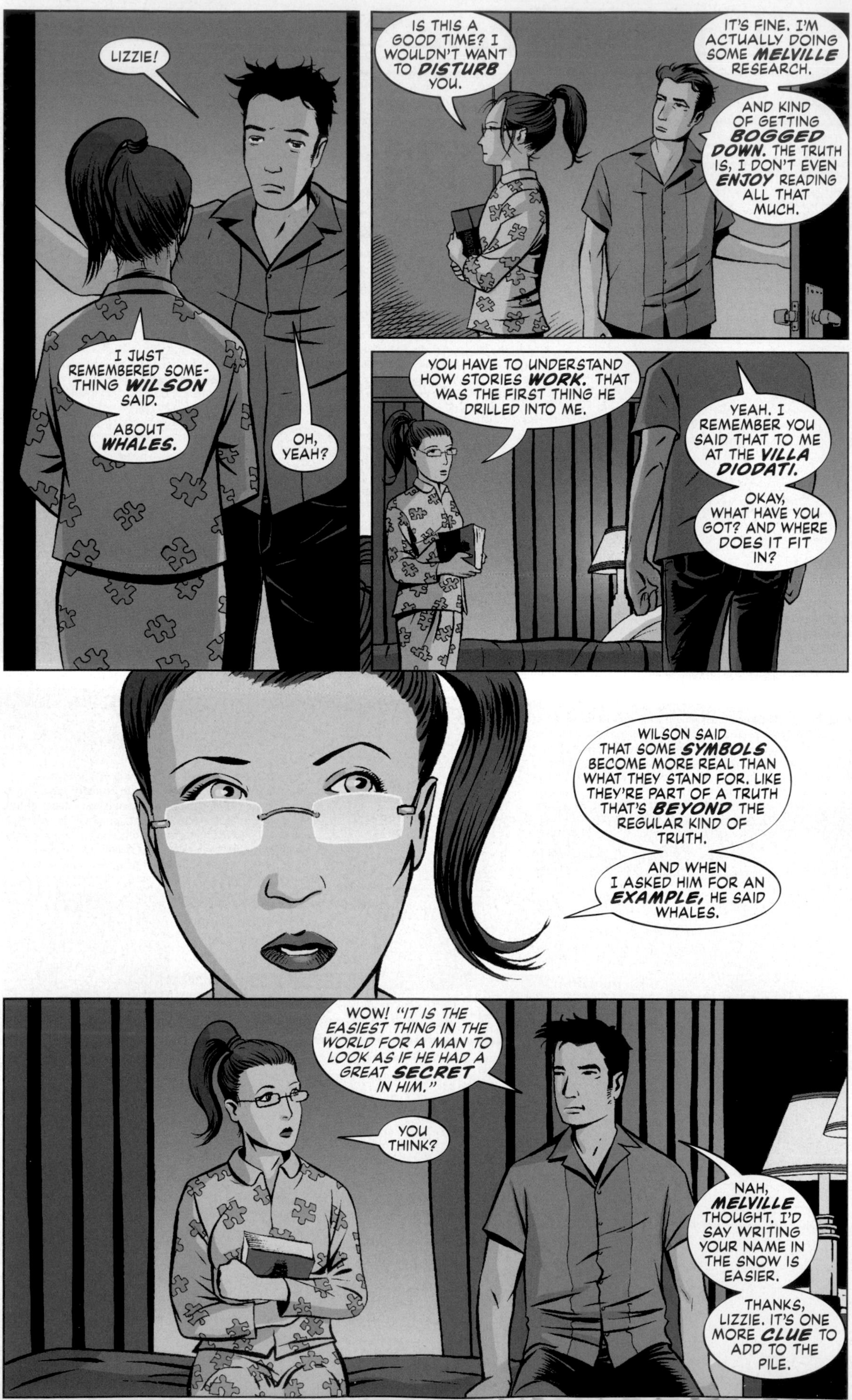
LIZZIE!
I JUST REMEMBERED SOMETHING WILSON SAID.
ABOUT WHALES.
OH, YEAH?
IS THIS A GOOD TIME? I WOULDN'T WANT TO DISTURB YOU.
IT'S FINE. I'M ACTUALLY DOING SOME MELVILLE RESEARCH.
AND KIND OF GETTING BOGGED DOWN. THE TRUTH IS, I DON'T EVEN ENJOY READING ALL THAT MUCH.
YOU HAVE TO UNDERSTAND HOW STORIES WORK. THAT WAS THE FIRST THING HE DRILLED INTO ME.
YEAH. I REMEMBER YOU SAID THAT TO ME AT THE VILLA DIODATI.
OKAY, WHAT HAVE YOU GOT? AND WHERE DOES IT FIT IN?
WILSON SAID THAT SOME SYMBOLS BECOME MORE REAL THAN WHAT THEY STAND FOR. LIKE THEY'RE PART OF A TRUTH THAT'S BEYOND THE REGULAR KIND OF TRUTH.
AND WHEN I ASKED HIM FOR AN EXAMPLE, HE SAID WHALES.
WOW! "IT IS THE EASIEST THING IN THE WORLD FOR A MAN TO LOOK AS IF HE HAD A GREAT SECRET IN HIM."
YOU THINK?
NAH, MELVILLE THOUGHT. I'D SAY WRITING YOUR NAME IN THE SNOW IS EASIER.
THANKS, LIZZIE. IT'S ONE MORE CLUE TO ADD TO THE PILE.

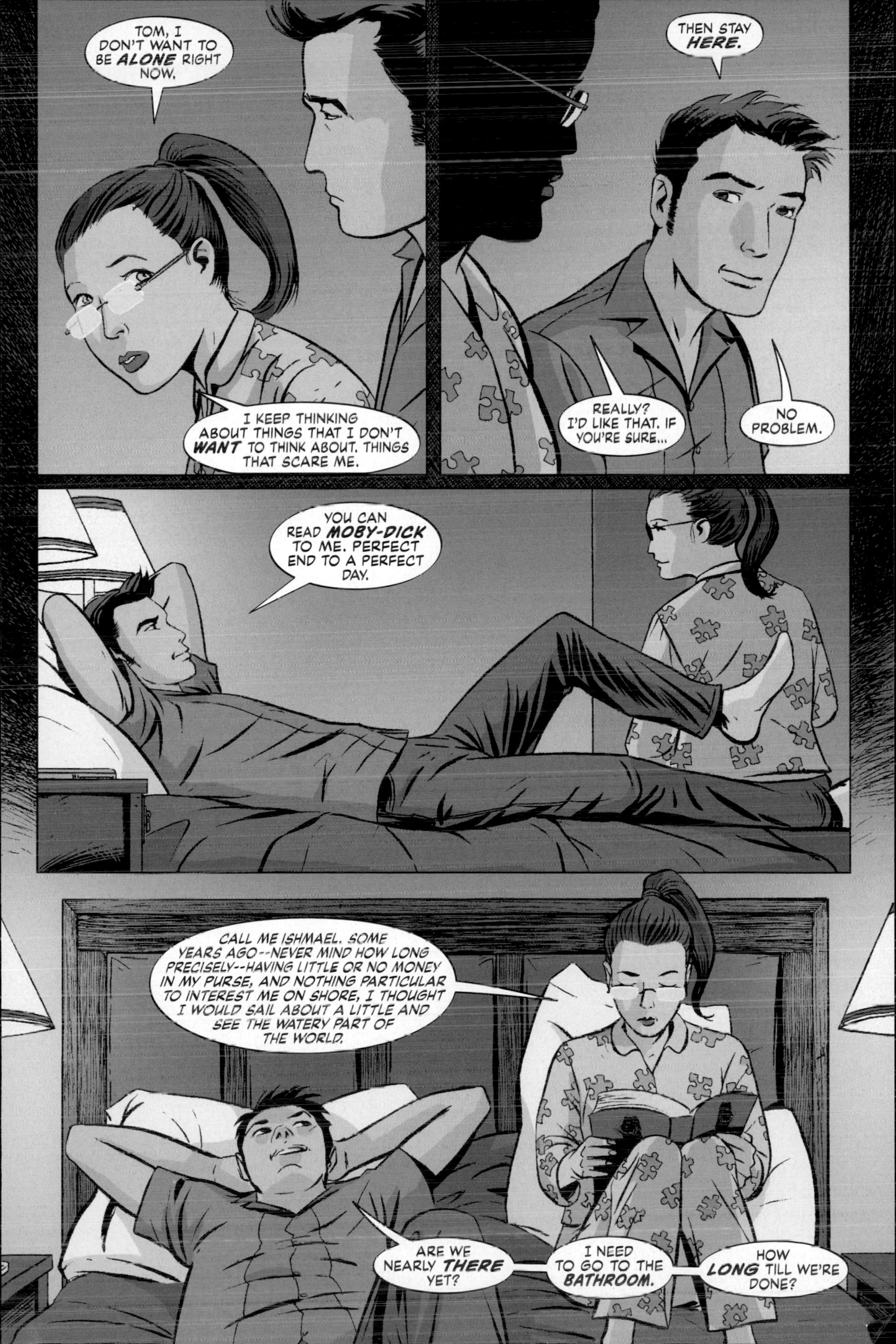
TOM, I DON'T WANT TO BE ALONE RIGHT NOW.
I KEEP THINKING ABOUT THINGS THAT I DON'T WANT TO THINK ABOUT. THINGS THAT SCARE ME.
THEN STAY HERE.
REALLY? I'D LIKE THAT. IF YOU'RE SURE...
NO PROBLEM.
YOU CAN READ MOBY-DICK TO ME. PERFECT END TO A PERFECT DAY.
CALL ME ISHMAEL. SOME YEARS AGO--NEVER MIND HOW LONG PRECISELY--HAVING LITTLE OR NO MONEY IN MY PURSE, AND NOTHING PARTICULAR TO INTEREST ME ON SHORE, I THOUGHT I WOULD SAIL ABOUT A LITTLE AND SEE THE WATERY PART OF THE WORLD.
ARE WE NEARLY THERE YET?
I NEED TO GO TO THE BATHROOM.
HOW LONG TILL WE'RE DONE?

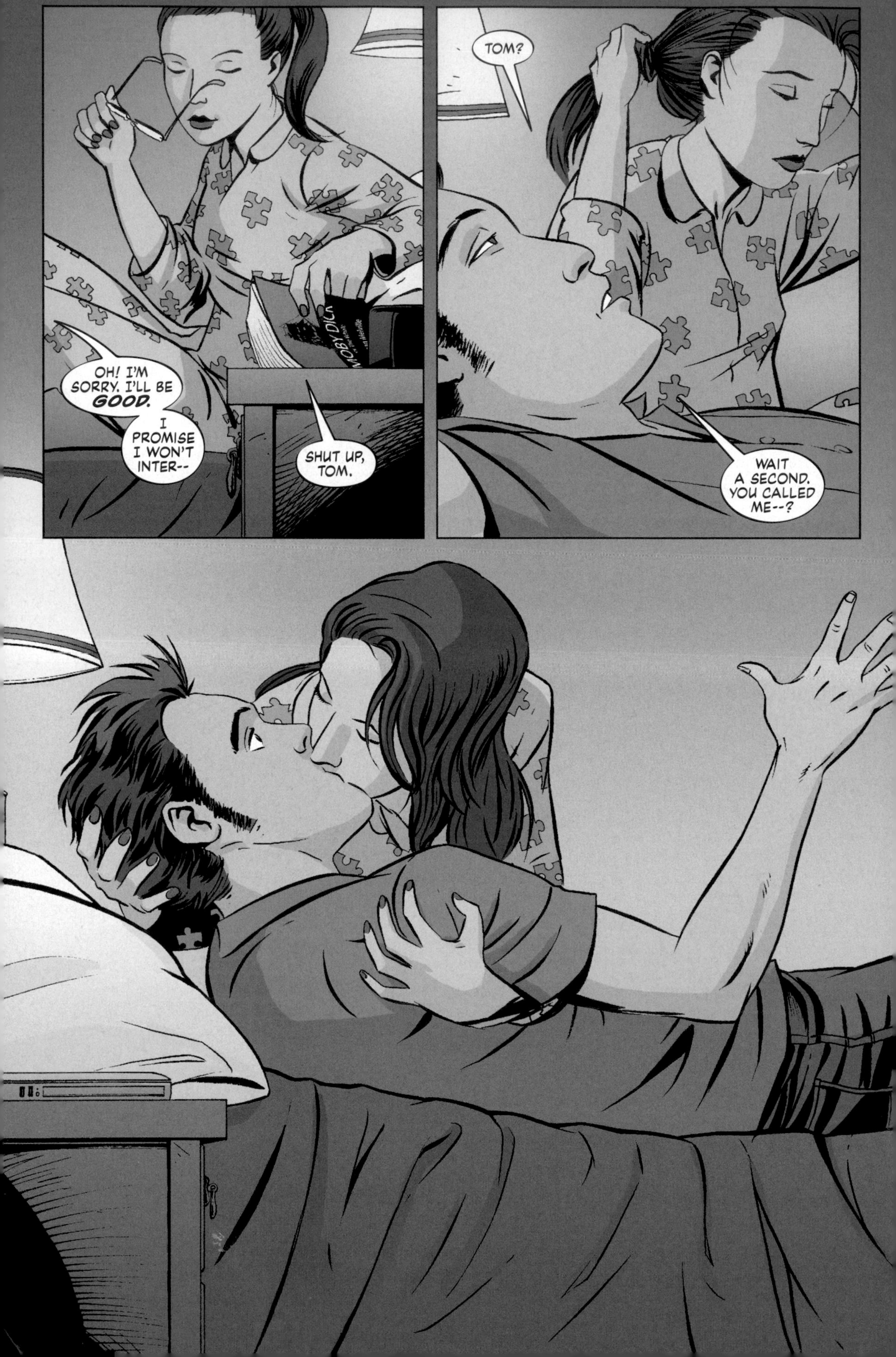
OH! I'M SORRY. I'LL BE GOOD.
I PROMISE I WON'T INTER--
SHUT UP, TOM.
TOM?
WAIT A SECOND. YOU CALLED ME--?

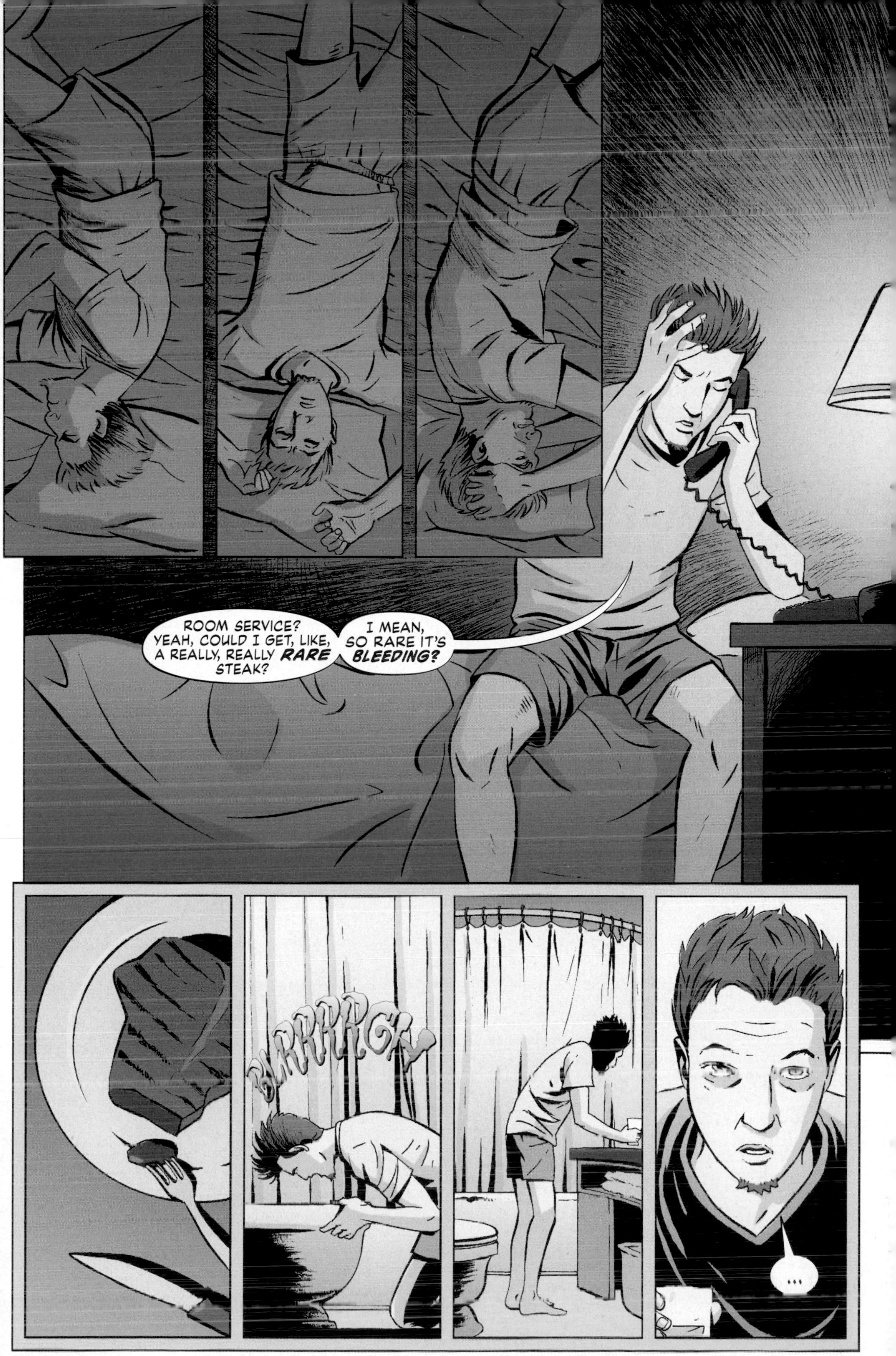
ROOM SERVICE? YEAH, COULD I GET, LIKE, A REALLY, REALLY RARE STEAK?
I MEAN, SO RARE IT'S BLEEDING?
BLRRRRGK
...

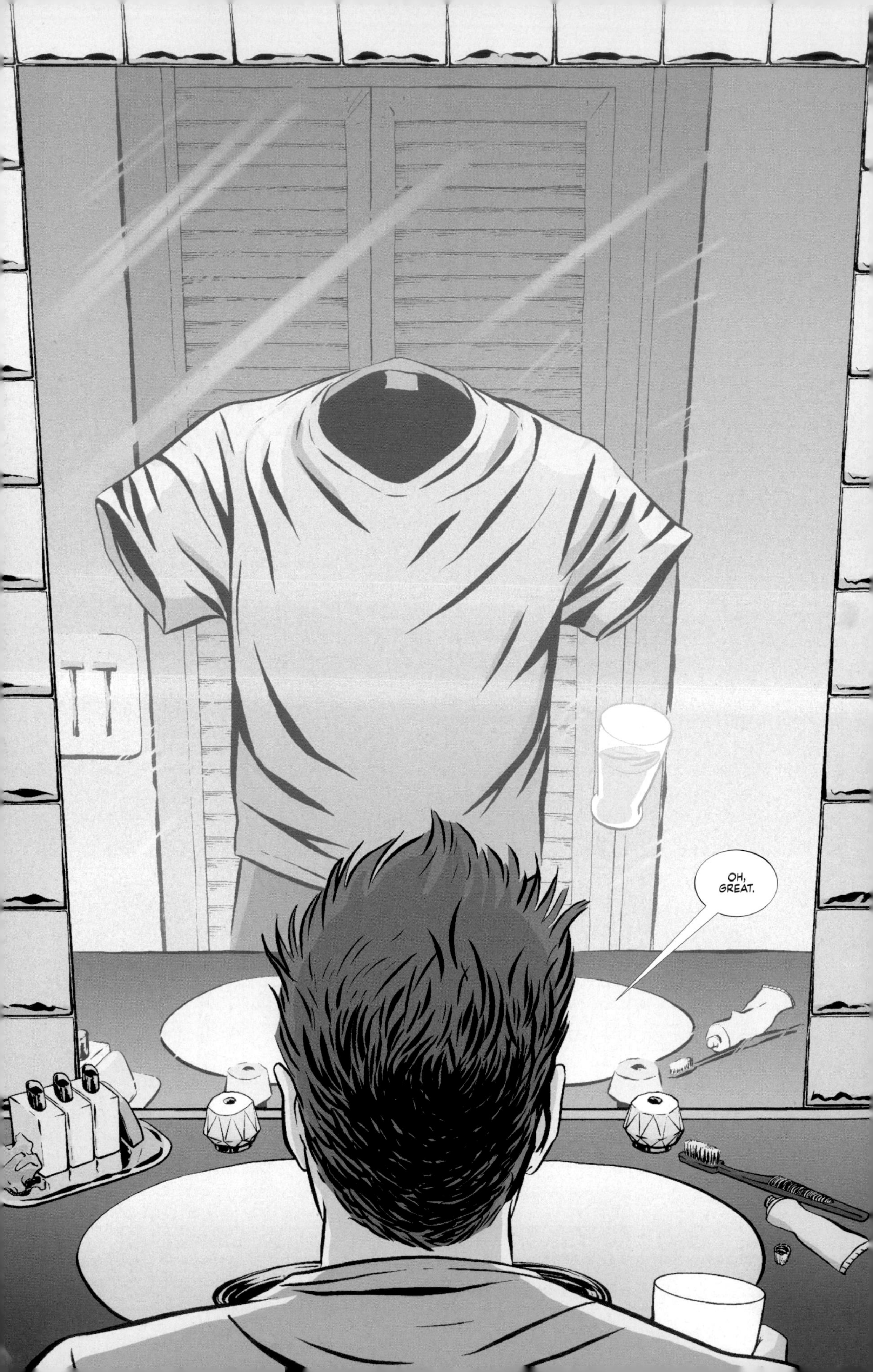
OH, GREAT.

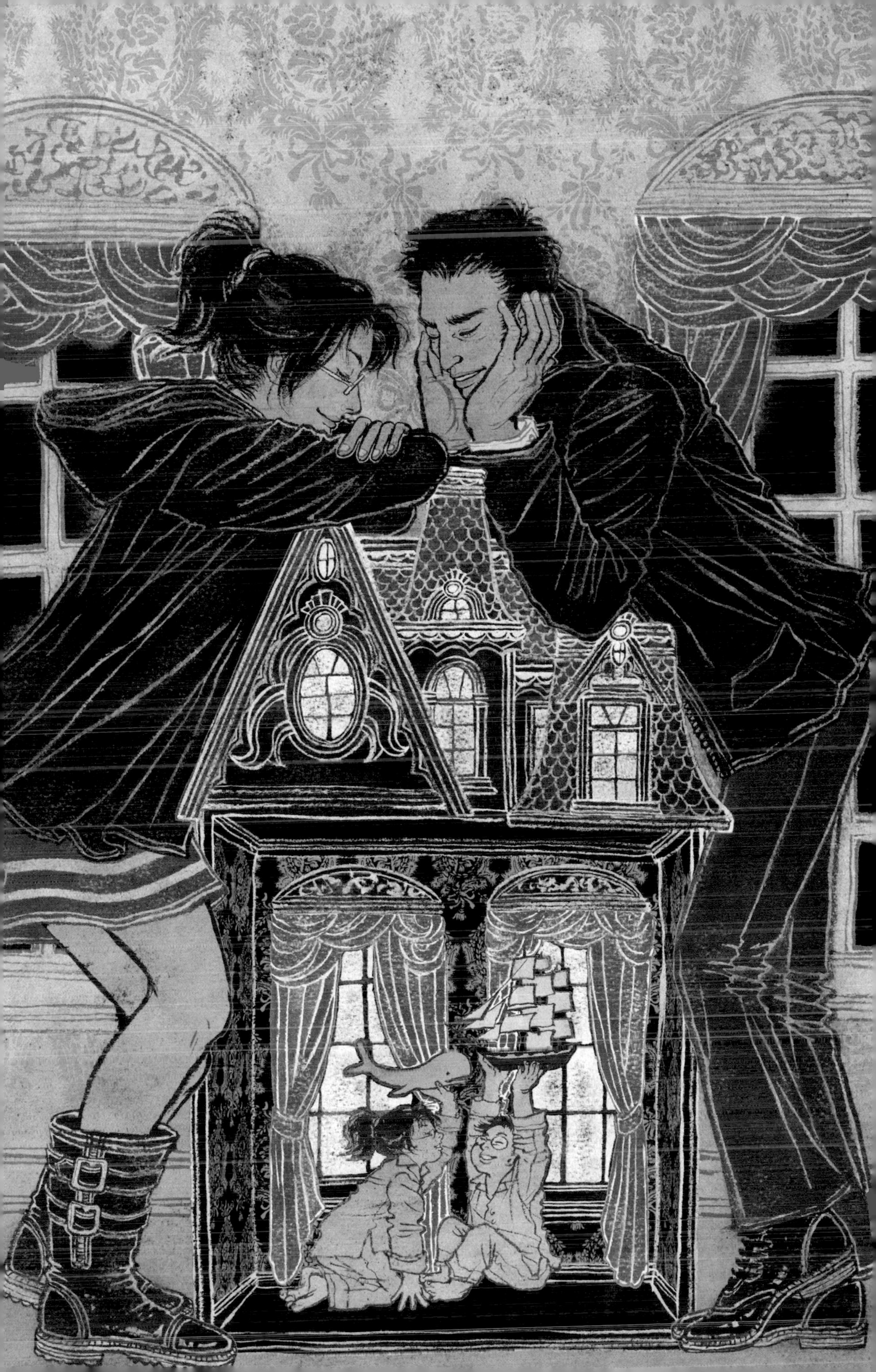

# Aftermath

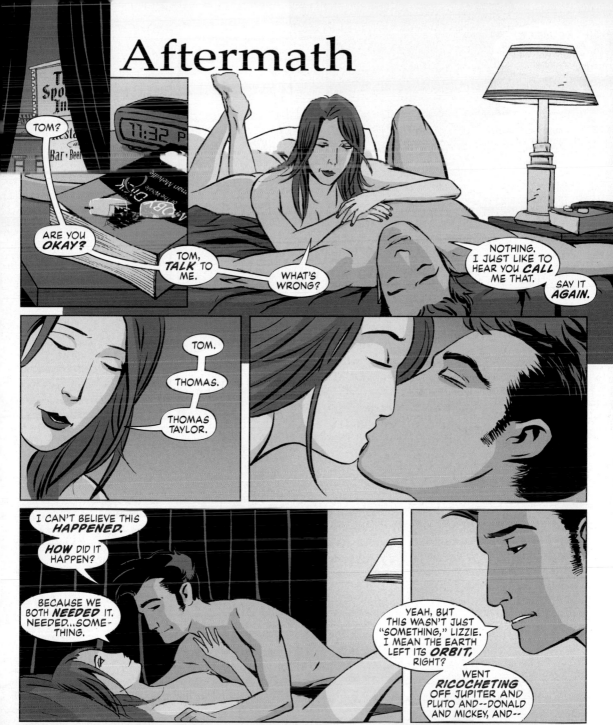

TOM?

ARE YOU *OKAY?*

TOM, *TALK* TO ME.

WHAT'S WRONG?

NOTHING. I JUST LIKE TO HEAR YOU *CALL* ME THAT. SAY IT *AGAIN.*

TOM.

THOMAS.

THOMAS TAYLOR.

I CAN'T BELIEVE THIS *HAPPENED.*

*HOW* DID IT HAPPEN?

BECAUSE WE BOTH *NEEDED* IT. NEEDED...SOME-THING.

YEAH, BUT THIS WASN'T JUST "SOMETHING," LIZZIE. I MEAN THE EARTH LEFT ITS *ORBIT,* RIGHT?

WENT *RICOCHETING* OFF JUPITER AND PLUTO AND--DONALD AND MICKEY, AND--

SHUSH.

YOU'RE BABBLING.

Mphlphlpgl!

CAN I USE YOUR BATHROOM?

YOU CAN USE *ANYTHING* THAT'S MINE.

THANK YOU, TOM.

YOU'RE VERY WELCOME.

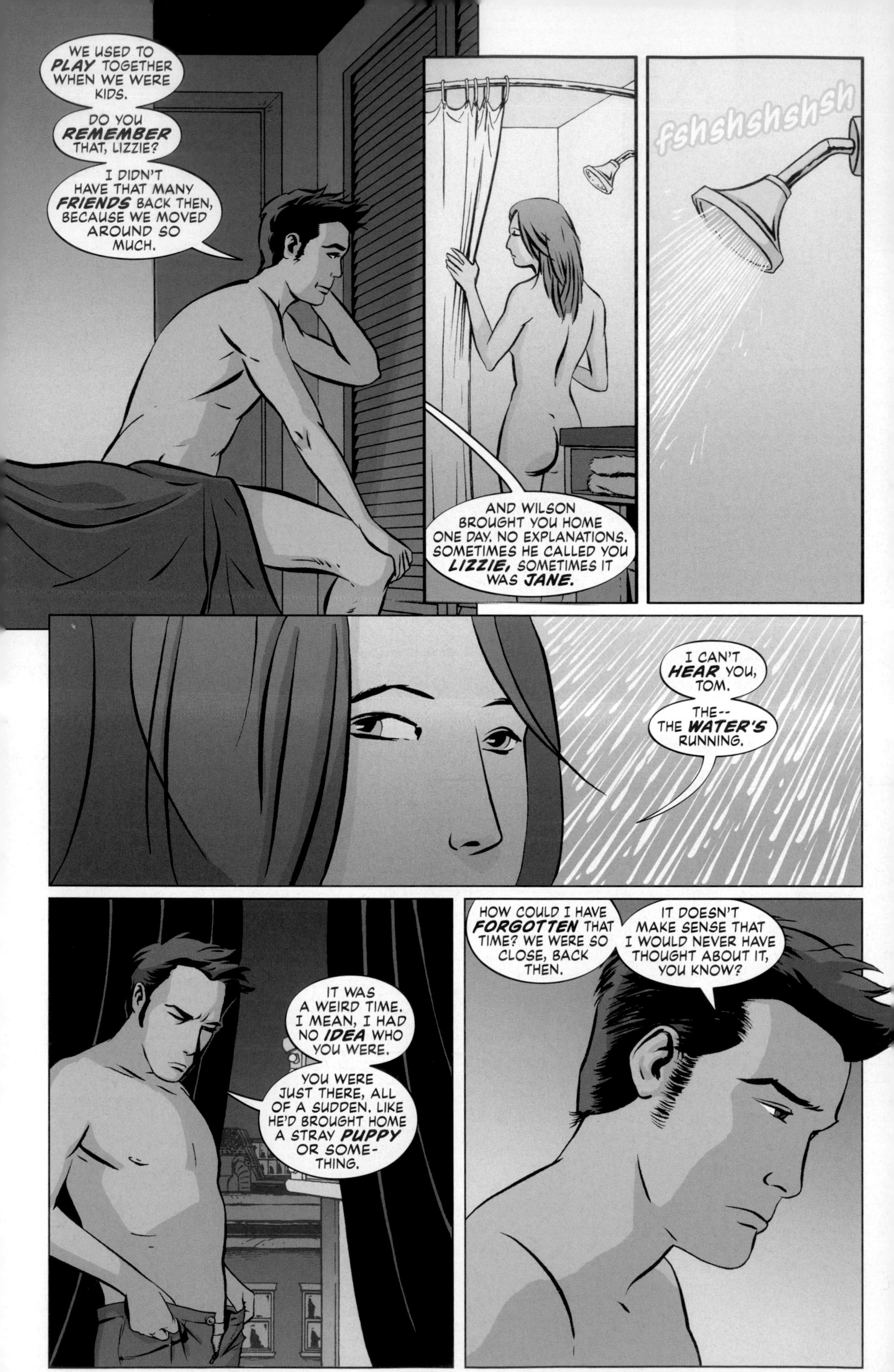
WE USED TO PLAY TOGETHER WHEN WE WERE KIDS.
DO YOU REMEMBER THAT, LIZZIE?
I DIDN'T HAVE THAT MANY FRIENDS BACK THEN, BECAUSE WE MOVED AROUND SO MUCH.
AND WILSON BROUGHT YOU HOME ONE DAY. NO EXPLANATIONS. SOMETIMES HE CALLED YOU LIZZIE, SOMETIMES IT WAS JANE.
fshshshshsh
I CAN'T HEAR YOU, TOM.
THE-- THE WATER'S RUNNING.
IT WAS A WEIRD TIME. I MEAN, I HAD NO IDEA WHO YOU WERE.
YOU WERE JUST THERE, ALL OF A SUDDEN. LIKE HE'D BROUGHT HOME A STRAY PUPPY OR SOMETHING.
HOW COULD I HAVE FORGOTTEN THAT TIME? WE WERE SO CLOSE, BACK THEN.
IT DOESN'T MAKE SENSE THAT I WOULD NEVER HAVE THOUGHT ABOUT IT, YOU KNOW?

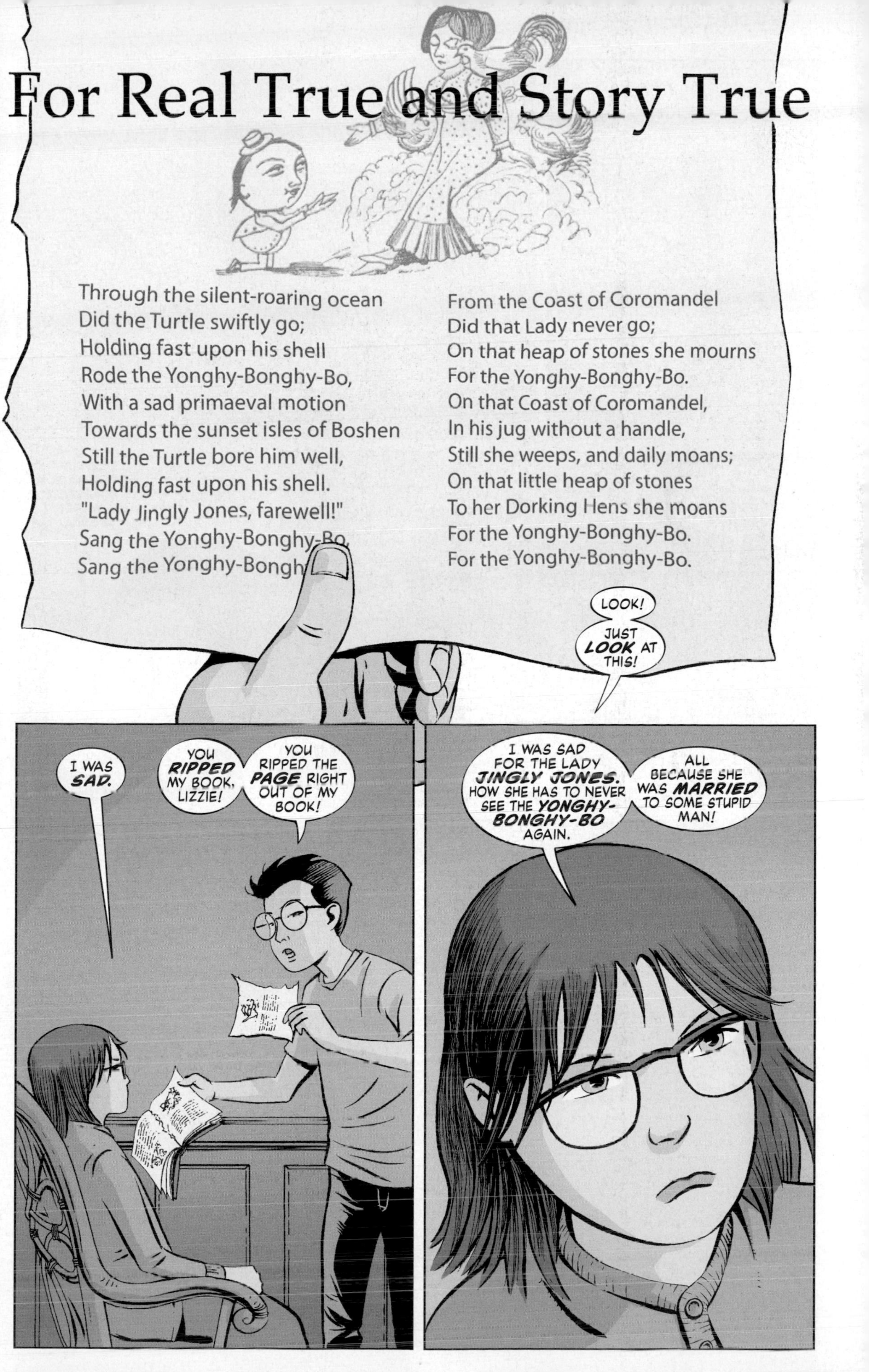
For Real True and Story True
Through the silent-roaring ocean
Did the Turtle swiftly go;
Holding fast upon his shell
Rode the Yonghy-Bonghy-Bo,
With a sad primaeval motion
Towards the sunset isles of Boshen
Still the Turtle bore him well,
Holding fast upon his shell.
"Lady Jingly Jones, farewell!"
Sang the Yonghy-Bonghy-Bo,
Sang the Yonghy-Bongh
From the Coast of Coromandel
Did that Lady never go;
On that heap of stones she mourns
For the Yonghy-Bonghy-Bo.
On that Coast of Coromandel,
In his jug without a handle,
Still she weeps, and daily moans;
On that little heap of stones
To her Dorking Hens she moans
For the Yonghy-Bonghy-Bo.
For the Yonghy-Bonghy-Bo.
LOOK!
JUST LOOK AT THIS!
YOU RIPPED MY BOOK, LIZZIE!
YOU RIPPED THE PAGE RIGHT OUT OF MY BOOK!
I WAS SAD.
I WAS SAD FOR THE LADY JINGLY JONES. HOW SHE HAS TO NEVER SEE THE YONGHY-BONGHY-BO AGAIN.
ALL BECAUSE SHE WAS MARRIED TO SOME STUPID MAN!

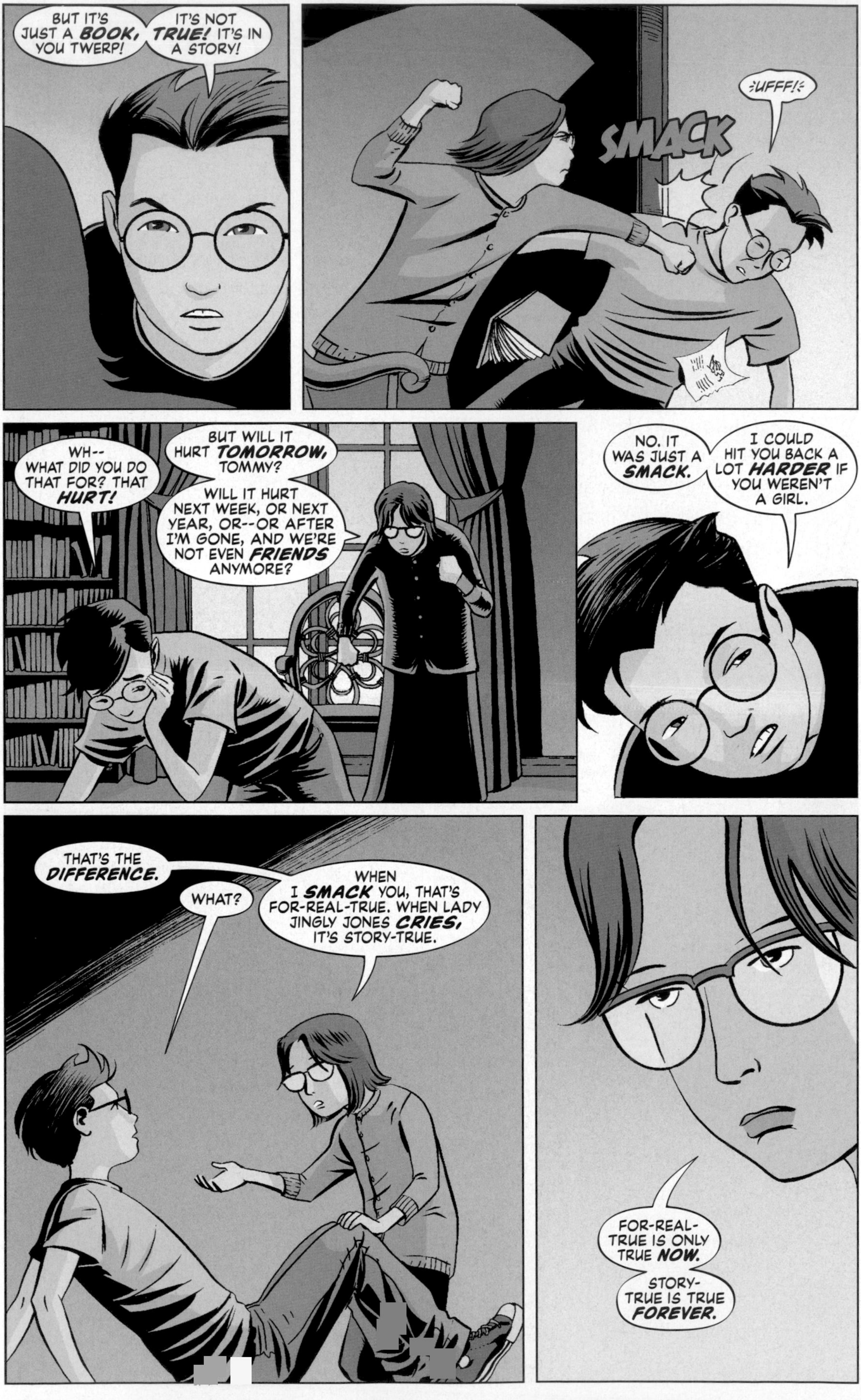
BUT IT'S JUST A BOOK, YOU TWERP!
IT'S NOT TRUE! IT'S IN A STORY!
UFFF!
SMACK
WH-- WHAT DID YOU DO THAT FOR? THAT HURT!
BUT WILL IT HURT TOMORROW, TOMMY?
WILL IT HURT NEXT WEEK, OR NEXT YEAR, OR--OR AFTER I'M GONE, AND WE'RE NOT EVEN FRIENDS ANYMORE?
NO. IT WAS JUST A SMACK.
I COULD HIT YOU BACK A LOT HARDER IF YOU WEREN'T A GIRL.
THAT'S THE DIFFERENCE.
WHAT?
WHEN I SMACK YOU, THAT'S FOR-REAL-TRUE. WHEN LADY JINGLY JONES CRIES, IT'S STORY-TRUE.
FOR-REAL-TRUE IS ONLY TRUE NOW.
STORY-TRUE IS TRUE FOREVER.

# Thar She Blows

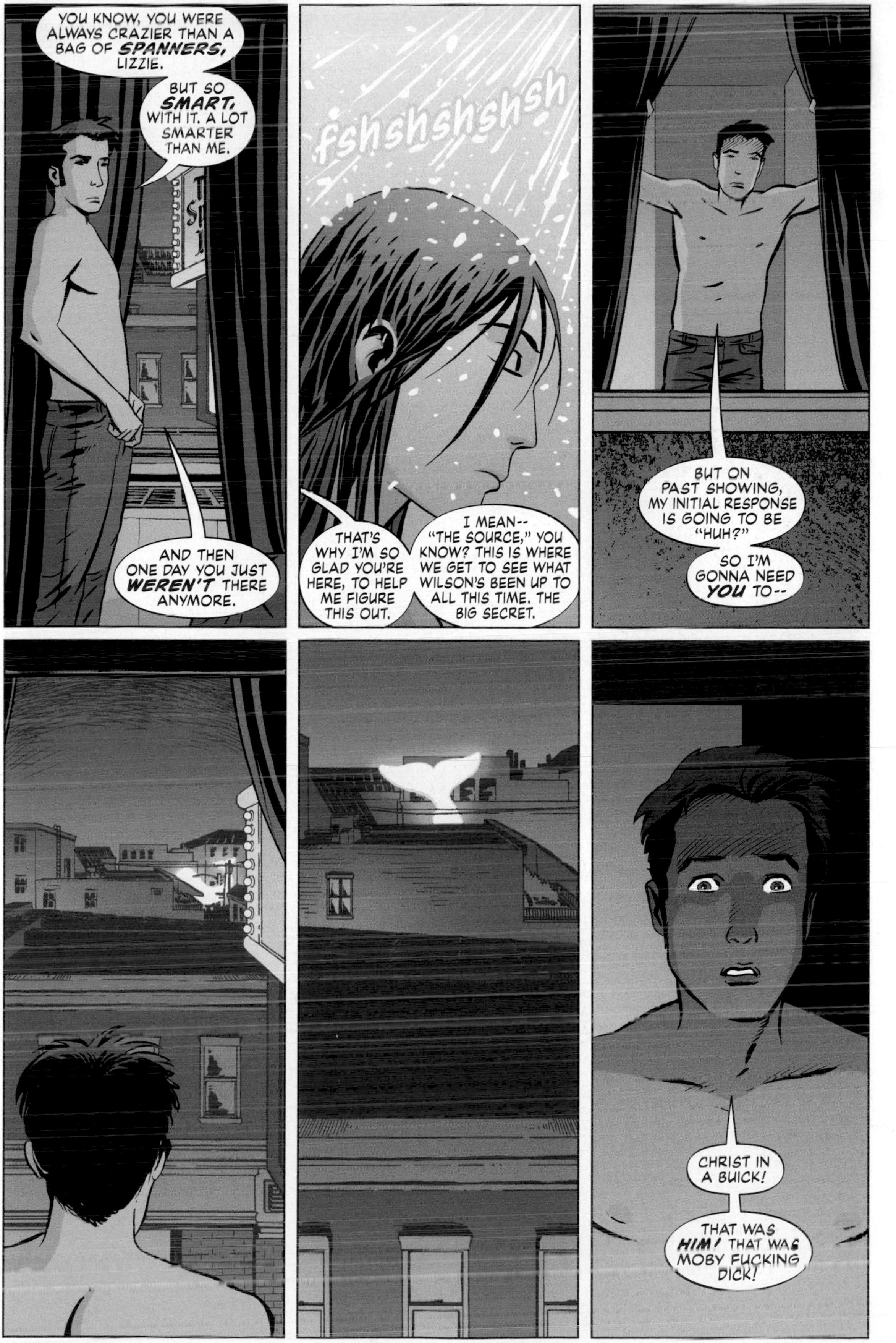
YOU KNOW, YOU WERE ALWAYS CRAZIER THAN A BAG OF SPANNERS, LIZZIE.
BUT SO SMART, WITH IT. A LOT SMARTER THAN ME.
AND THEN ONE DAY YOU JUST WEREN'T THERE ANYMORE.
fshshshshsh
THAT'S WHY I'M SO GLAD YOU'RE HERE, TO HELP ME FIGURE THIS OUT.
I MEAN-- "THE SOURCE," YOU KNOW? THIS IS WHERE WE GET TO SEE WHAT WILSON'S BEEN UP TO ALL THIS TIME. THE BIG SECRET.
BUT ON PAST SHOWING, MY INITIAL RESPONSE IS GOING TO BE "HUH?"
SO I'M GONNA NEED YOU TO--
CHRIST IN A BUICK!
THAT WAS HIM! THAT WAS MOBY FUCKING DICK!

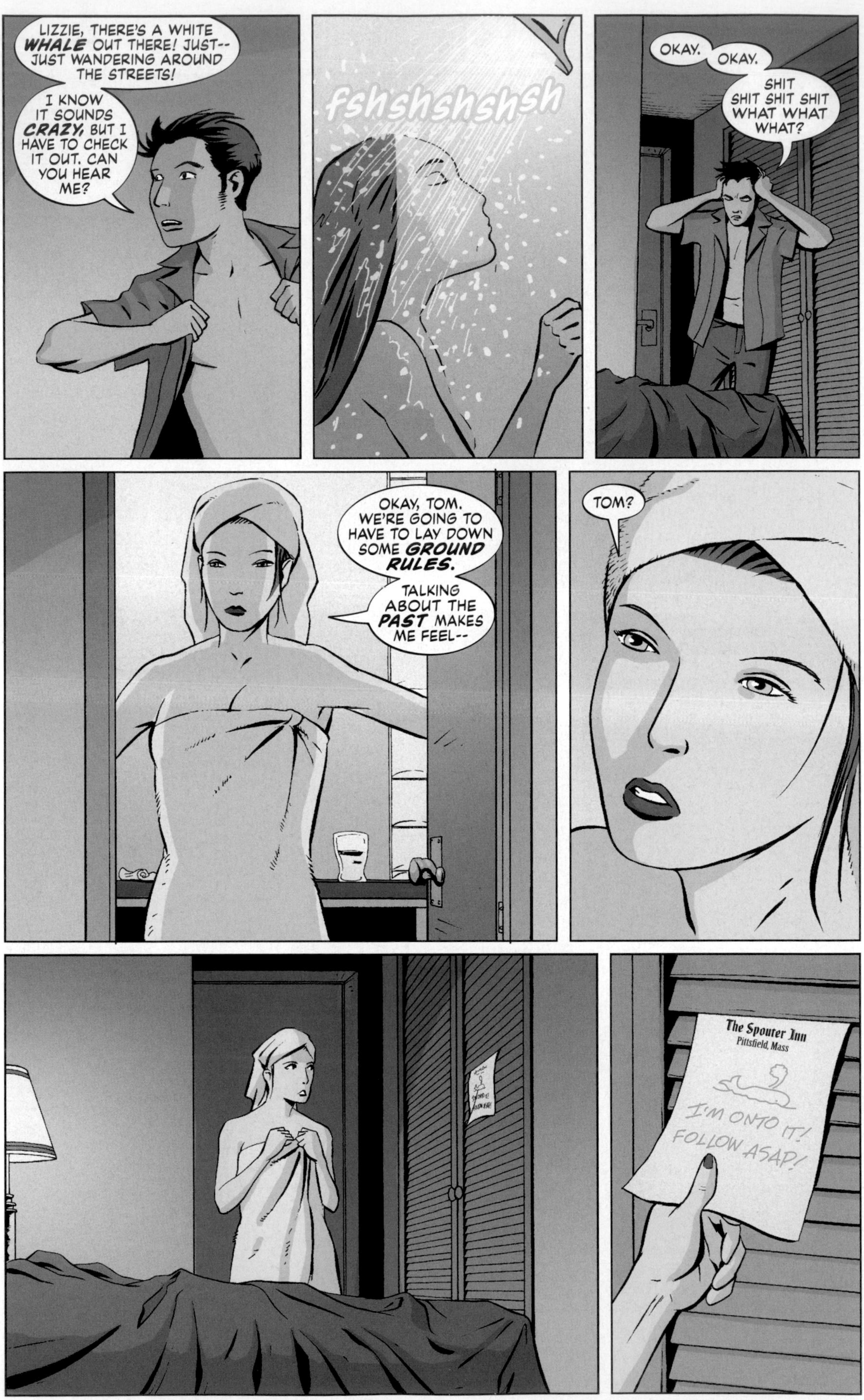
LIZZIE, THERE'S A WHITE WHALE OUT THERE! JUST--JUST WANDERING AROUND THE STREETS!
I KNOW IT SOUNDS CRAZY, BUT I HAVE TO CHECK IT OUT. CAN YOU HEAR ME?
fshshshshshsh
OKAY.
OKAY.
SHIT SHIT SHIT SHIT WHAT WHAT WHAT?
OKAY, TOM. WE'RE GOING TO HAVE TO LAY DOWN SOME GROUND RULES.
TALKING ABOUT THE PAST MAKES ME FEEL--
TOM?
The Spouter Inn
Pittsfield, Mass
I'M ONTO IT! FOLLOW ASAP!

# Very Like A Whale

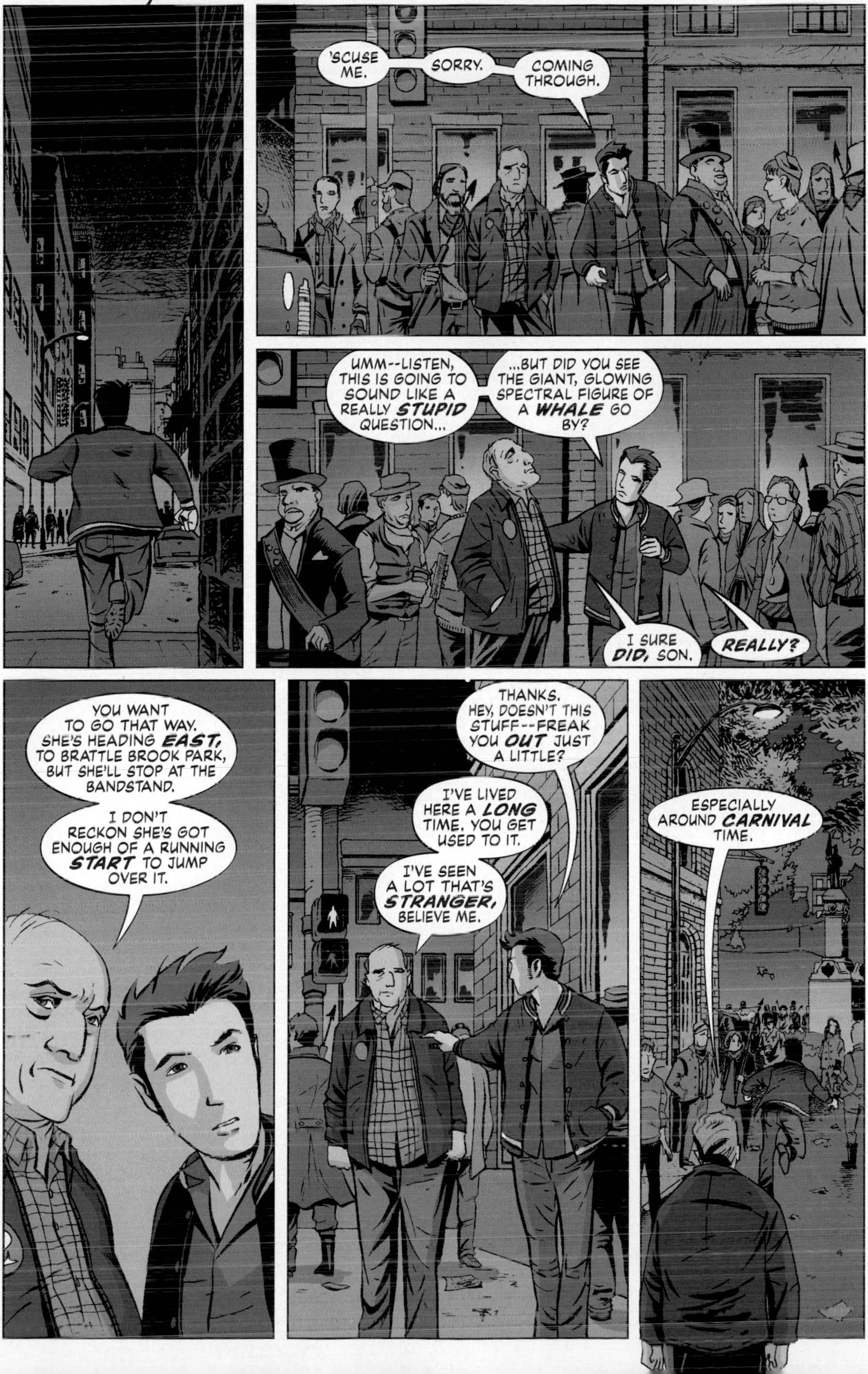

'SCUSE ME.
SORRY.
COMING THROUGH.
UMM--LISTEN, THIS IS GOING TO SOUND LIKE A REALLY STUPID QUESTION...
...BUT DID YOU SEE THE GIANT, GLOWING SPECTRAL FIGURE OF A WHALE GO BY?
I SURE DID, SON.
REALLY?
YOU WANT TO GO THAT WAY. SHE'S HEADING EAST, TO BRATTLE BROOK PARK, BUT SHE'LL STOP AT THE BANDSTAND.
I DON'T RECKON SHE'S GOT ENOUGH OF A RUNNING START TO JUMP OVER IT.
THANKS. HEY, DOESN'T THIS STUFF--FREAK YOU OUT JUST A LITTLE?
I'VE LIVED HERE A LONG TIME. YOU GET USED TO IT.
I'VE SEEN A LOT THAT'S STRANGER, BELIEVE ME.
ESPECIALLY AROUND CARNIVAL TIME.

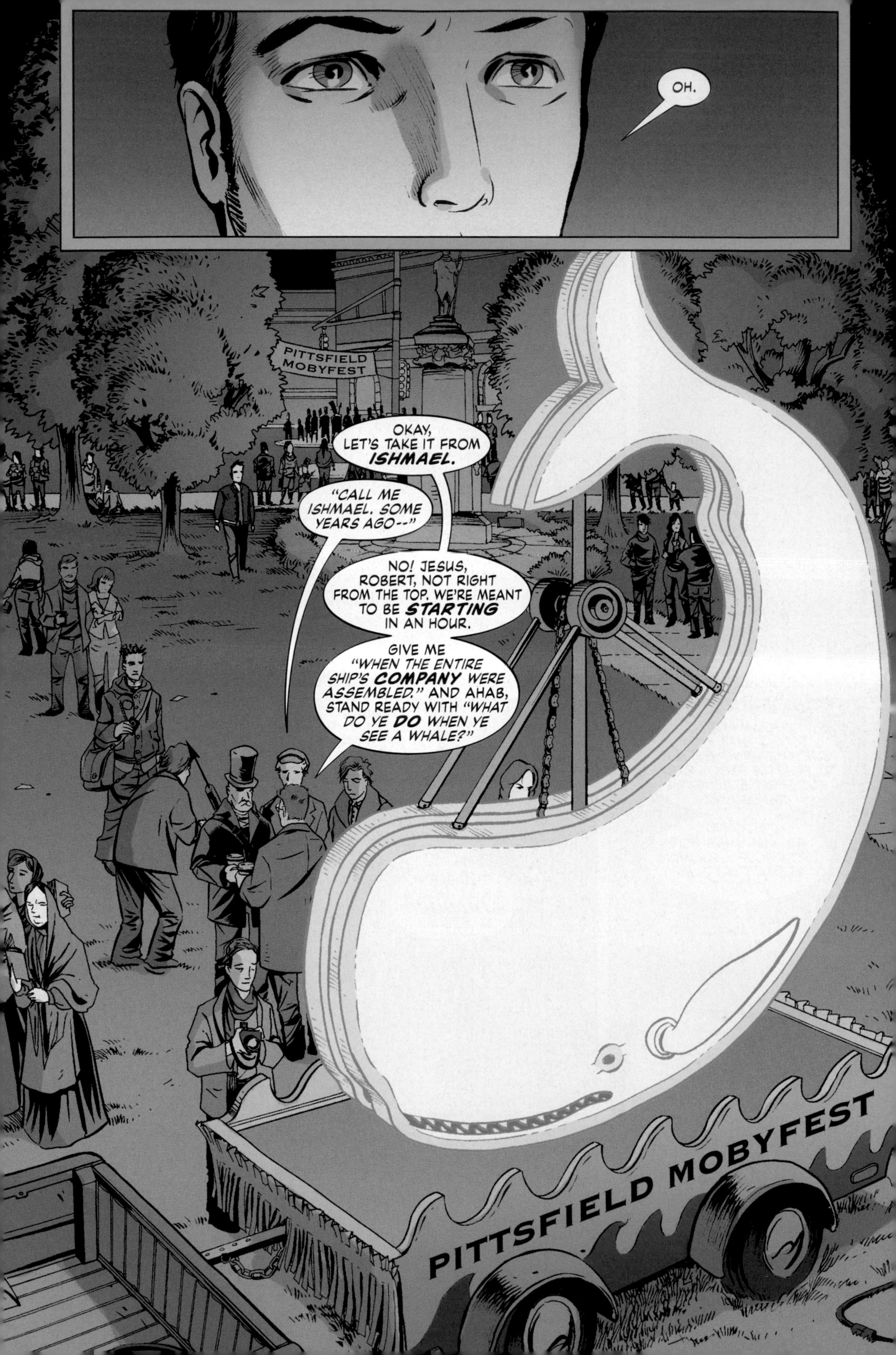
OH.
PITTSFIELD MOBYFEST
OKAY, LET'S TAKE IT FROM *ISHMAEL.*
"CALL ME ISHMAEL. SOME YEARS AGO--"
NO! JESUS, ROBERT, NOT RIGHT FROM THE TOP. WE'RE MEANT TO BE *STARTING* IN AN HOUR.
GIVE ME "WHEN THE ENTIRE SHIP'S **COMPANY** WERE ASSEMBLED," AND AHAB, STAND READY WITH "WHAT DO YE **DO** WHEN YE SEE A WHALE?"
PITTSFIELD MOBYFEST

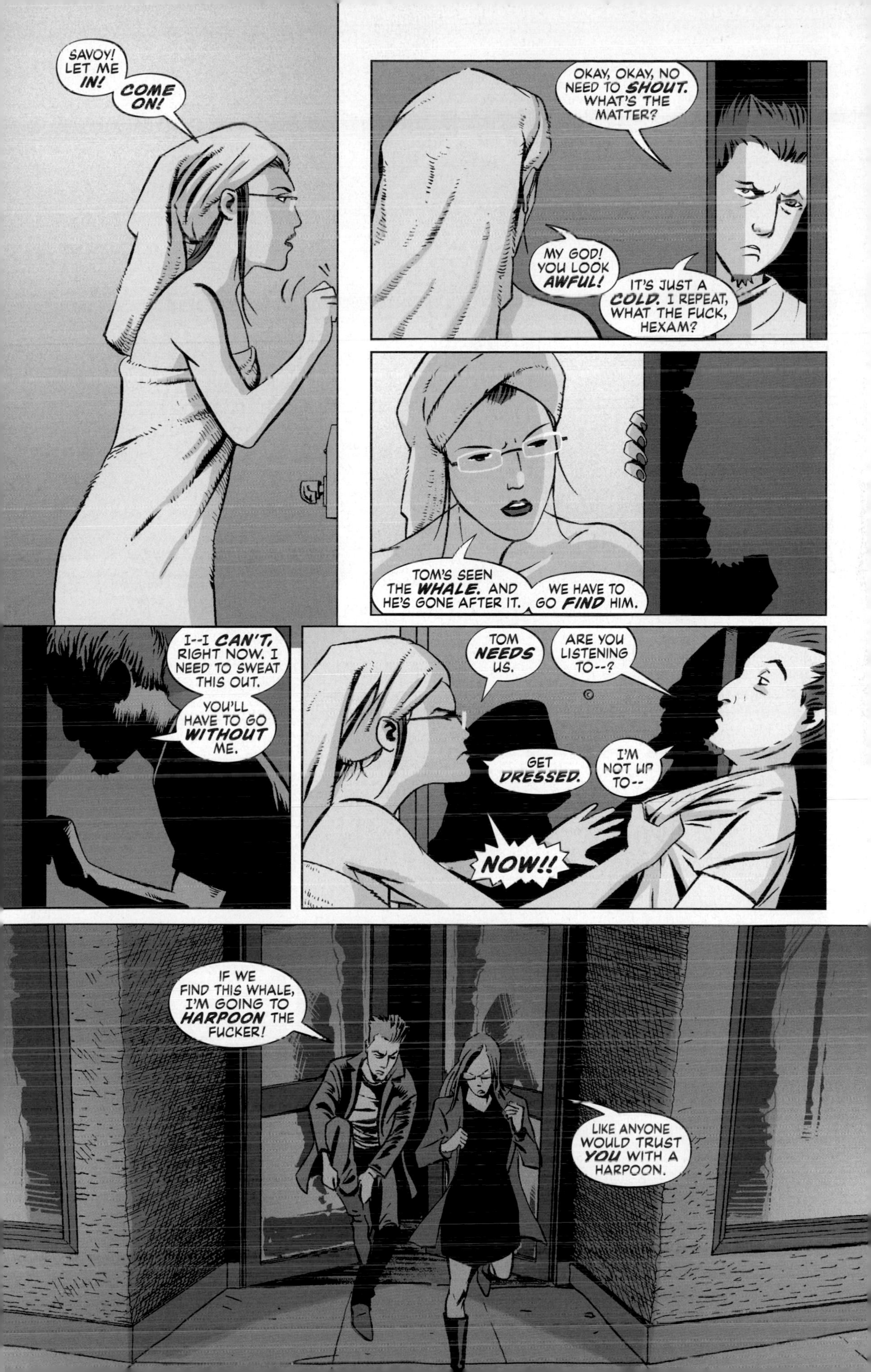
SAVOY! LET ME IN!
COME ON!
OKAY, OKAY, NO NEED TO SHOUT. WHAT'S THE MATTER?
MY GOD! YOU LOOK AWFUL!
IT'S JUST A COLD. I REPEAT, WHAT THE FUCK, HEXAM?
TOM'S SEEN THE WHALE. AND HE'S GONE AFTER IT.
WE HAVE TO GO FIND HIM.
I--I CAN'T, RIGHT NOW. I NEED TO SWEAT THIS OUT.
YOU'LL HAVE TO GO WITHOUT ME.
TOM NEEDS US.
ARE YOU LISTENING TO--?
GET DRESSED.
I'M NOT UP TO--
NOW!!
IF WE FIND THIS WHALE, I'M GOING TO HARPOON THE FUCKER!
LIKE ANYONE WOULD TRUST YOU WITH A HARPOON.

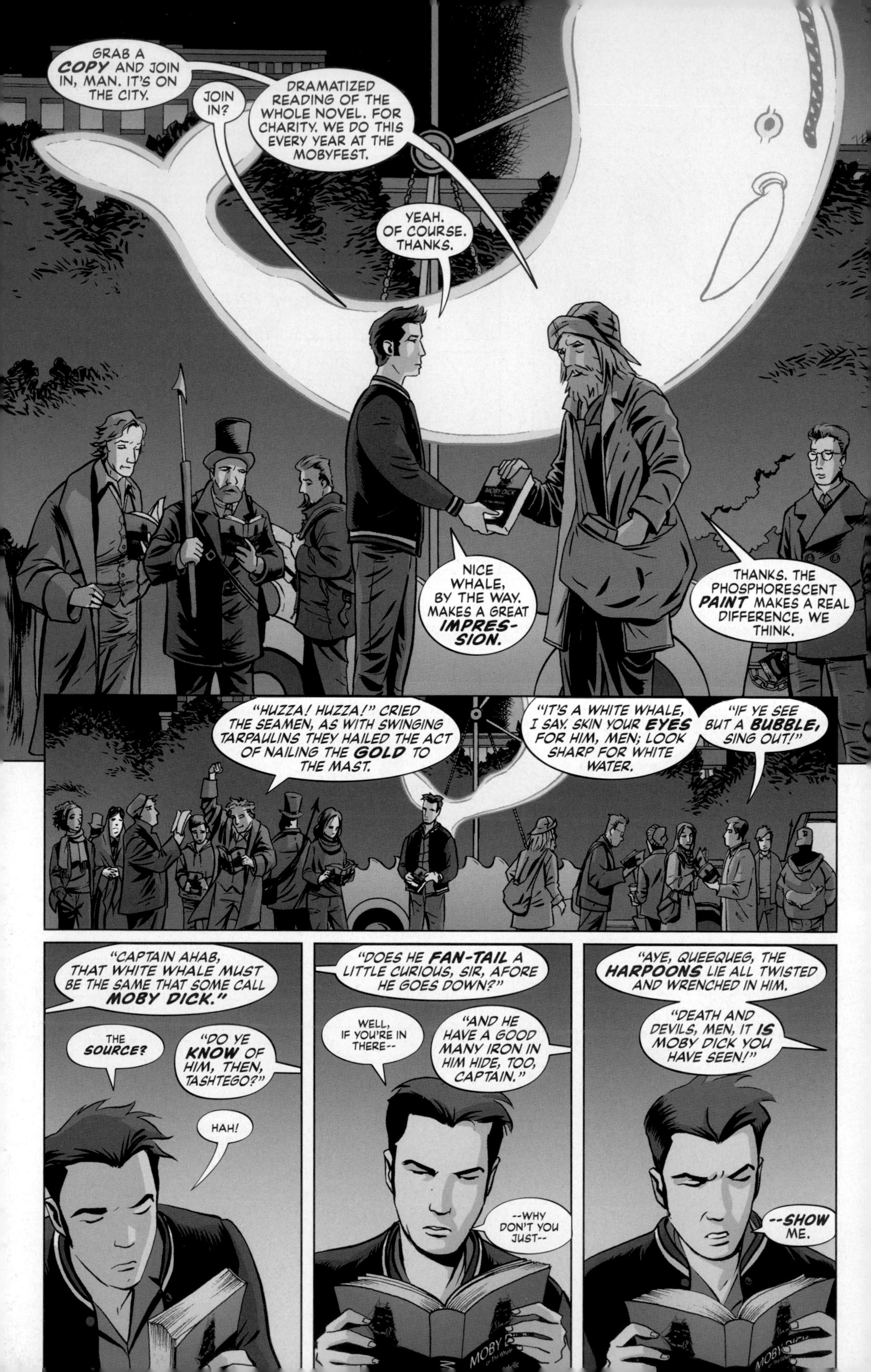

GRAB A COPY AND JOIN IN, MAN. IT'S ON THE CITY.
JOIN IN?
DRAMATIZED READING OF THE WHOLE NOVEL. FOR CHARITY. WE DO THIS EVERY YEAR AT THE MOBYFEST.
YEAH. OF COURSE. THANKS.
MOBY DICK
NICE WHALE, BY THE WAY. MAKES A GREAT IMPRESSION.
THANKS. THE PHOSPHORESCENT PAINT MAKES A REAL DIFFERENCE, WE THINK.
"HUZZA! HUZZA!" CRIED THE SEAMEN, AS WITH SWINGING TARPAULINS THEY HAILED THE ACT OF NAILING THE GOLD TO THE MAST.
"IT'S A WHITE WHALE, I SAY. SKIN YOUR EYES FOR HIM, MEN; LOOK SHARP FOR WHITE WATER.
"IF YE SEE BUT A BUBBLE, SING OUT!"
"CAPTAIN AHAB, THAT WHITE WHALE MUST BE THE SAME THAT SOME CALL MOBY DICK."
THE SOURCE?
"DO YE KNOW OF HIM, THEN, TASHTEGO?"
HAH!
"DOES HE FAN-TAIL A LITTLE CURIOUS, SIR, AFORE HE GOES DOWN?"
WELL, IF YOU'RE IN THERE--
"AND HE HAVE A GOOD MANY IRON IN HIM HIDE, TOO, CAPTAIN."
--WHY DON'T YOU JUST--
"AYE, QUEEQUEG, THE HARPOONS LIE ALL TWISTED AND WRENCHED IN HIM.
"DEATH AND DEVILS, MEN, IT IS MOBY DICK YOU HAVE SEEN!"
--SHOW ME.

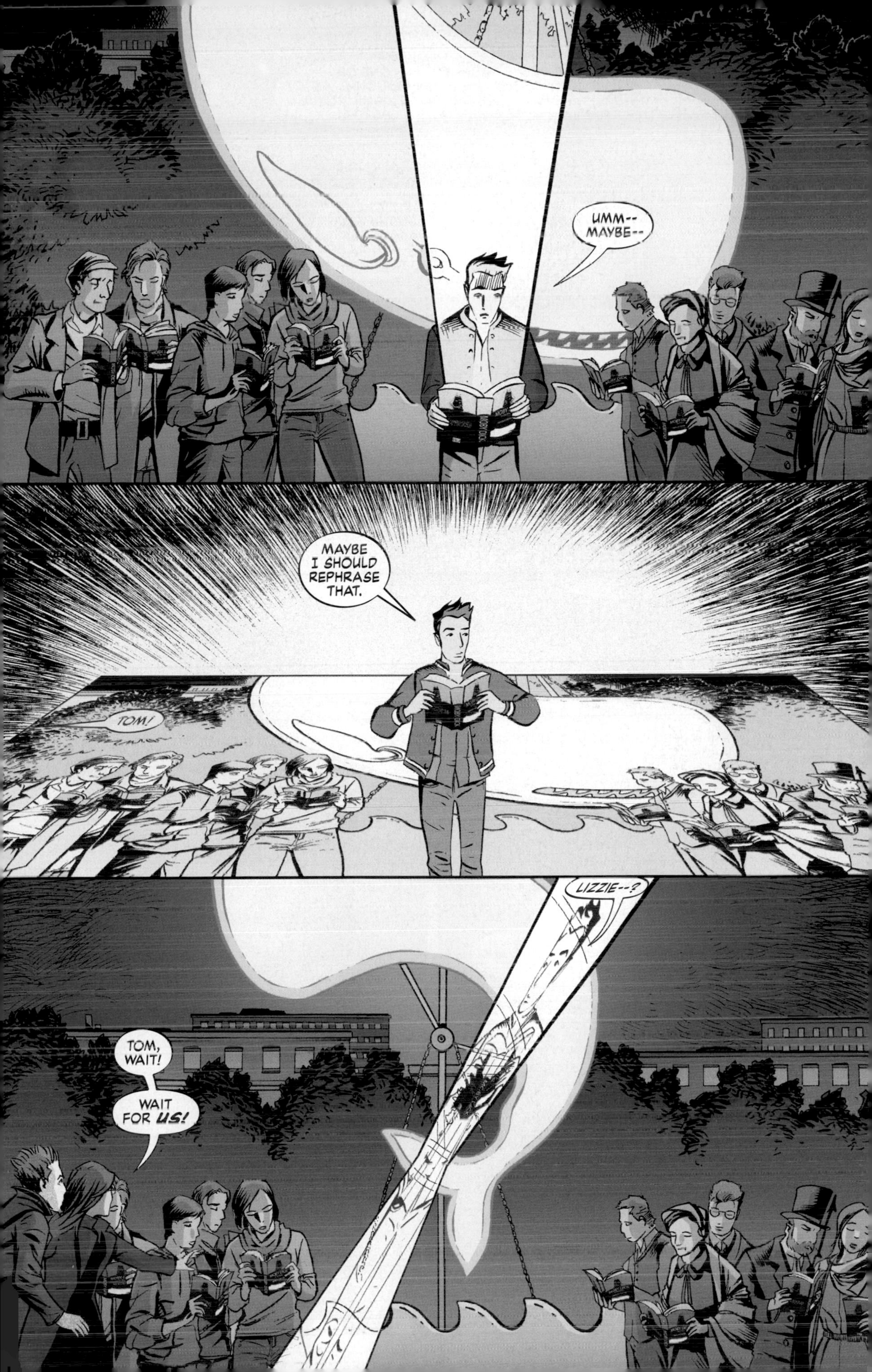
UMM-- MAYBE--
MAYBE I SHOULD REPHRASE THAT.
TOM!
LIZZIE--?
TOM, WAIT!
WAIT FOR US!

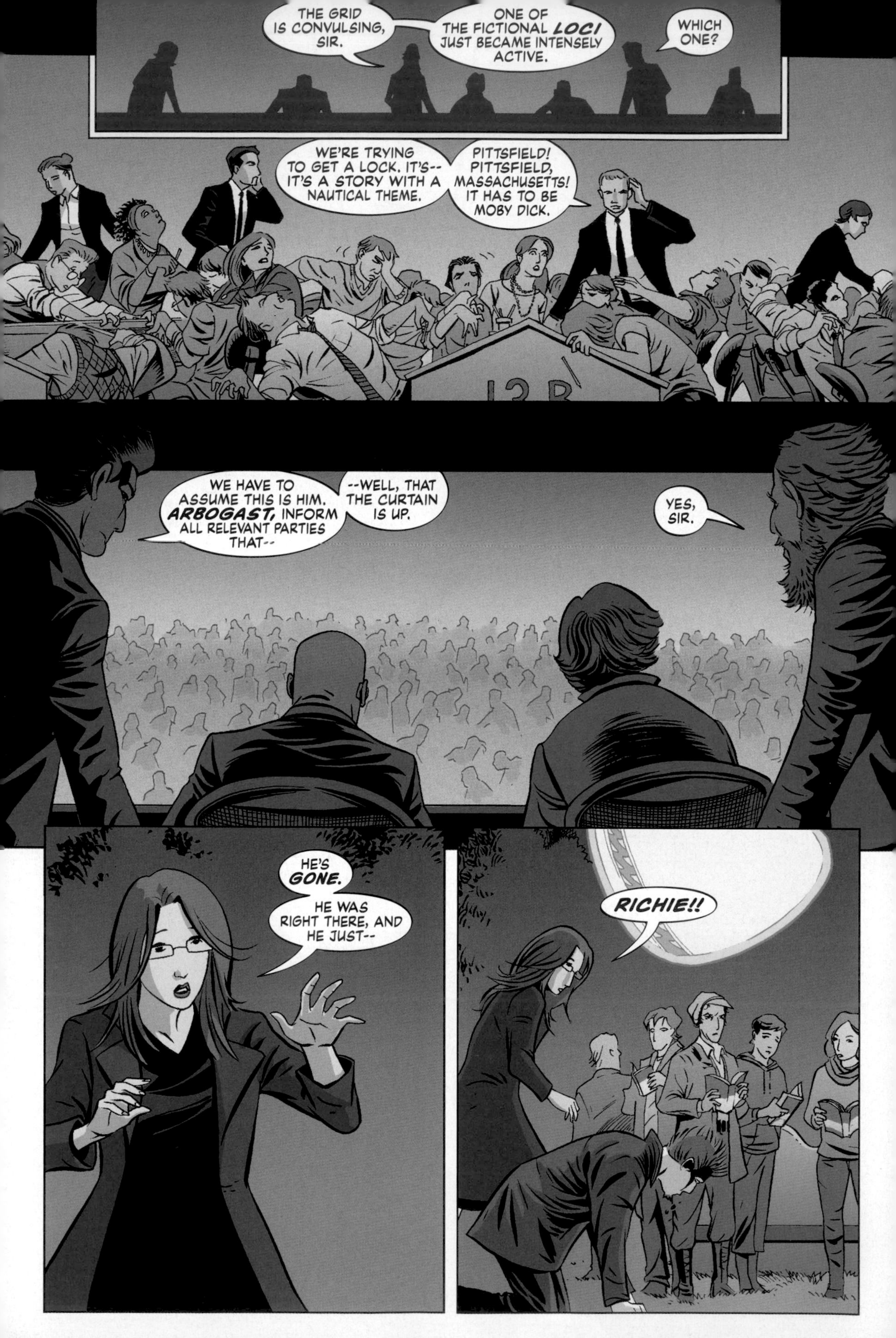
THE GRID IS CONVULSING, SIR.
ONE OF THE FICTIONAL LOCI JUST BECAME INTENSELY ACTIVE.
WHICH ONE?
WE'RE TRYING TO GET A LOCK. IT'S-- IT'S A STORY WITH A NAUTICAL THEME.
PITTSFIELD! PITTSFIELD, MASSACHUSETTS! IT HAS TO BE MOBY DICK.
12 B
WE HAVE TO ASSUME THIS IS HIM. ARBOGAST, INFORM ALL RELEVANT PARTIES THAT--
--WELL, THAT THE CURTAIN IS UP.
YES, SIR.
HE'S GONE.
HE WAS RIGHT THERE, AND HE JUST--
RICHIE!!

# String Theory

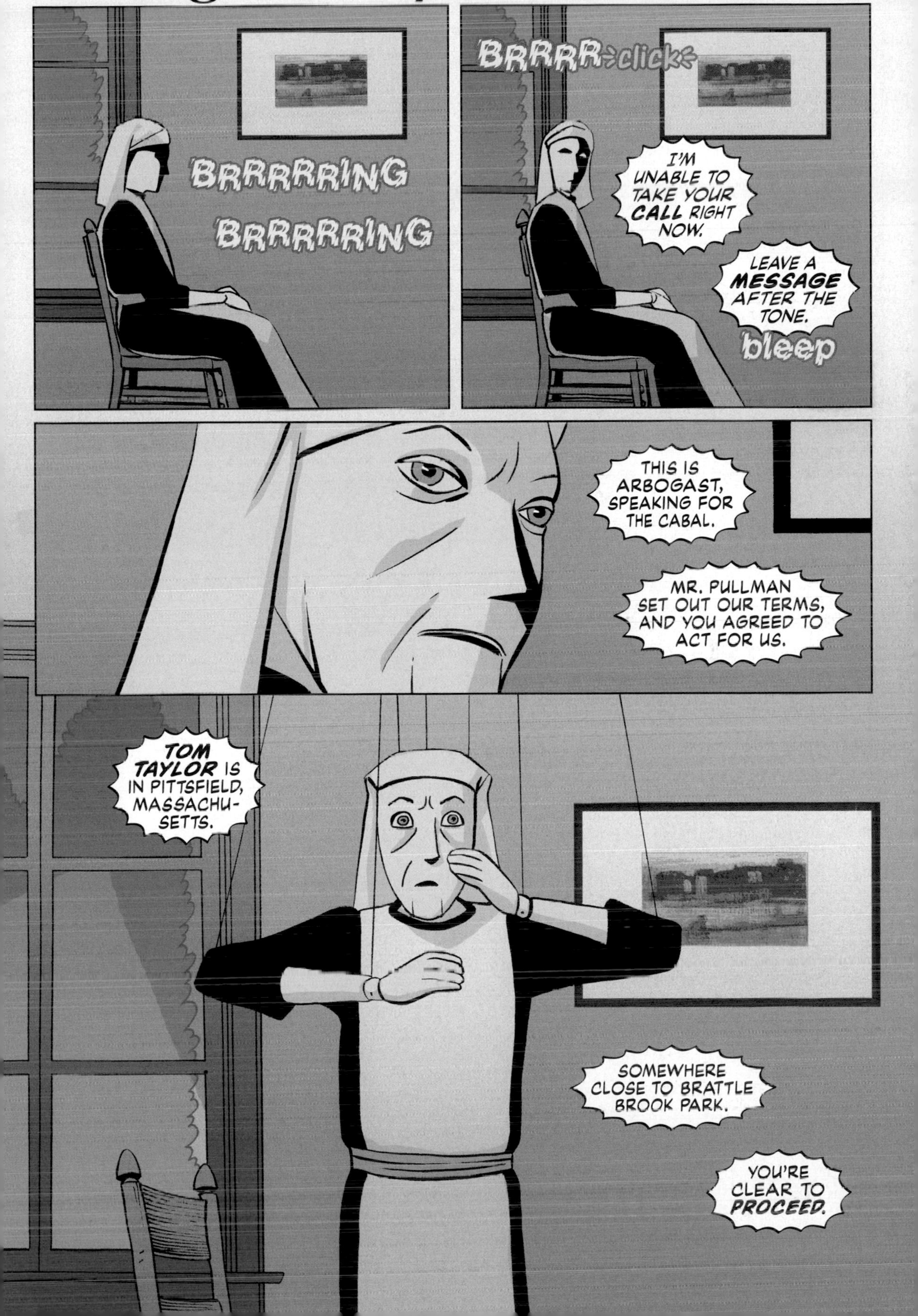
BRRRRRING
BRRRRRING
BRRRR-click
I'M UNABLE TO TAKE YOUR CALL RIGHT NOW.
LEAVE A MESSAGE AFTER THE TONE.
bleep
THIS IS ARBOGAST, SPEAKING FOR THE CABAL.
MR. PULLMAN SET OUT OUR TERMS, AND YOU AGREED TO ACT FOR US.
TOM TAYLOR IS IN PITTSFIELD, MASSACHU-SETTS.
SOMEWHERE CLOSE TO BRATTLE BROOK PARK.
YOU'RE CLEAR TO PROCEED.

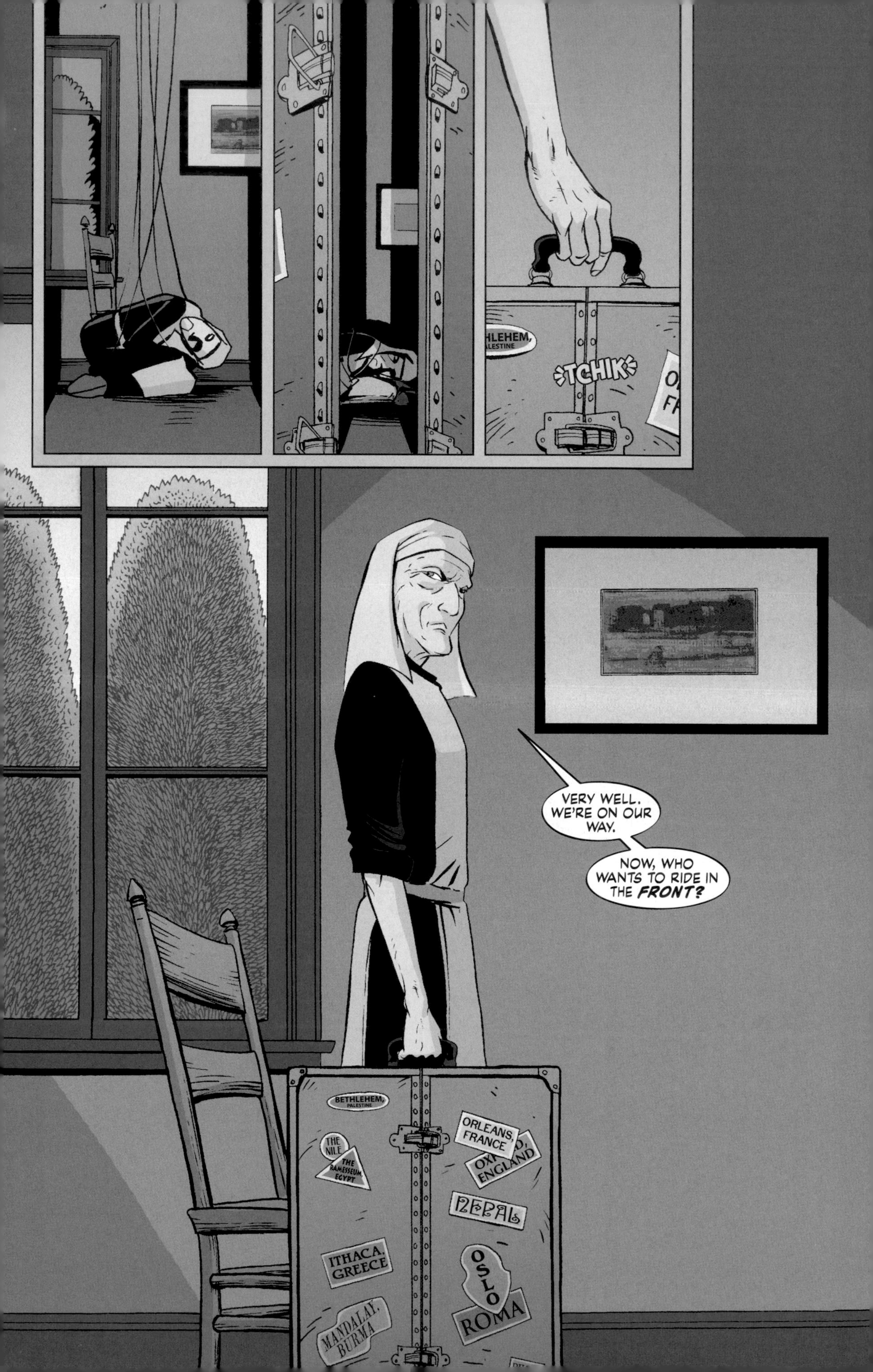

BETHLEHEM, PALESTINE
TCHIK
VERY WELL. WE'RE ON OUR WAY.
NOW, WHO WANTS TO RIDE IN THE *FRONT?*
BETHLEHEM, PALESTINE
ORLEANS, FRANCE
THE NILE
THE RAMESSEUM, EGYPT
ENGLAND
NEPAL
ITHACA, GREECE
OSLO
ROMA
MANDALAY, BURMA

# Call Him Ishmael

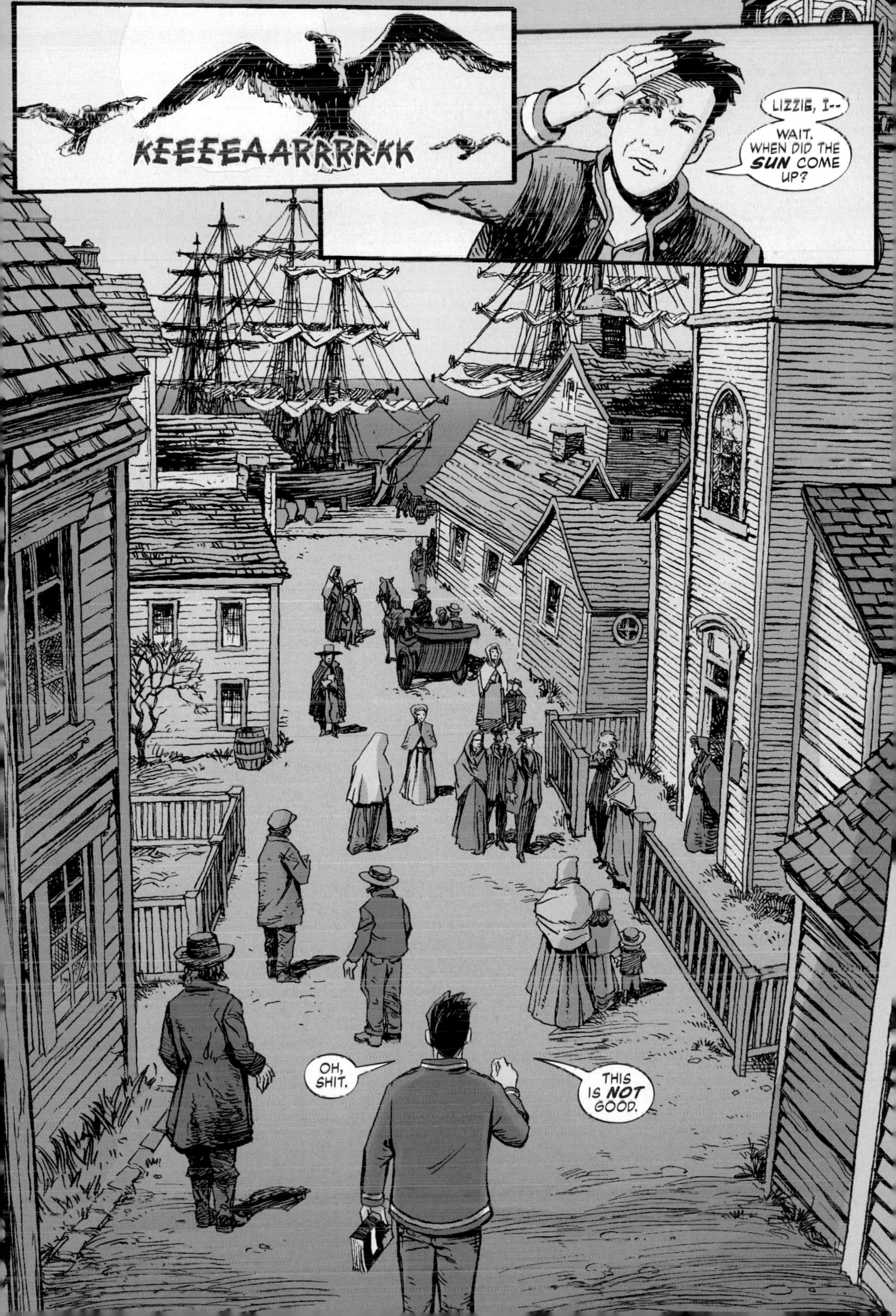
KEEEEAARRRRKK
LIZZIE, I--
WAIT. WHEN DID THE SUN COME UP?
OH, SHIT.
THIS IS NOT GOOD.

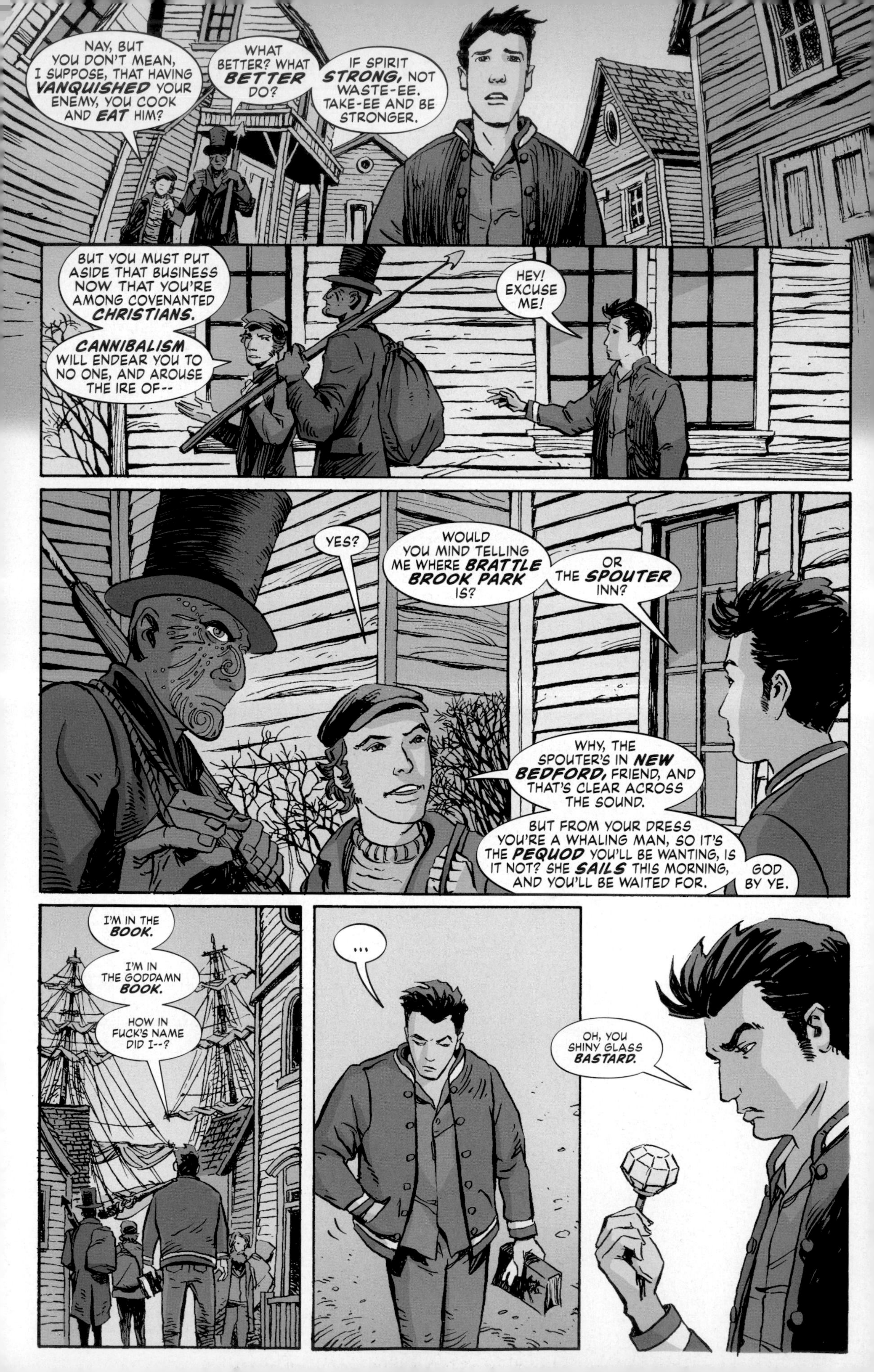
NAY, BUT YOU DON'T MEAN, I SUPPOSE, THAT HAVING VANQUISHED YOUR ENEMY, YOU COOK AND EAT HIM?
WHAT BETTER? WHAT BETTER DO?
IF SPIRIT STRONG, NOT WASTE-EE. TAKE-EE AND BE STRONGER.
BUT YOU MUST PUT ASIDE THAT BUSINESS NOW THAT YOU'RE AMONG COVENANTED CHRISTIANS.
CANNIBALISM WILL ENDEAR YOU TO NO ONE, AND AROUSE THE IRE OF--
HEY! EXCUSE ME!
YES?
WOULD YOU MIND TELLING ME WHERE BRATTLE BROOK PARK IS?
OR THE SPOUTER INN?
WHY, THE SPOUTER'S IN NEW BEDFORD, FRIEND, AND THAT'S CLEAR ACROSS THE SOUND.
BUT FROM YOUR DRESS YOU'RE A WHALING MAN, SO IT'S THE PEQUOD YOU'LL BE WANTING, IS IT NOT? SHE SAILS THIS MORNING, AND YOU'LL BE WAITED FOR.
GOD BY YE.
I'M IN THE BOOK.
I'M IN THE GODDAMN BOOK.
HOW IN FUCK'S NAME DID I--?
...
OH, YOU SHINY GLASS BASTARD.

# Vampire State of Mind

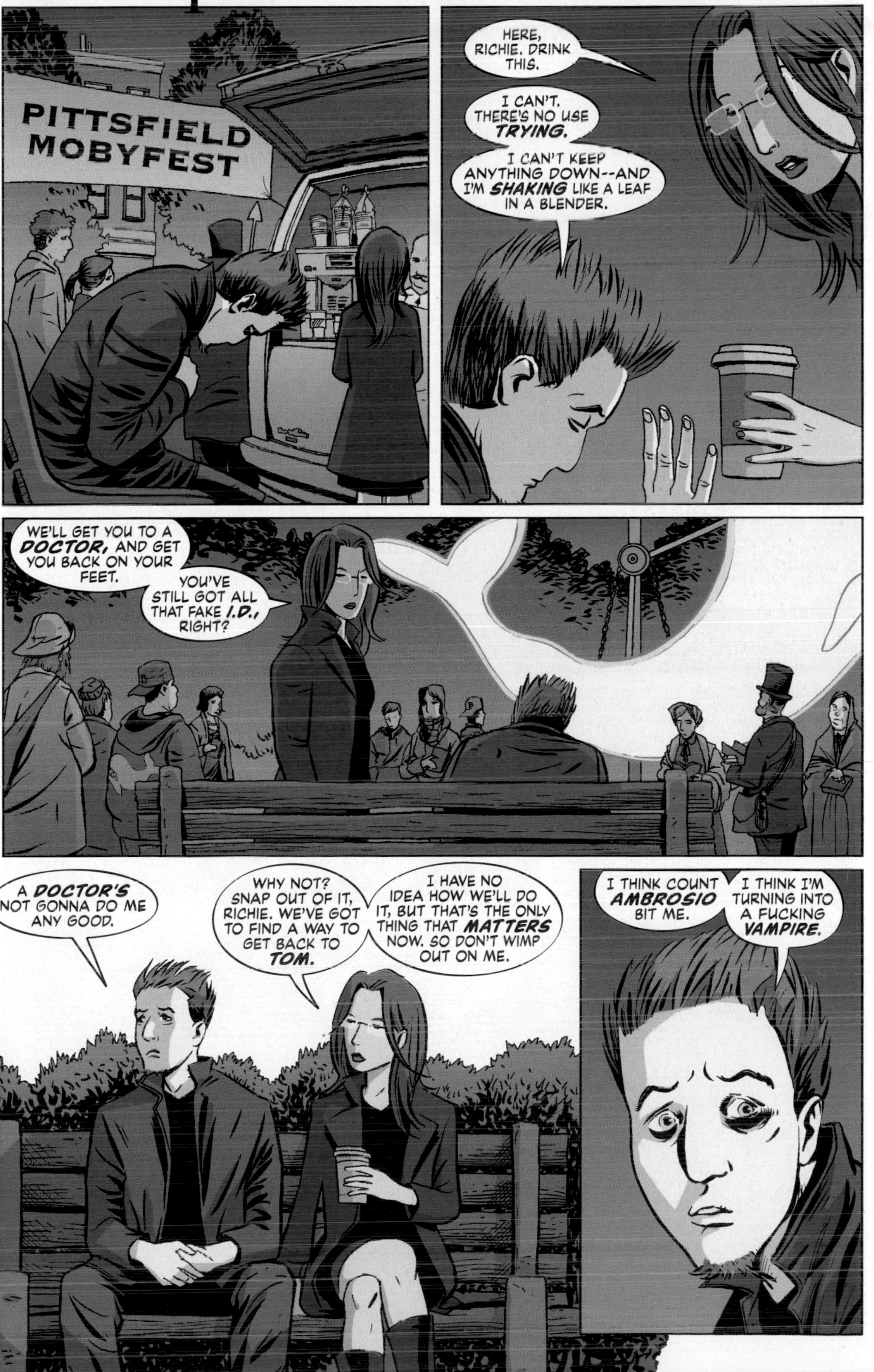

PITTSFIELD MOBYFEST
HERE, RICHIE. DRINK THIS.
I CAN'T. THERE'S NO USE TRYING.
I CAN'T KEEP ANYTHING DOWN--AND I'M SHAKING LIKE A LEAF IN A BLENDER.
WE'LL GET YOU TO A DOCTOR, AND GET YOU BACK ON YOUR FEET.
YOU'VE STILL GOT ALL THAT FAKE I.D., RIGHT?
A DOCTOR'S NOT GONNA DO ME ANY GOOD.
WHY NOT? SNAP OUT OF IT, RICHIE. WE'VE GOT TO FIND A WAY TO GET BACK TO TOM.
I HAVE NO IDEA HOW WE'LL DO IT, BUT THAT'S THE ONLY THING THAT MATTERS NOW. SO DON'T WIMP OUT ON ME.
I THINK COUNT AMBROSIO BIT ME.
I THINK I'M TURNING INTO A FUCKING VAMPIRE.

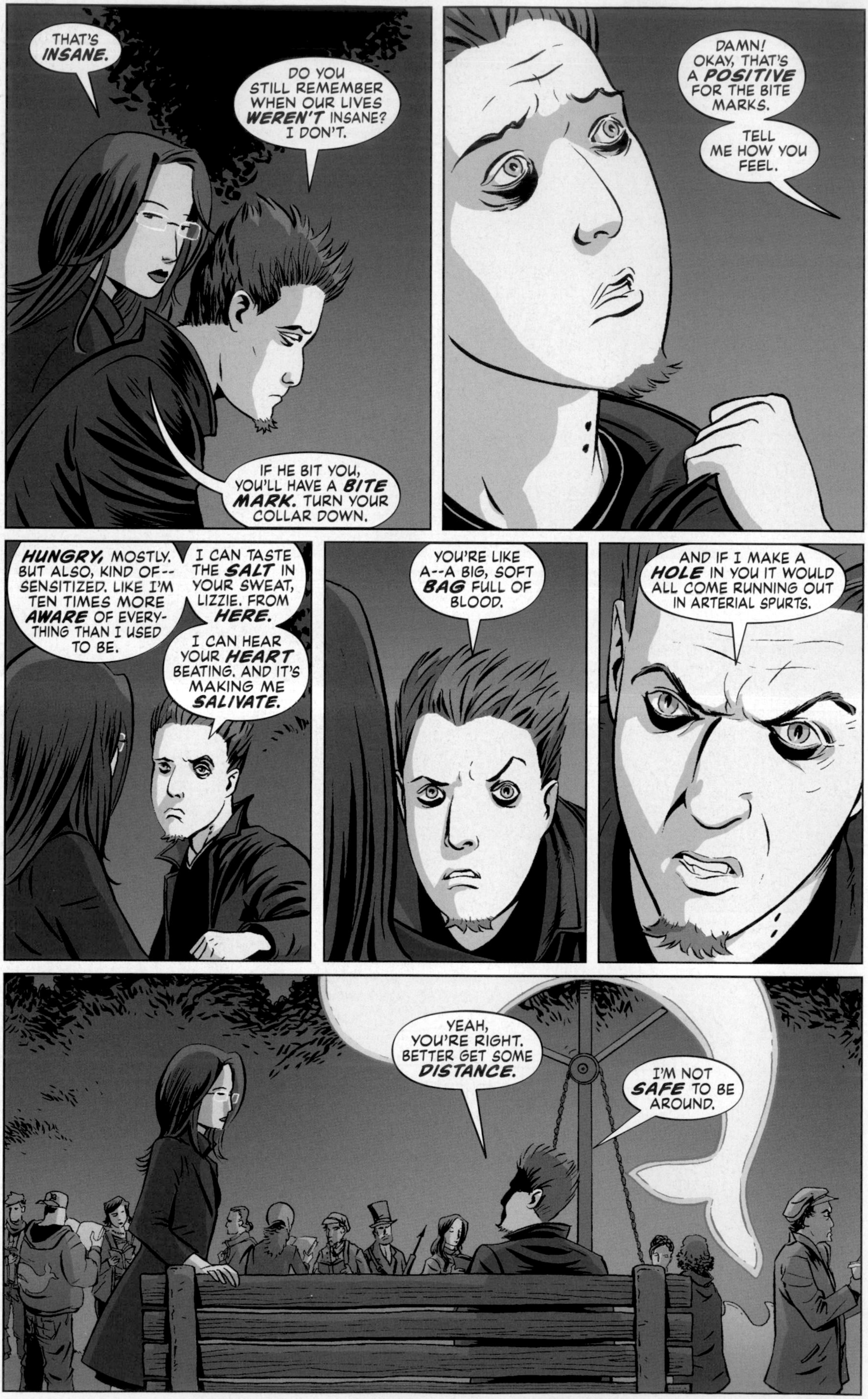
THAT'S INSANE.
DO YOU STILL REMEMBER WHEN OUR LIVES WEREN'T INSANE? I DON'T.
IF HE BIT YOU, YOU'LL HAVE A BITE MARK. TURN YOUR COLLAR DOWN.
DAMN! OKAY, THAT'S A POSITIVE FOR THE BITE MARKS.
TELL ME HOW YOU FEEL.
HUNGRY, MOSTLY. BUT ALSO, KIND OF--SENSITIZED. LIKE I'M TEN TIMES MORE AWARE OF EVERYTHING THAN I USED TO BE.
I CAN TASTE THE SALT IN YOUR SWEAT, LIZZIE. FROM HERE.
I CAN HEAR YOUR HEART BEATING. AND IT'S MAKING ME SALIVATE.
YOU'RE LIKE A--A BIG, SOFT BAG FULL OF BLOOD.
AND IF I MAKE A HOLE IN YOU IT WOULD ALL COME RUNNING OUT IN ARTERIAL SPURTS.
YEAH, YOU'RE RIGHT. BETTER GET SOME DISTANCE.
I'M NOT SAFE TO BE AROUND.

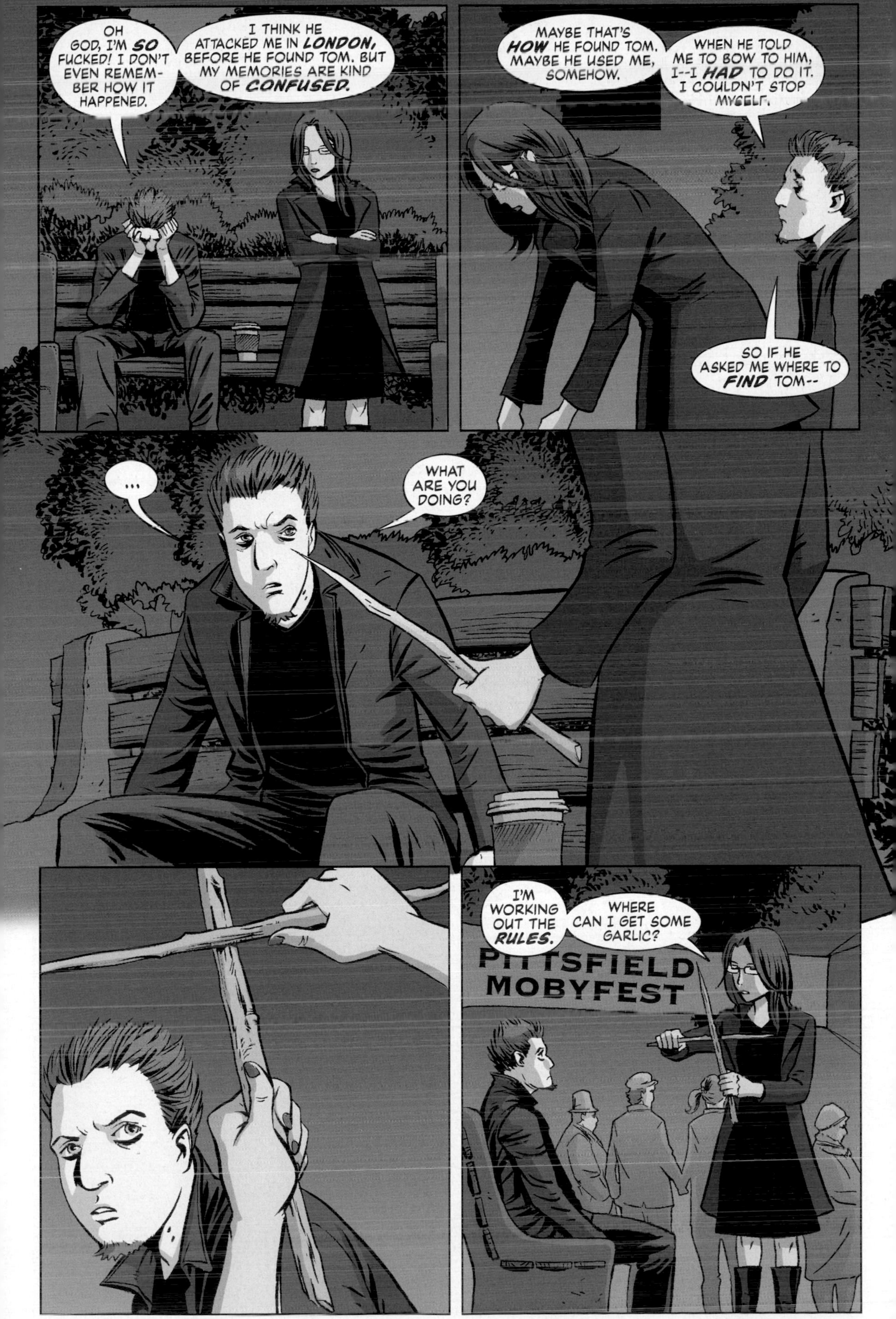
OH GOD, I'M SO FUCKED! I DON'T EVEN REMEMBER HOW IT HAPPENED.
I THINK HE ATTACKED ME IN LONDON, BEFORE HE FOUND TOM. BUT MY MEMORIES ARE KIND OF CONFUSED.
MAYBE THAT'S HOW HE FOUND TOM. MAYBE HE USED ME, SOMEHOW.
WHEN HE TOLD ME TO BOW TO HIM, I--I HAD TO DO IT. I COULDN'T STOP MYSELF.
SO IF HE ASKED ME WHERE TO FIND TOM--
...
WHAT ARE YOU DOING?
I'M WORKING OUT THE RULES.
WHERE CAN I GET SOME GARLIC?
PITTSFIELD MOBYFEST

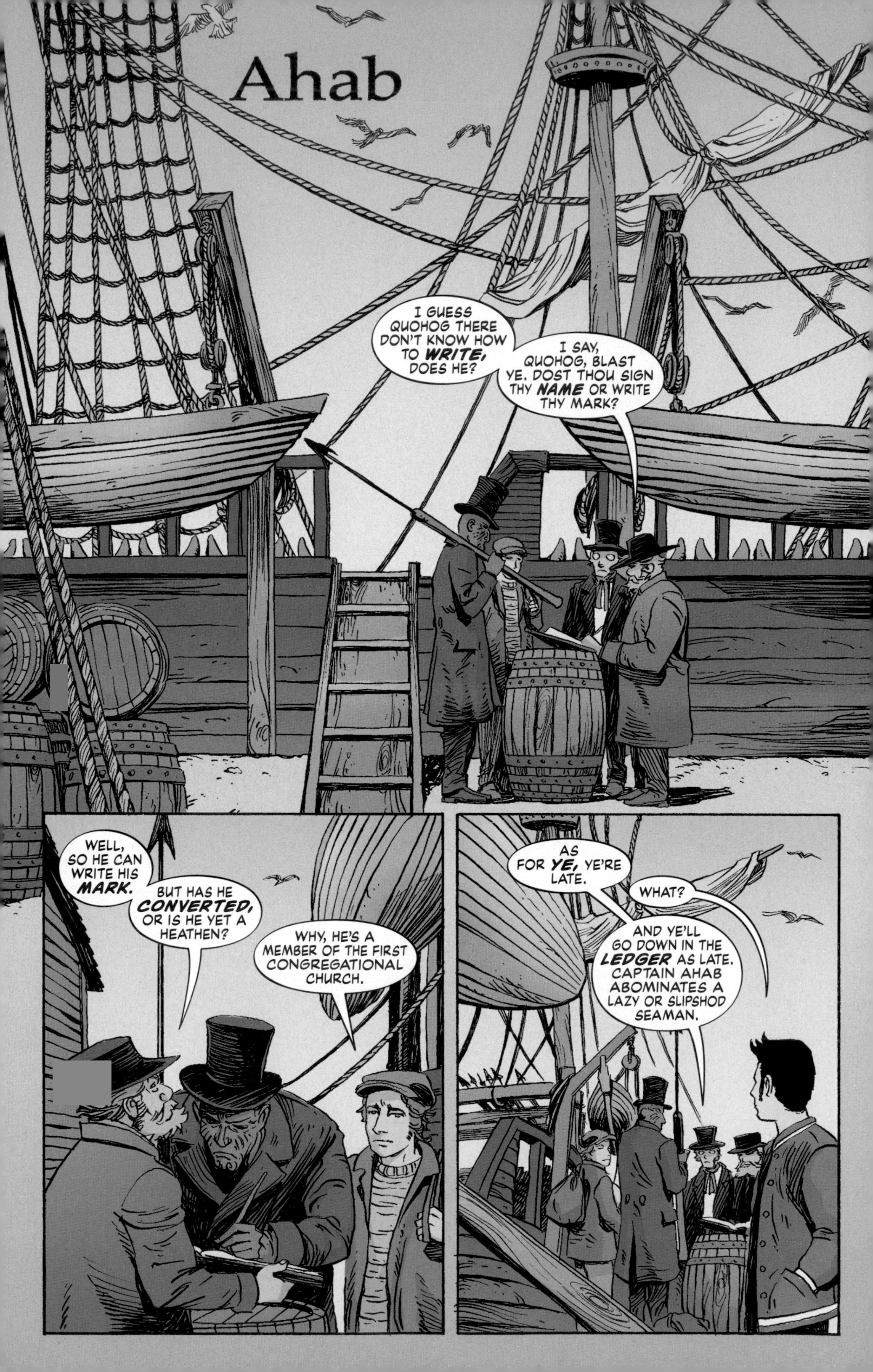
Ahab
I GUESS QUOHOG THERE DON'T KNOW HOW TO WRITE, DOES HE?
I SAY, QUOHOG, BLAST YE. DOST THOU SIGN THY NAME OR WRITE THY MARK?
WELL, SO HE CAN WRITE HIS MARK.
BUT HAS HE CONVERTED, OR IS HE YET A HEATHEN?
WHY, HE'S A MEMBER OF THE FIRST CONGREGATIONAL CHURCH.
AS FOR YE, YE'RE LATE.
WHAT?
AND YE'LL GO DOWN IN THE LEDGER AS LATE. CAPTAIN AHAB ABOMINATES A LAZY OR SLIPSHOD SEAMAN.

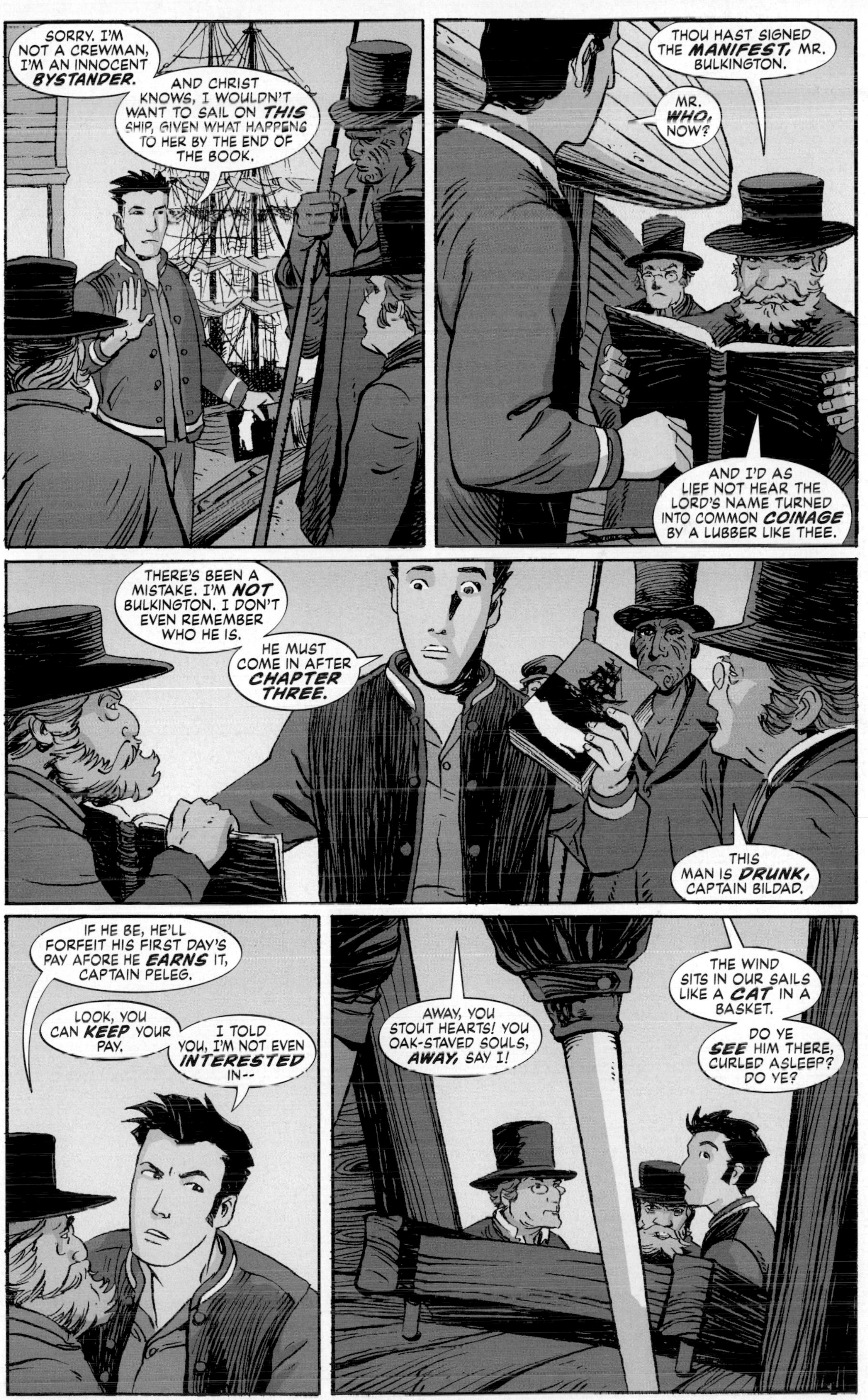
SORRY. I'M NOT A CREWMAN, I'M AN INNOCENT BYSTANDER.
AND CHRIST KNOWS, I WOULDN'T WANT TO SAIL ON THIS SHIP, GIVEN WHAT HAPPENS TO HER BY THE END OF THE BOOK.
THOU HAST SIGNED THE MANIFEST, MR. BULKINGTON.
MR. WHO, NOW?
AND I'D AS LIEF NOT HEAR THE LORD'S NAME TURNED INTO COMMON COINAGE BY A LUBBER LIKE THEE.
THERE'S BEEN A MISTAKE. I'M NOT BULKINGTON. I DON'T EVEN REMEMBER WHO HE IS.
HE MUST COME IN AFTER CHAPTER THREE.
THIS MAN IS DRUNK, CAPTAIN BILDAD.
IF HE BE, HE'LL FORFEIT HIS FIRST DAY'S PAY AFORE HE EARNS IT, CAPTAIN PELEG.
LOOK, YOU CAN KEEP YOUR PAY.
I TOLD YOU, I'M NOT EVEN INTERESTED IN--
AWAY, YOU STOUT HEARTS! YOU OAK-STAVED SOULS, AWAY, SAY I!
THE WIND SITS IN OUR SAILS LIKE A CAT IN A BASKET.
DO YE SEE HIM THERE, CURLED ASLEEP? DO YE?

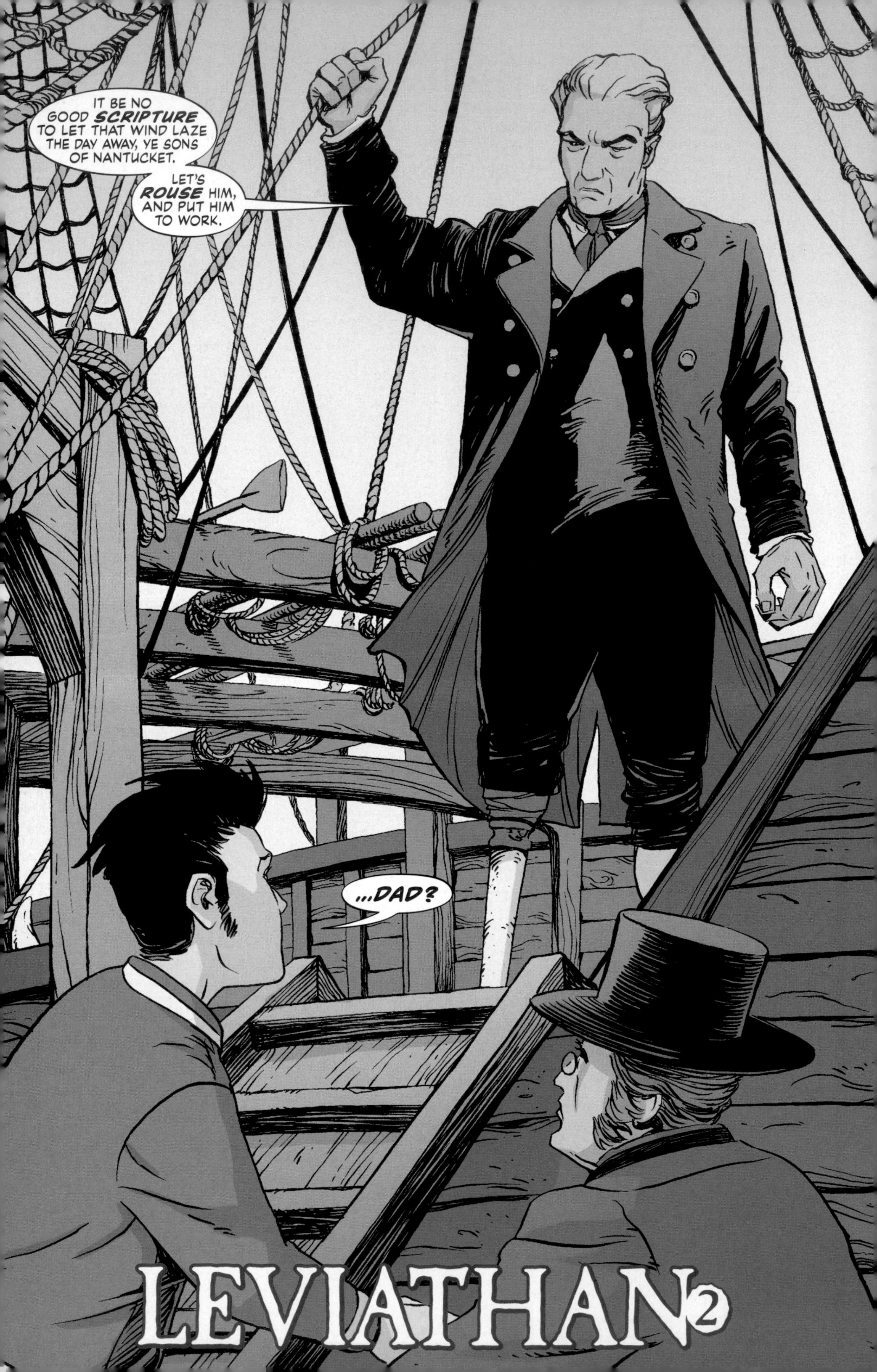
IT BE NO GOOD SCRIPTURE TO LET THAT WIND LAZE THE DAY AWAY, YE SONS OF NANTUCKET.
LET'S ROUSE HIM, AND PUT HIM TO WORK.
...DAD?
LEVIATHAN 2

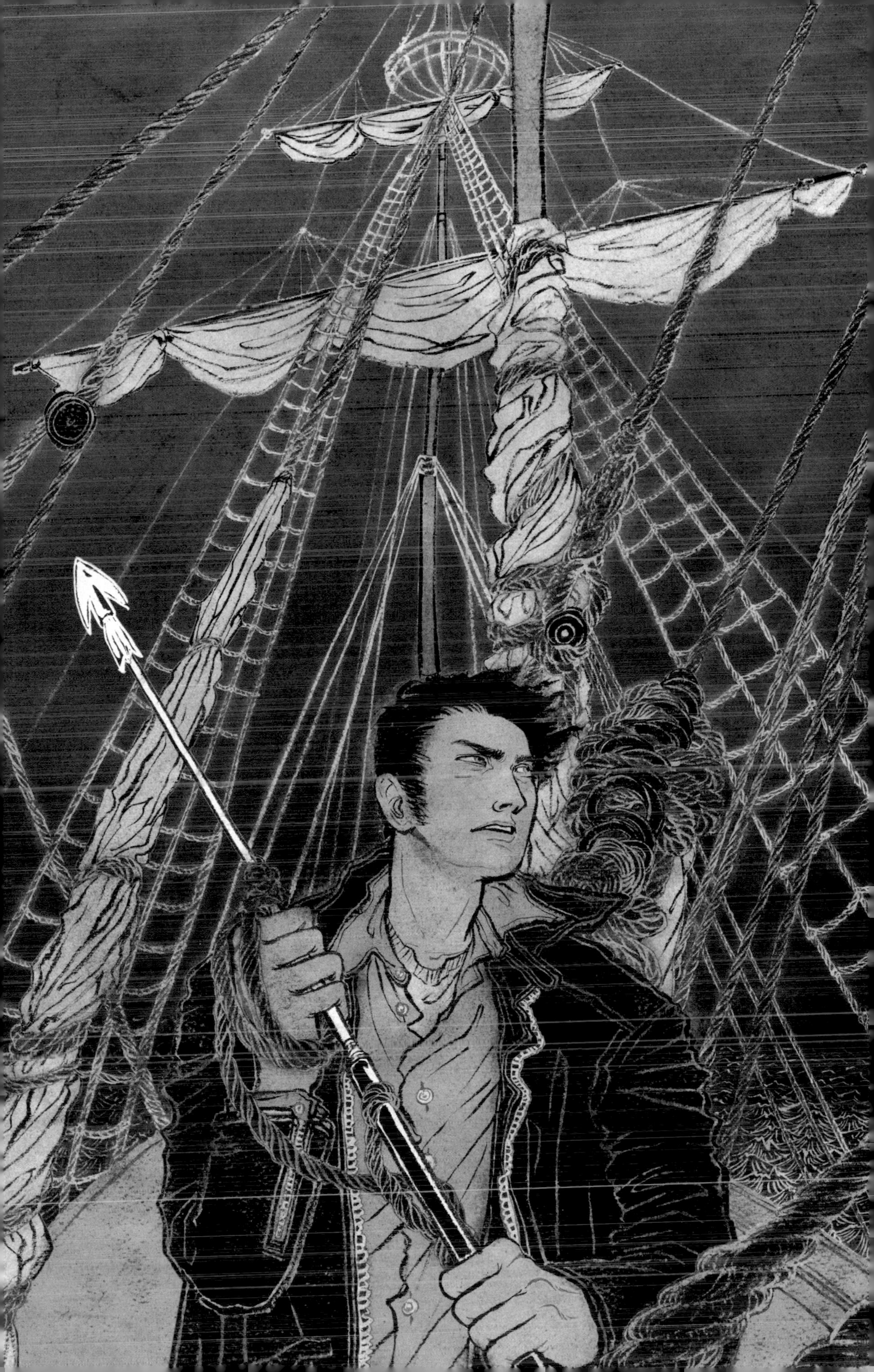

# A Failure to Communicate

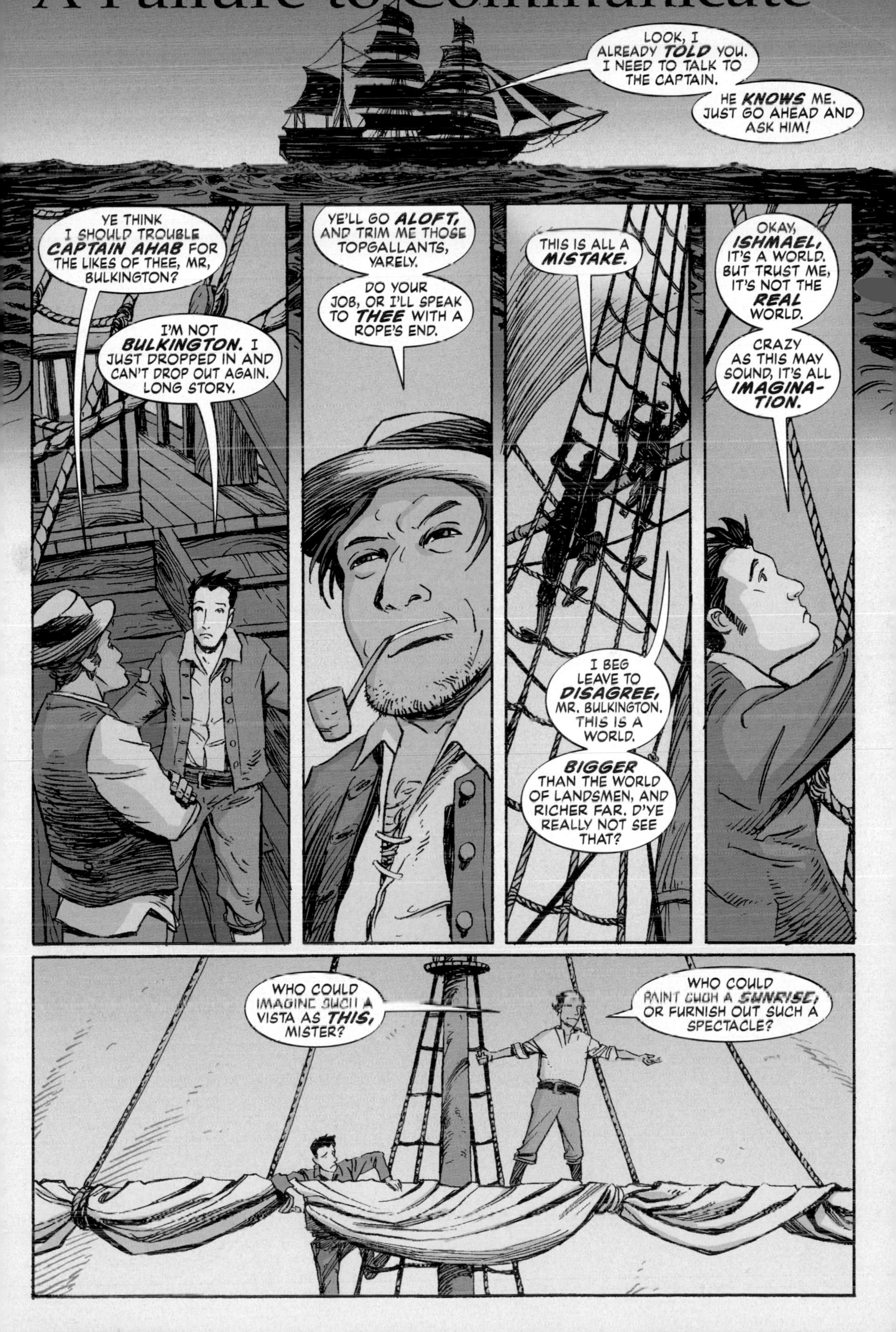

LOOK, I ALREADY TOLD YOU. I NEED TO TALK TO THE CAPTAIN.
HE KNOWS ME. JUST GO AHEAD AND ASK HIM!
YE THINK I SHOULD TROUBLE CAPTAIN AHAB FOR THE LIKES OF THEE, MR, BULKINGTON?
I'M NOT BULKINGTON. I JUST DROPPED IN AND CAN'T DROP OUT AGAIN. LONG STORY.
YE'LL GO ALOFT, AND TRIM ME THOSE TOPGALLANTS, YARELY.
DO YOUR JOB, OR I'LL SPEAK TO THEE WITH A ROPE'S END.
THIS IS ALL A MISTAKE.
I BEG LEAVE TO DISAGREE, MR. BULKINGTON. THIS IS A WORLD.
BIGGER THAN THE WORLD OF LANDSMEN, AND RICHER FAR. D'YE REALLY NOT SEE THAT?
OKAY, ISHMAEL, IT'S A WORLD. BUT TRUST ME, IT'S NOT THE REAL WORLD.
CRAZY AS THIS MAY SOUND, IT'S ALL IMAGINATION.
WHO COULD IMAGINE SUCH A VISTA AS THIS, MISTER?
WHO COULD PAINT SUCH A SUNRISE, OR FURNISH OUT SUCH A SPECTACLE?

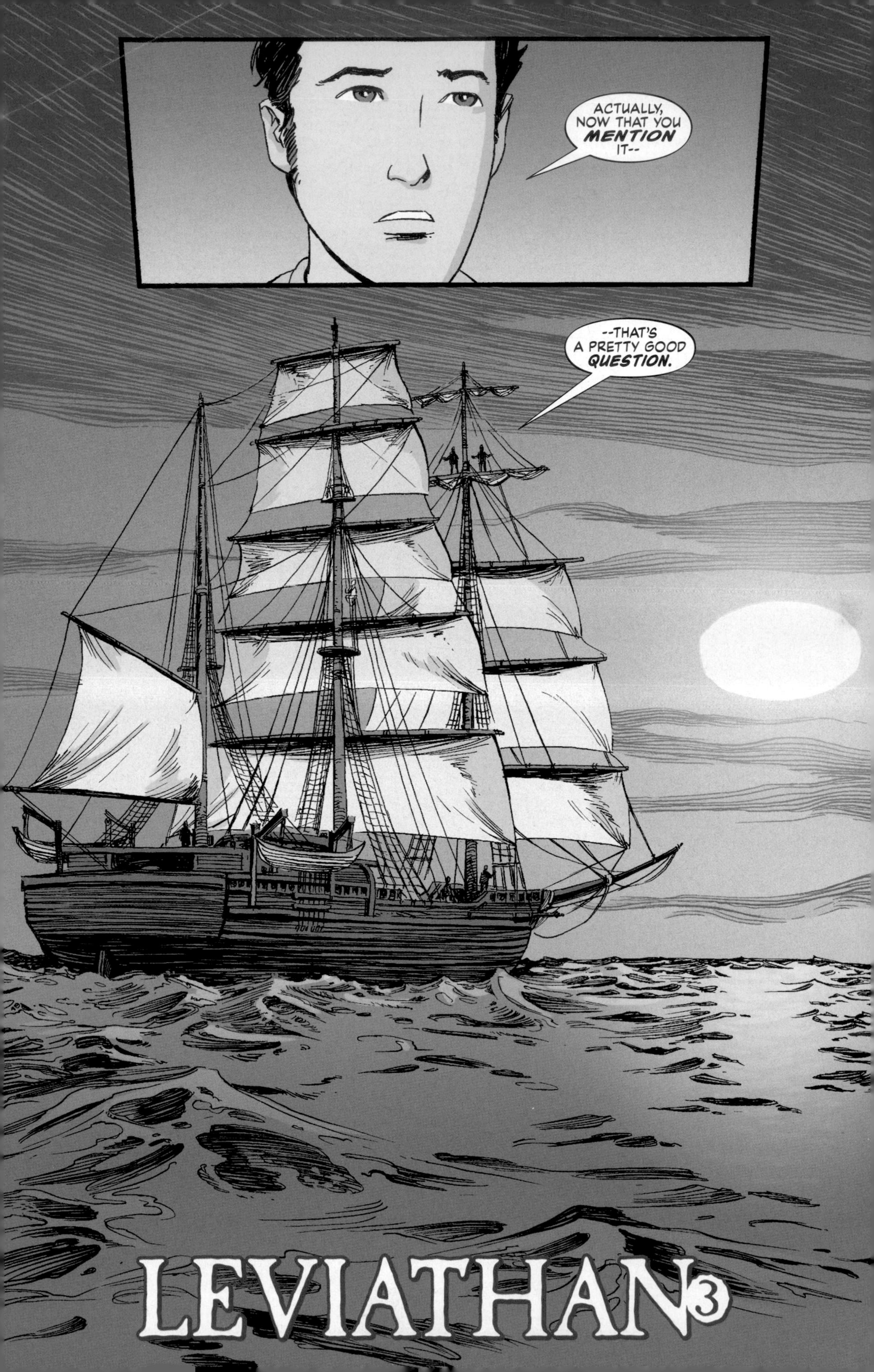
ACTUALLY, NOW THAT YOU MENTION IT--
--THAT'S A PRETTY GOOD QUESTION.
LEVIATHAN 3

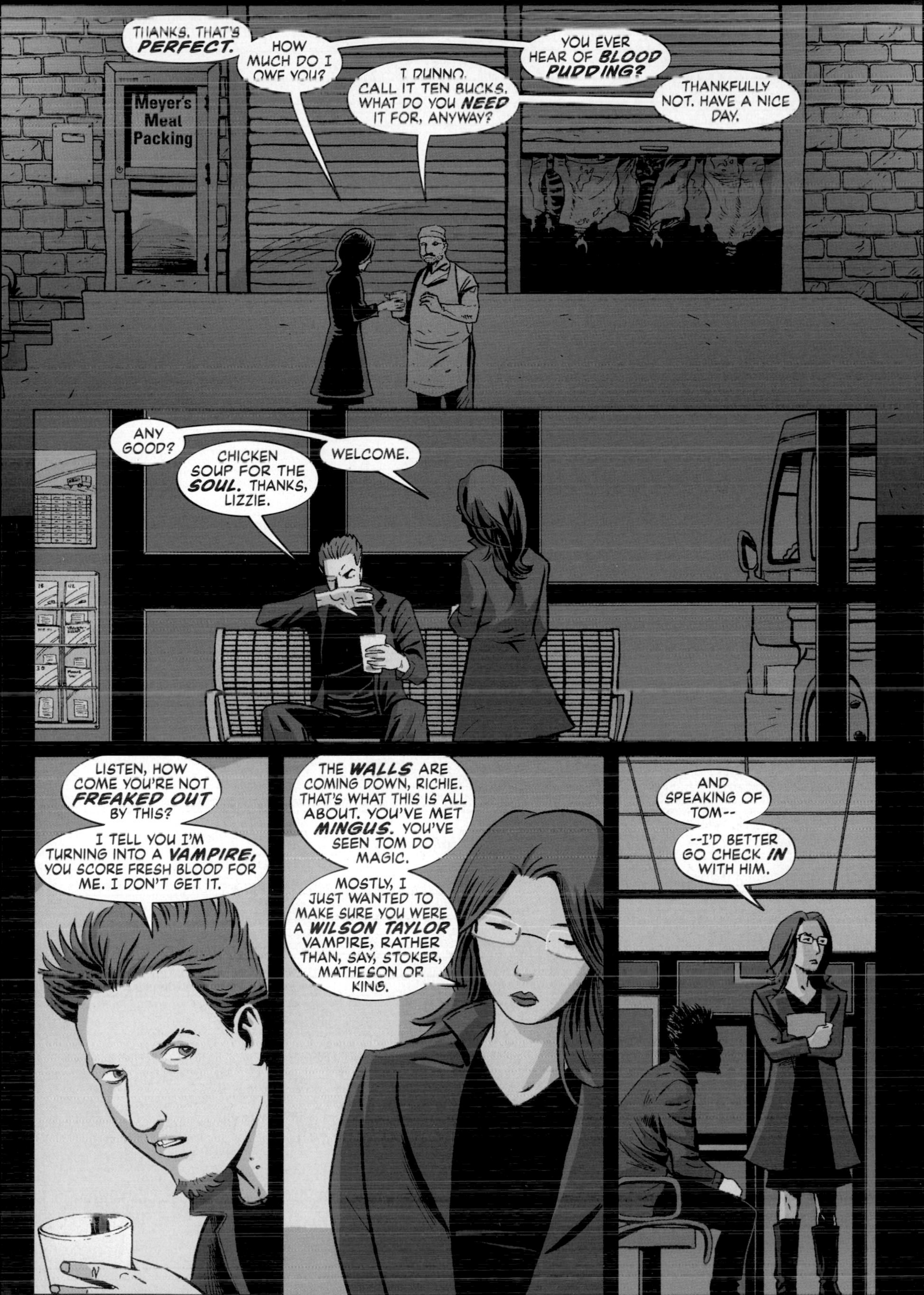
THANKS. THAT'S **PERFECT.**
HOW MUCH DO I OWE YOU?
I DUNNO. CALL IT TEN BUCKS. WHAT DO YOU **NEED** IT FOR, ANYWAY?
YOU EVER HEAR OF **BLOOD PUDDING?**
THANKFULLY NOT. HAVE A NICE DAY.
Meyer's Meat Packing
ANY GOOD?
CHICKEN SOUP FOR THE **SOUL.** THANKS, LIZZIE.
WELCOME.
LISTEN, HOW COME YOU'RE NOT **FREAKED OUT** BY THIS?
I TELL YOU I'M TURNING INTO A **VAMPIRE,** YOU SCORE FRESH BLOOD FOR ME. I DON'T GET IT.
THE **WALLS** ARE COMING DOWN, RICHIE. THAT'S WHAT THIS IS ALL ABOUT. YOU'VE MET **MINGUS.** YOU'VE SEEN TOM DO MAGIC.
MOSTLY, I JUST WANTED TO MAKE SURE YOU WERE A **WILSON TAYLOR** VAMPIRE, RATHER THAN, SAY, STOKER, MATHESON OR KING.
AND SPEAKING OF TOM--
--I'D BETTER GO CHECK **IN** WITH HIM.

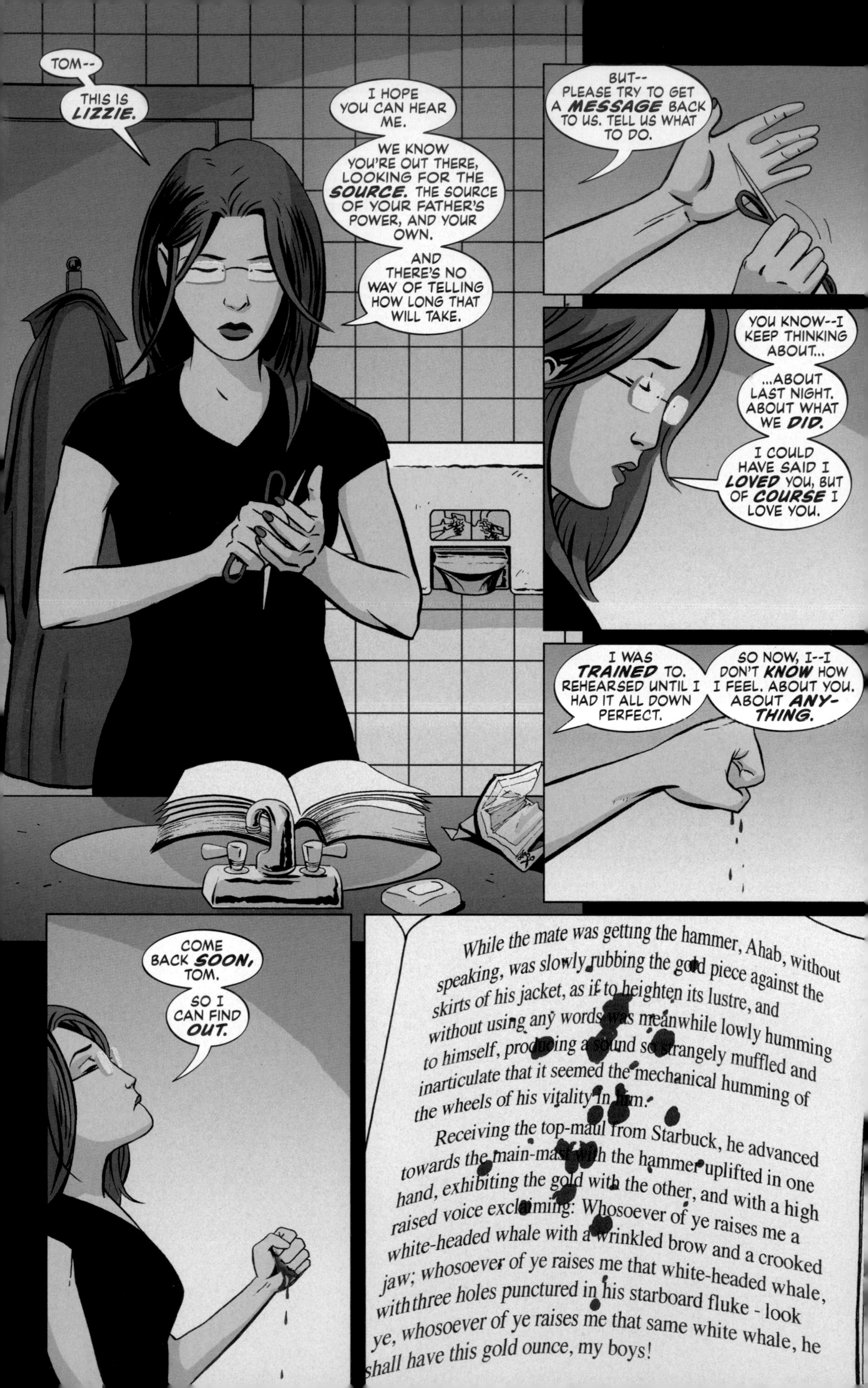
TOM--
THIS IS LIZZIE.
I HOPE YOU CAN HEAR ME.
WE KNOW YOU'RE OUT THERE, LOOKING FOR THE SOURCE. THE SOURCE OF YOUR FATHER'S POWER, AND YOUR OWN.
AND THERE'S NO WAY OF TELLING HOW LONG THAT WILL TAKE.
BUT-- PLEASE TRY TO GET A MESSAGE BACK TO US. TELL US WHAT TO DO.
YOU KNOW--I KEEP THINKING ABOUT...
...ABOUT LAST NIGHT. ABOUT WHAT WE DID.
I COULD HAVE SAID I LOVED YOU, BUT OF COURSE I LOVE YOU.
I WAS TRAINED TO. REHEARSED UNTIL I HAD IT ALL DOWN PERFECT.
SO NOW, I--I DON'T KNOW HOW I FEEL. ABOUT YOU. ABOUT ANY-THING.
COME BACK SOON, TOM.
SO I CAN FIND OUT.
While the mate was getting the hammer, Ahab, without speaking, was slowly rubbing the gold piece against the skirts of his jacket, as if to heighten its lustre, and without using any words was meanwhile lowly humming to himself, producing a sound so strangely muffled and inarticulate that it seemed the mechanical humming of the wheels of his vitality in him.
Receiving the top-maul from Starbuck, he advanced towards the main-mast with the hammer uplifted in one hand, exhibiting the gold with the other, and with a high raised voice exclaiming: Whosoever of ye raises me a white-headed whale with a wrinkled brow and a crooked jaw; whosoever of ye raises me that white-headed whale with three holes punctured in his starboard fluke - look ye, whosoever of ye raises me that same white whale, he shall have this gold ounce, my boys!

# The Gold Dubloon

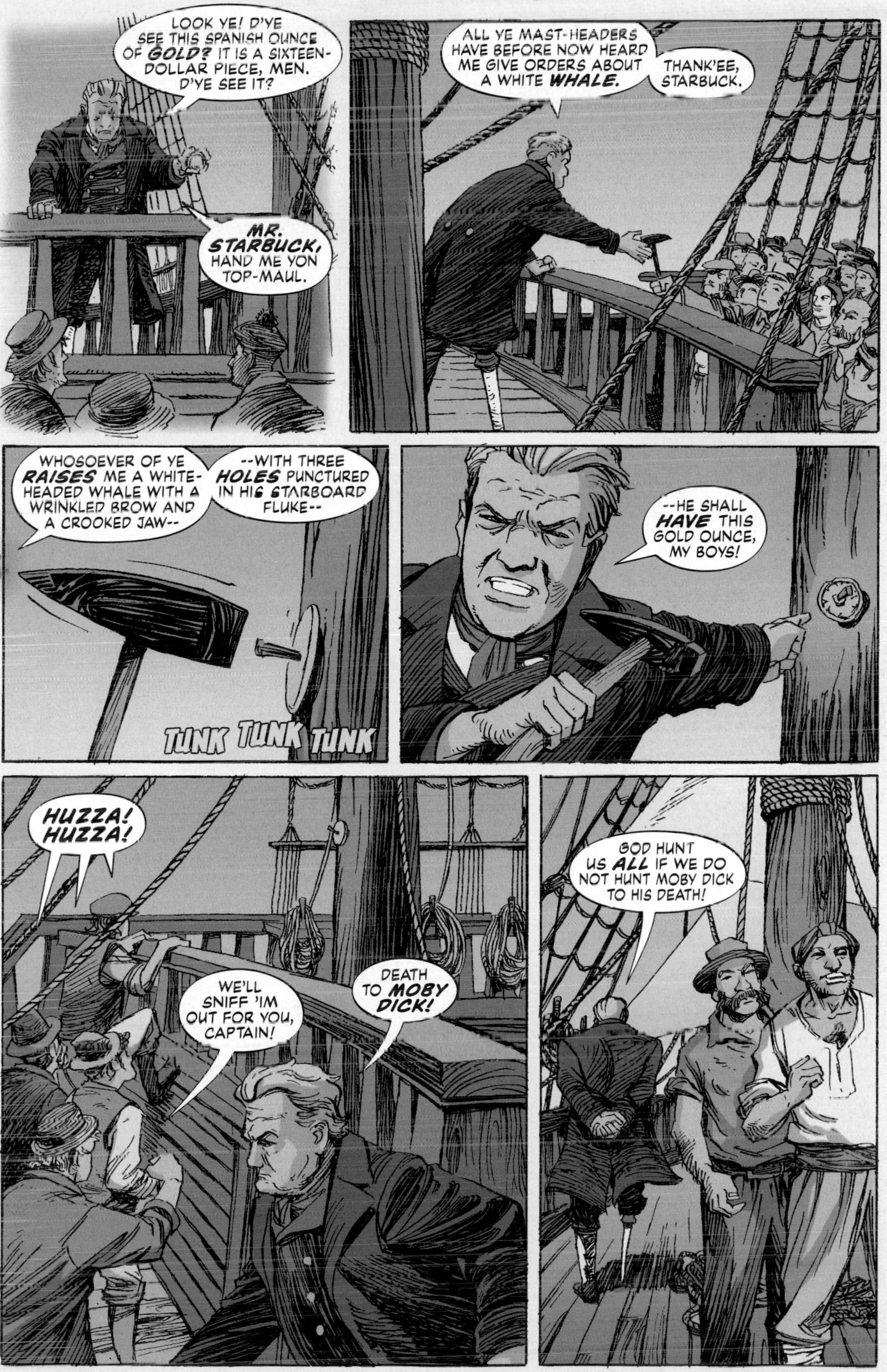
LOOK YE! D'YE SEE THIS SPANISH OUNCE OF GOLD? IT IS A SIXTEEN-DOLLAR PIECE, MEN. D'YE SEE IT?
MR. STARBUCK, HAND ME YON TOP-MAUL.
ALL YE MAST-HEADERS HAVE BEFORE NOW HEARD ME GIVE ORDERS ABOUT A WHITE WHALE.
THANK'EE, STARBUCK.
WHOSOEVER OF YE RAISES ME A WHITE-HEADED WHALE WITH A WRINKLED BROW AND A CROOKED JAW--
--WITH THREE HOLES PUNCTURED IN HIS STARBOARD FLUKE--
TUNK TUNK TUNK
--HE SHALL HAVE THIS GOLD OUNCE, MY BOYS!
HUZZA! HUZZA!
WE'LL SNIFF 'IM OUT FOR YOU, CAPTAIN!
DEATH TO MOBY DICK!
GOD HUNT US ALL IF WE DO NOT HUNT MOBY DICK TO HIS DEATH!

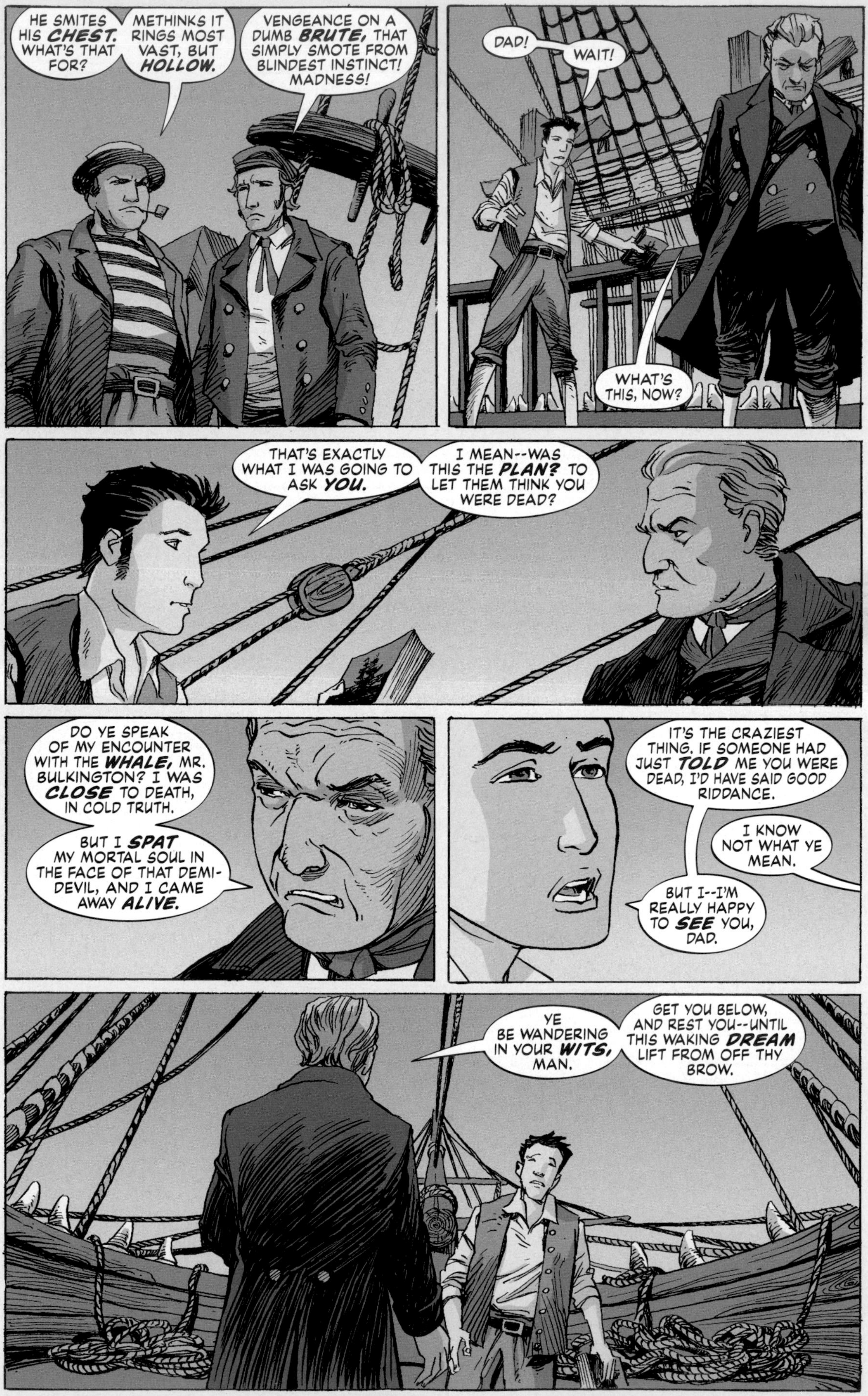
HE SMITES HIS CHEST. WHAT'S THAT FOR?
METHINKS IT RINGS MOST VAST, BUT HOLLOW.
VENGEANCE ON A DUMB BRUTE, THAT SIMPLY SMOTE FROM BLINDEST INSTINCT! MADNESS!
DAD!
WAIT!
WHAT'S THIS, NOW?
THAT'S EXACTLY WHAT I WAS GOING TO ASK YOU.
I MEAN--WAS THIS THE PLAN? TO LET THEM THINK YOU WERE DEAD?
DO YE SPEAK OF MY ENCOUNTER WITH THE WHALE, MR. BULKINGTON? I WAS CLOSE TO DEATH, IN COLD TRUTH.
BUT I SPAT MY MORTAL SOUL IN THE FACE OF THAT DEMI-DEVIL, AND I CAME AWAY ALIVE.
IT'S THE CRAZIEST THING. IF SOMEONE HAD JUST TOLD ME YOU WERE DEAD, I'D HAVE SAID GOOD RIDDANCE.
I KNOW NOT WHAT YE MEAN.
BUT I--I'M REALLY HAPPY TO SEE YOU, DAD.
YE BE WANDERING IN YOUR WITS, MAN.
GET YOU BELOW, AND REST YOU--UNTIL THIS WAKING DREAM LIFT FROM OFF THY BROW.

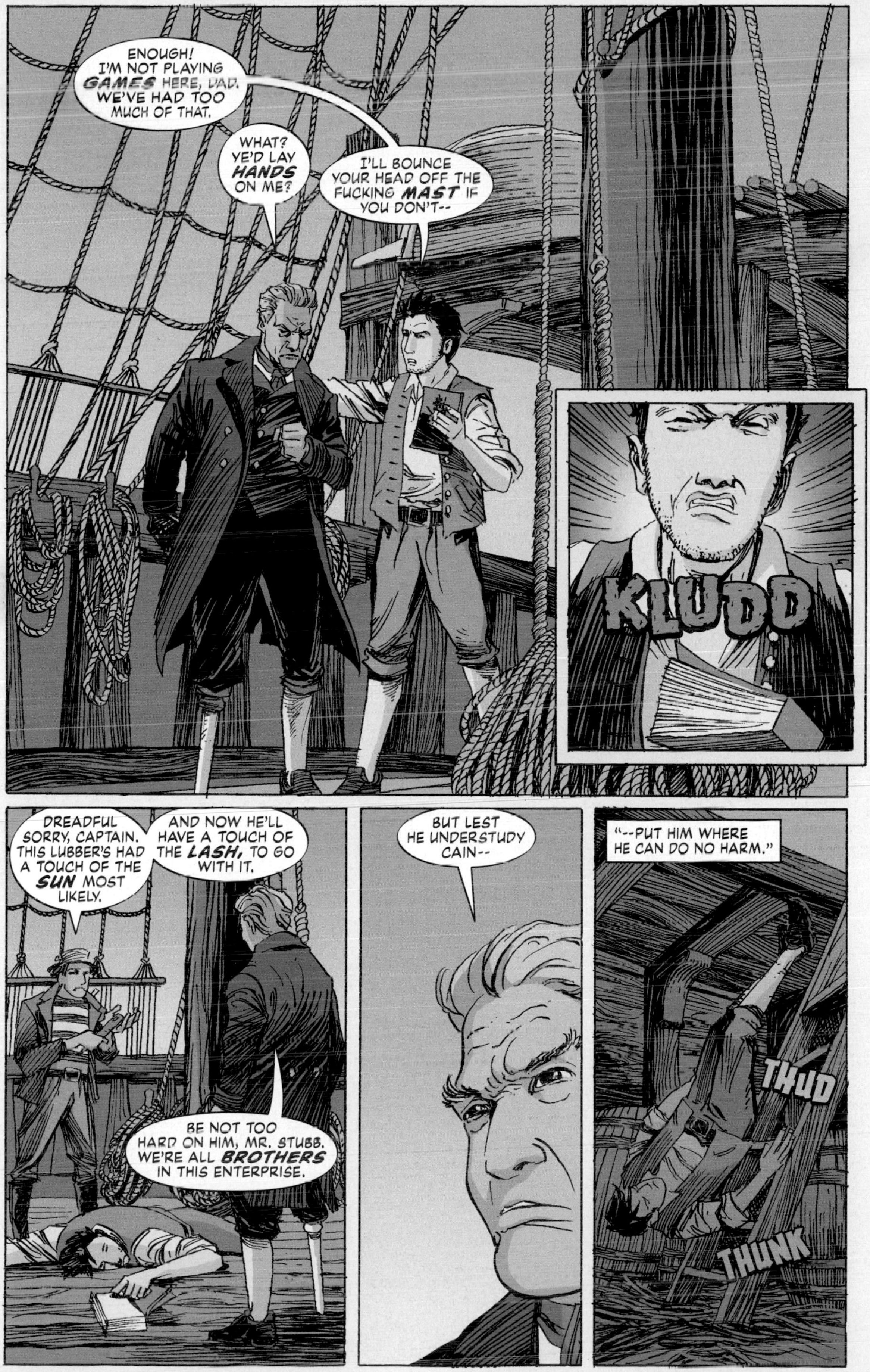
ENOUGH! I'M NOT PLAYING GAMES HERE, DAD. WE'VE HAD TOO MUCH OF THAT.
WHAT? YE'D LAY HANDS ON ME?
I'LL BOUNCE YOUR HEAD OFF THE FUCKING MAST IF YOU DON'T--
KLUDD
DREADFUL SORRY, CAPTAIN. THIS LUBBER'S HAD A TOUCH OF THE SUN MOST LIKELY.
AND NOW HE'LL HAVE A TOUCH OF THE LASH, TO GO WITH IT.
BE NOT TOO HARD ON HIM, MR. STUBB. WE'RE ALL BROTHERS IN THIS ENTERPRISE.
BUT LEST HE UNDERSTUDY CAIN--
"--PUT HIM WHERE HE CAN DO NO HARM."
THUD
THUNK

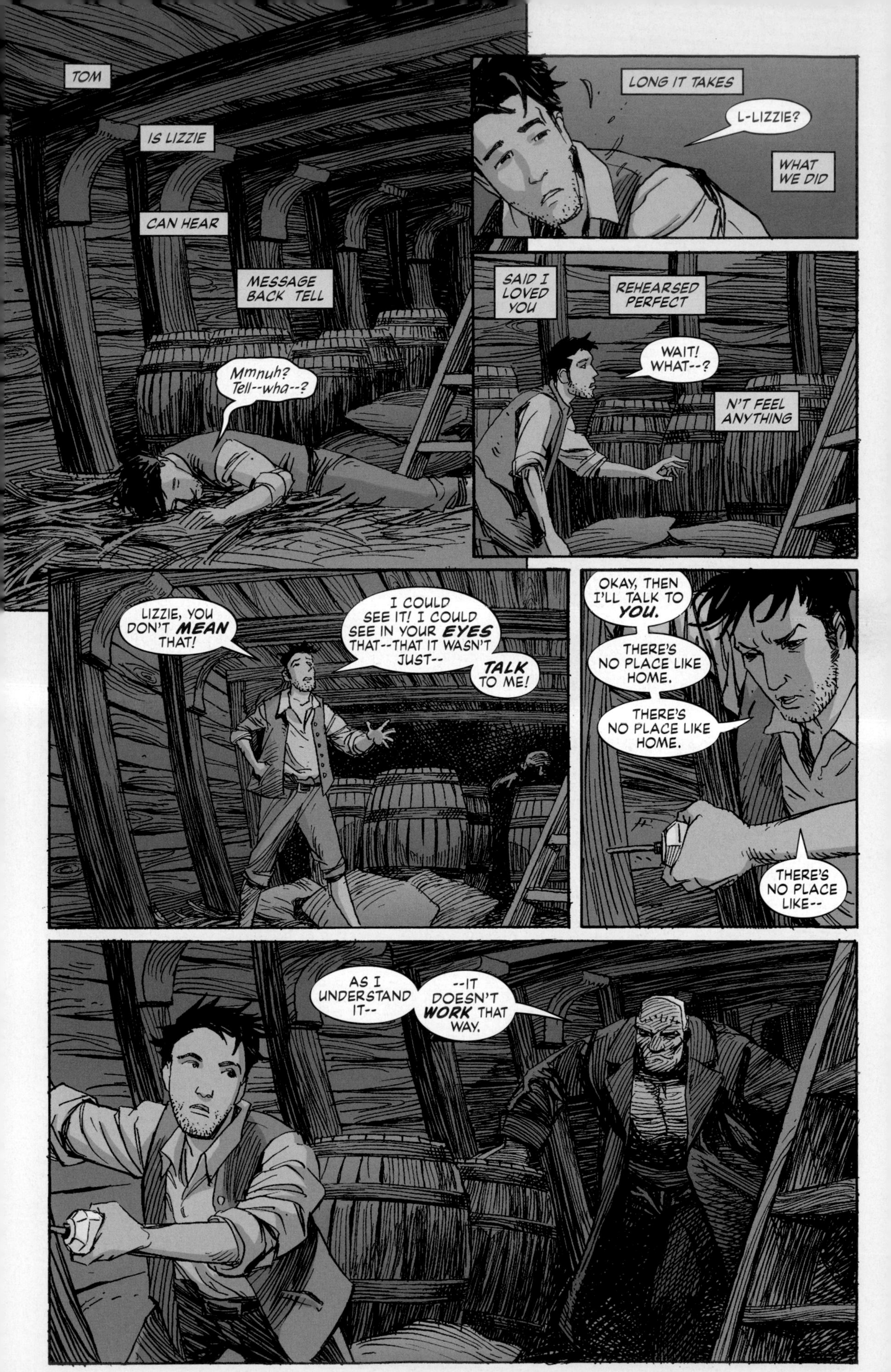
TOM
IS LIZZIE
CAN HEAR
MESSAGE BACK TELL
Mmnuh? Tell--wha--?
LONG IT TAKES
L-LIZZIE?
WHAT WE DID
SAID I LOVED YOU
REHEARSED PERFECT
WAIT! WHAT--?
N'T FEEL ANYTHING
LIZZIE, YOU DON'T MEAN THAT!
I COULD SEE IT! I COULD SEE IN YOUR EYES THAT--THAT IT WASN'T JUST--
TALK TO ME!
OKAY, THEN I'LL TALK TO YOU.
THERE'S NO PLACE LIKE HOME.
THERE'S NO PLACE LIKE HOME.
THERE'S NO PLACE LIKE--
AS I UNDERSTAND IT--
--IT DOESN'T WORK THAT WAY.

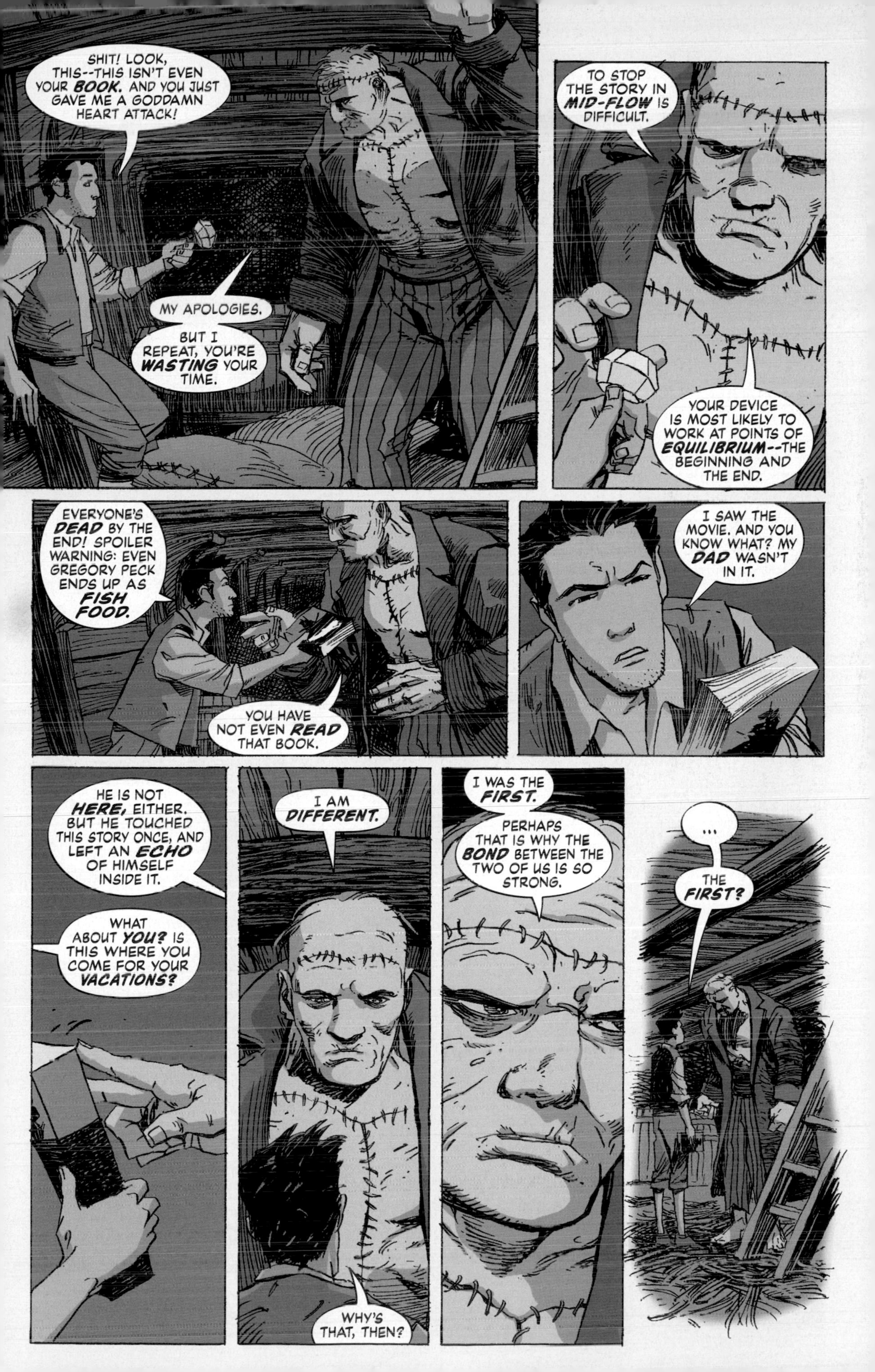
SHIT! LOOK, THIS--THIS ISN'T EVEN YOUR BOOK. AND YOU JUST GAVE ME A GODDAMN HEART ATTACK!
MY APOLOGIES.
BUT I REPEAT, YOU'RE WASTING YOUR TIME.
TO STOP THE STORY IN MID-FLOW IS DIFFICULT.
YOUR DEVICE IS MOST LIKELY TO WORK AT POINTS OF EQUILIBRIUM--THE BEGINNING AND THE END.
EVERYONE'S DEAD BY THE END! SPOILER WARNING: EVEN GREGORY PECK ENDS UP AS FISH FOOD.
YOU HAVE NOT EVEN READ THAT BOOK.
I SAW THE MOVIE. AND YOU KNOW WHAT? MY DAD WASN'T IN IT.
HE IS NOT HERE, EITHER. BUT HE TOUCHED THIS STORY ONCE, AND LEFT AN ECHO OF HIMSELF INSIDE IT.
WHAT ABOUT YOU? IS THIS WHERE YOU COME FOR YOUR VACATIONS?
I AM DIFFERENT.
WHY'S THAT, THEN?
I WAS THE FIRST.
PERHAPS THAT IS WHY THE BOND BETWEEN THE TWO OF US IS SO STRONG.
...
THE FIRST?

# Very Like James Whale

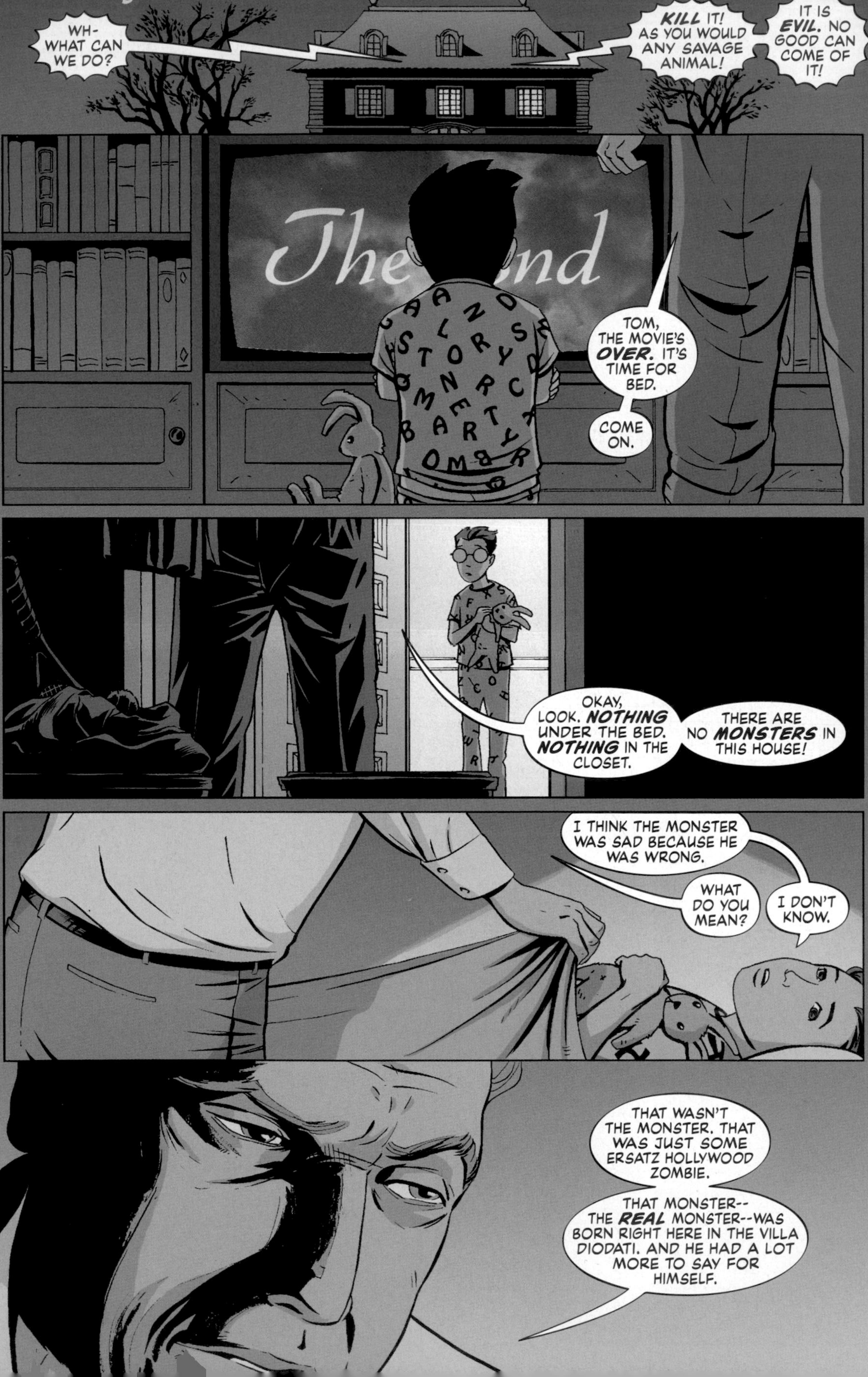
WH- WHAT CAN WE DO?
KILL IT! AS YOU WOULD ANY SAVAGE ANIMAL!
IT IS EVIL. NO GOOD CAN COME OF IT!
The End
TOM, THE MOVIE'S OVER. IT'S TIME FOR BED.
COME ON.
OKAY, LOOK. NOTHING UNDER THE BED. NOTHING IN THE CLOSET.
THERE ARE NO MONSTERS IN THIS HOUSE!
I THINK THE MONSTER WAS SAD BECAUSE HE WAS WRONG.
WHAT DO YOU MEAN?
I DON'T KNOW.
THAT WASN'T THE MONSTER. THAT WAS JUST SOME ERSATZ HOLLYWOOD ZOMBIE.
THAT MONSTER-- THE REAL MONSTER--WAS BORN RIGHT HERE IN THE VILLA DIODATI. AND HE HAD A LOT MORE TO SAY FOR HIMSELF.

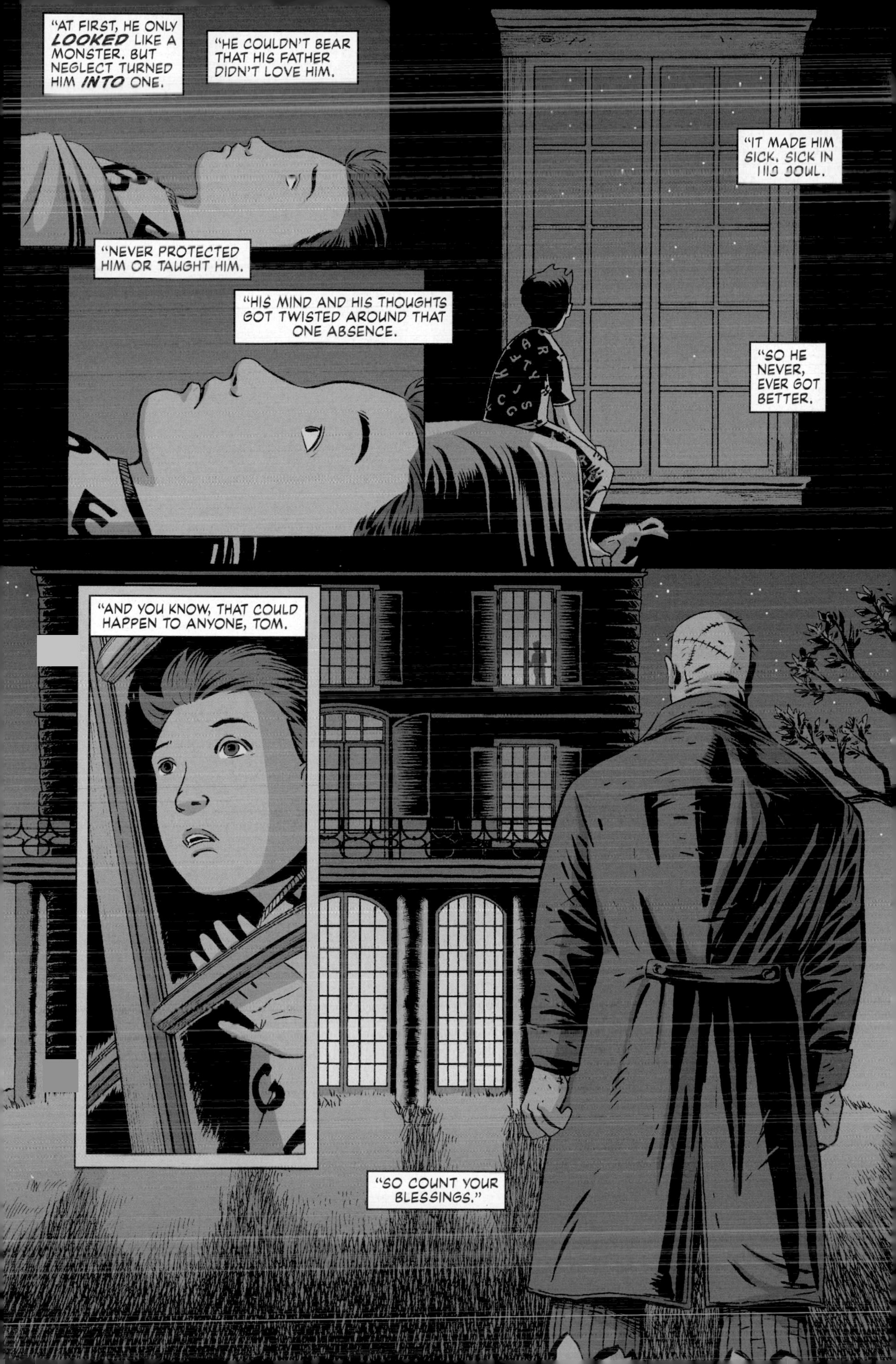
"AT FIRST, HE ONLY *LOOKED* LIKE A MONSTER. BUT NEGLECT TURNED HIM *INTO* ONE.
"HE COULDN'T BEAR THAT HIS FATHER DIDN'T LOVE HIM.
"NEVER PROTECTED HIM OR TAUGHT HIM.
"HIS MIND AND HIS THOUGHTS GOT TWISTED AROUND THAT ONE ABSENCE.
"IT MADE HIM SICK. SICK IN HIS SOUL.
"SO HE NEVER, EVER GOT BETTER.
"AND YOU KNOW, THAT COULD HAPPEN TO ANYONE, TOM.
"SO COUNT YOUR BLESSINGS."

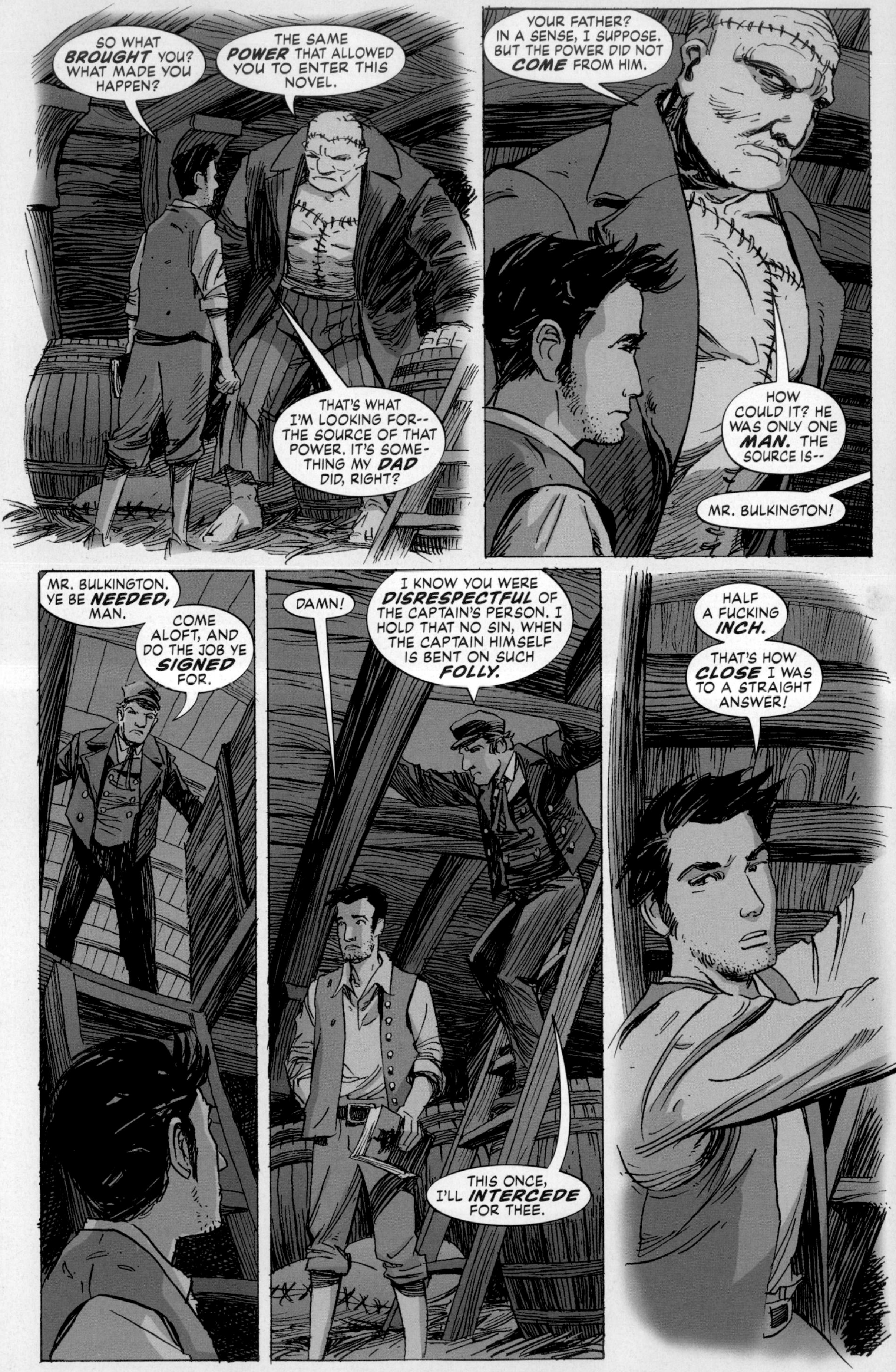
SO WHAT BROUGHT YOU? WHAT MADE YOU HAPPEN?
THE SAME POWER THAT ALLOWED YOU TO ENTER THIS NOVEL.
THAT'S WHAT I'M LOOKING FOR-- THE SOURCE OF THAT POWER. IT'S SOMETHING MY DAD DID, RIGHT?
YOUR FATHER? IN A SENSE, I SUPPOSE. BUT THE POWER DID NOT COME FROM HIM.
HOW COULD IT? HE WAS ONLY ONE MAN. THE SOURCE IS--
MR. BULKINGTON!
MR. BULKINGTON. YE BE NEEDED, MAN.
COME ALOFT, AND DO THE JOB YE SIGNED FOR.
DAMN!
I KNOW YOU WERE DISRESPECTFUL OF THE CAPTAIN'S PERSON. I HOLD THAT NO SIN, WHEN THE CAPTAIN HIMSELF IS BENT ON SUCH FOLLY.
THIS ONCE, I'LL INTERCEDE FOR THEE.
HALF A FUCKING INCH.
THAT'S HOW CLOSE I WAS TO A STRAIGHT ANSWER!

# Enter, Stage Left

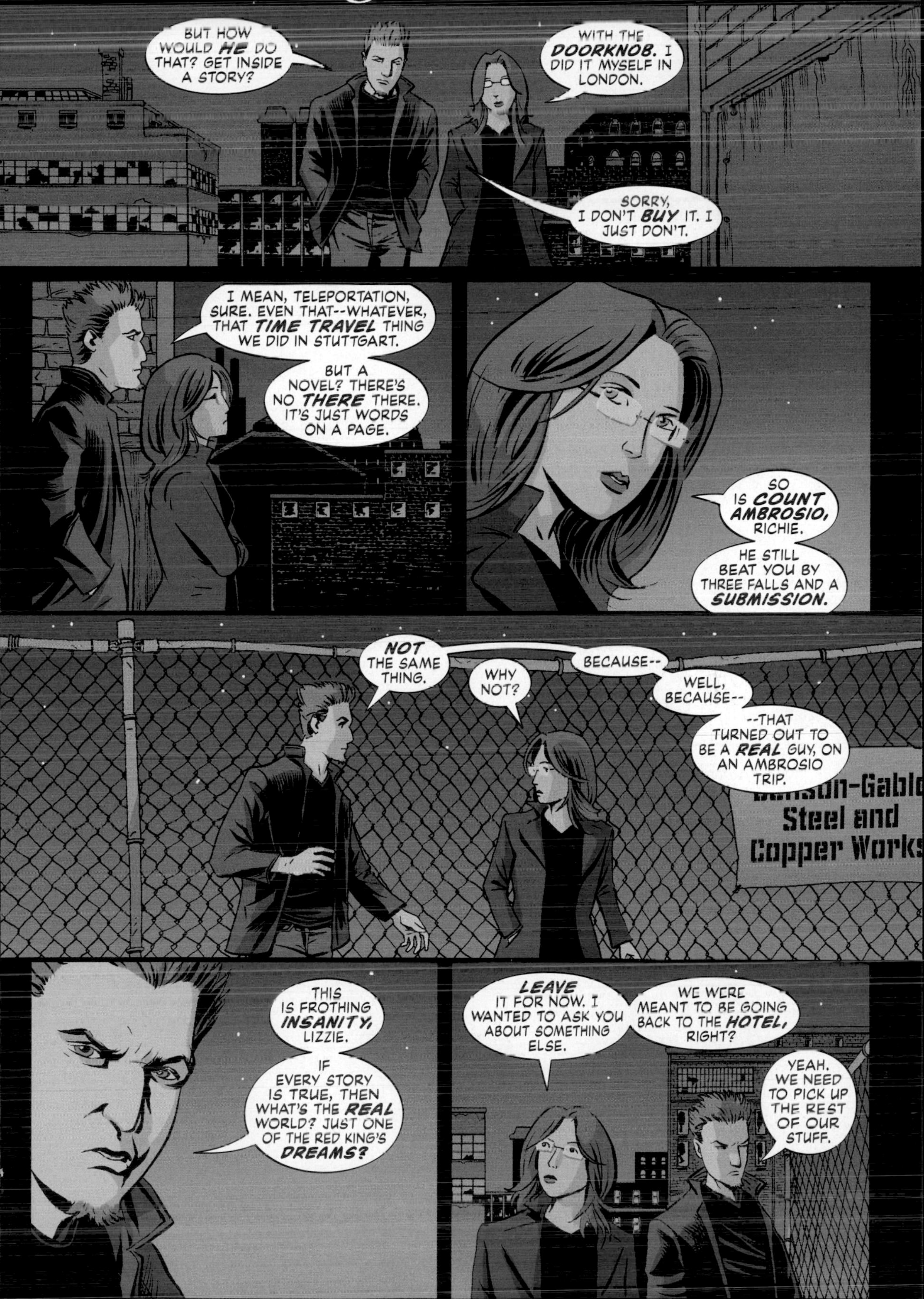
BUT HOW WOULD HE DO THAT? GET INSIDE A STORY?
WITH THE DOORKNOB. I DID IT MYSELF IN LONDON.
SORRY, I DON'T BUY IT. I JUST DON'T.
I MEAN, TELEPORTATION, SURE. EVEN THAT--WHATEVER, THAT TIME TRAVEL THING WE DID IN STUTTGART.
BUT A NOVEL? THERE'S NO THERE THERE. IT'S JUST WORDS ON A PAGE.
SO IS COUNT AMBROSIO, RICHIE.
HE STILL BEAT YOU BY THREE FALLS AND A SUBMISSION.
NOT THE SAME THING.
WHY NOT?
BECAUSE--
WELL, BECAUSE--
--THAT TURNED OUT TO BE A REAL GUY, ON AN AMBROSIO TRIP.
Steel and
Copper
THIS IS FROTHING INSANITY, LIZZIE.
IF EVERY STORY IS TRUE, THEN WHAT'S THE REAL WORLD? JUST ONE OF THE RED KING'S DREAMS?
LEAVE IT FOR NOW. I WANTED TO ASK YOU ABOUT SOMETHING ELSE.
WE WERE MEANT TO BE GOING BACK TO THE HOTEL, RIGHT?
YEAH. WE NEED TO PICK UP THE REST OF OUR STUFF.

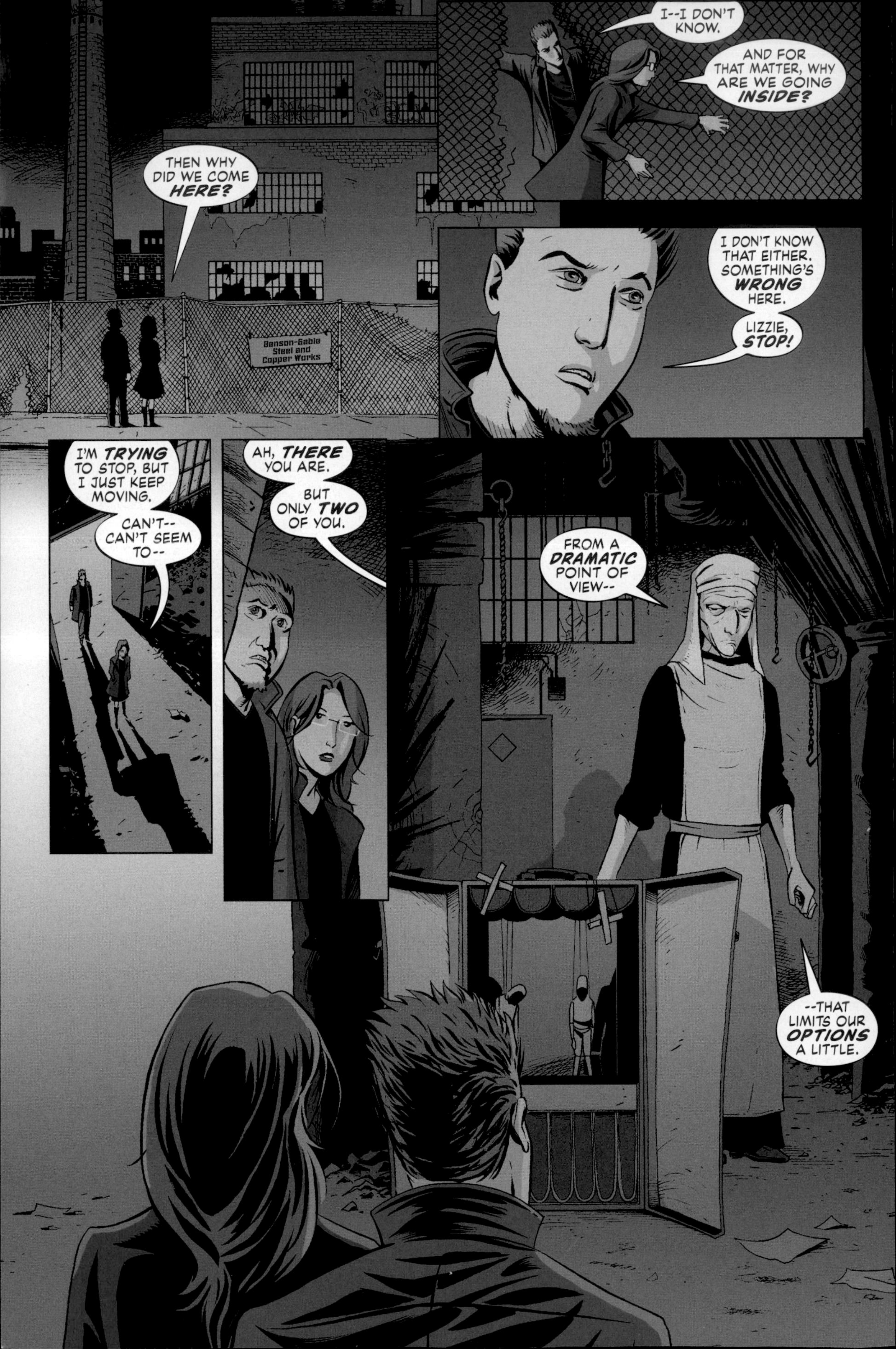
THEN WHY DID WE COME HERE?
I--I DON'T KNOW.
AND FOR THAT MATTER, WHY ARE WE GOING INSIDE?
Benson-Gable Steel and Copper Works
I DON'T KNOW THAT EITHER. SOMETHING'S WRONG HERE.
LIZZIE, STOP!
I'M TRYING TO STOP, BUT I JUST KEEP MOVING.
CAN'T-- CAN'T SEEM TO--
AH, THERE YOU ARE.
BUT ONLY TWO OF YOU.
FROM A DRAMATIC POINT OF VIEW--
--THAT LIMITS OUR OPTIONS A LITTLE.

# A Skein of Voices

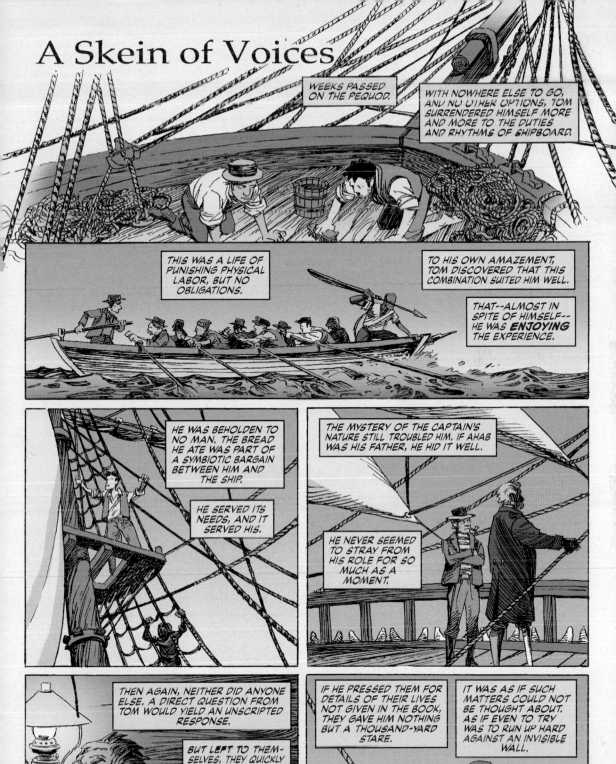

WEEKS PASSED ON THE PEQUOD.

WITH NOWHERE ELSE TO GO, AND NO OTHER OPTIONS, TOM SURRENDERED HIMSELF MORE AND MORE TO THE DUTIES AND RHYTHMS OF SHIPBOARD.

THIS WAS A LIFE OF PUNISHING PHYSICAL LABOR, BUT NO OBLIGATIONS.

TO HIS OWN AMAZEMENT, TOM DISCOVERED THAT THIS COMBINATION SUITED HIM WELL.

THAT--ALMOST IN SPITE OF HIMSELF-- HE WAS **ENJOYING** THE EXPERIENCE.

HE WAS BEHOLDEN TO NO MAN. THE BREAD HE ATE WAS PART OF A SYMBIOTIC BARGAIN BETWEEN HIM AND THE SHIP.

HE SERVED ITS NEEDS, AND IT SERVED HIS.

THE MYSTERY OF THE CAPTAIN'S NATURE STILL TROUBLED HIM. IF AHAB WAS HIS FATHER, HE HID IT WELL.

HE NEVER SEEMED TO STRAY FROM HIS ROLE FOR SO MUCH AS A MOMENT.

THEN AGAIN, NEITHER DID ANYONE ELSE. A DIRECT QUESTION FROM TOM WOULD YIELD AN UNSCRIPTED RESPONSE.

BUT LEFT TO THEM-SELVES, THEY QUICKLY DEFAULTED BACK TO SPEECHES TAKEN VERBATIM FROM THE BOOK.

IF HE PRESSED THEM FOR DETAILS OF THEIR LIVES NOT GIVEN IN THE BOOK, THEY GAVE HIM NOTHING BUT A THOUSAND-YARD STARE.

IT WAS AS IF SUCH MATTERS COULD NOT BE THOUGHT ABOUT. AS IF EVEN TO TRY WAS TO RUN UP HARD AGAINST AN INVISIBLE WALL.

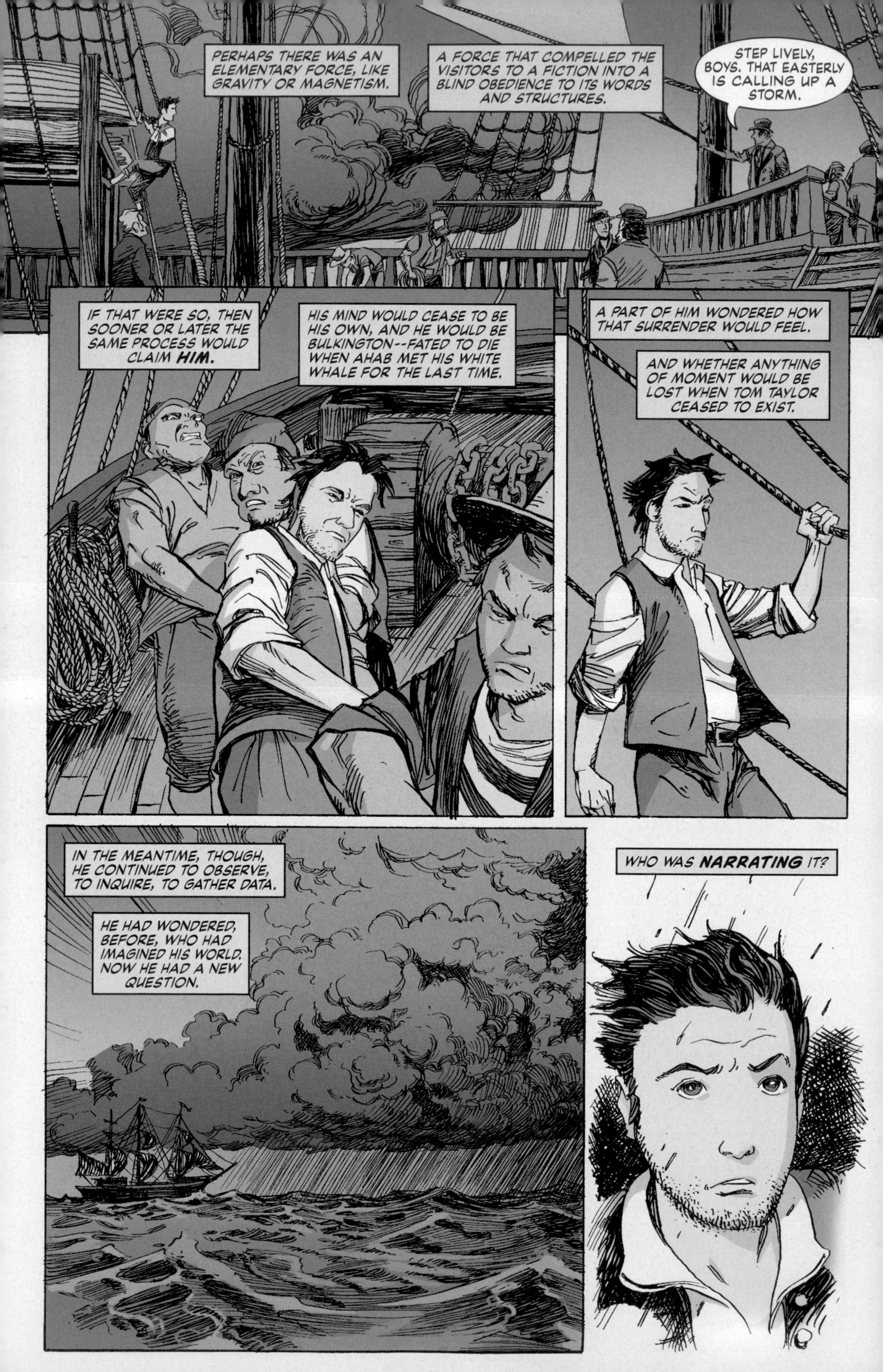
PERHAPS THERE WAS AN ELEMENTARY FORCE, LIKE GRAVITY OR MAGNETISM.
A FORCE THAT COMPELLED THE VISITORS TO A FICTION INTO A BLIND OBEDIENCE TO ITS WORDS AND STRUCTURES.
STEP LIVELY, BOYS. THAT EASTERLY IS CALLING UP A STORM.
IF THAT WERE SO, THEN SOONER OR LATER THE SAME PROCESS WOULD CLAIM **HIM.**
HIS MIND WOULD CEASE TO BE HIS OWN, AND HE WOULD BE BULKINGTON--FATED TO DIE WHEN AHAB MET HIS WHITE WHALE FOR THE LAST TIME.
A PART OF HIM WONDERED HOW THAT SURRENDER WOULD FEEL.
AND WHETHER ANYTHING OF MOMENT WOULD BE LOST WHEN TOM TAYLOR CEASED TO EXIST.
IN THE MEANTIME, THOUGH, HE CONTINUED TO OBSERVE, TO INQUIRE, TO GATHER DATA.
HE HAD WONDERED, BEFORE, WHO HAD IMAGINED HIS WORLD. NOW HE HAD A NEW QUESTION.
WHO WAS **NARRATING** IT?

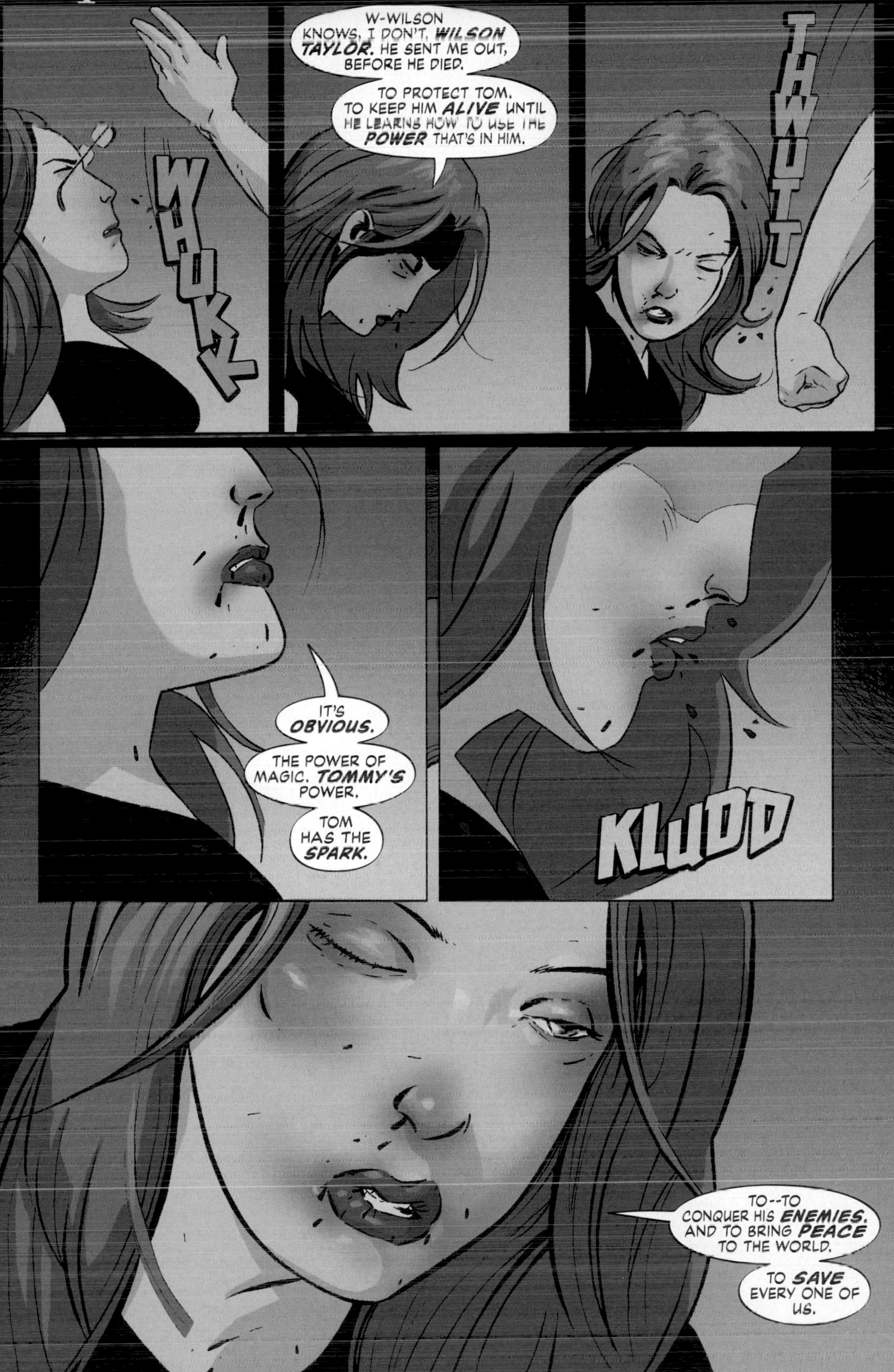
WHUKK
W-WILSON KNOWS, I DON'T. WILSON TAYLOR. HE SENT ME OUT, BEFORE HE DIED.
TO PROTECT TOM. TO KEEP HIM ALIVE UNTIL HE LEARNS HOW TO USE THE POWER THAT'S IN HIM.
THWUTT
IT'S OBVIOUS.
THE POWER OF MAGIC. TOMMY'S POWER.
TOM HAS THE SPARK.
KLUDD
TO--TO CONQUER HIS ENEMIES. AND TO BRING PEACE TO THE WORLD.
TO SAVE EVERY ONE OF US.

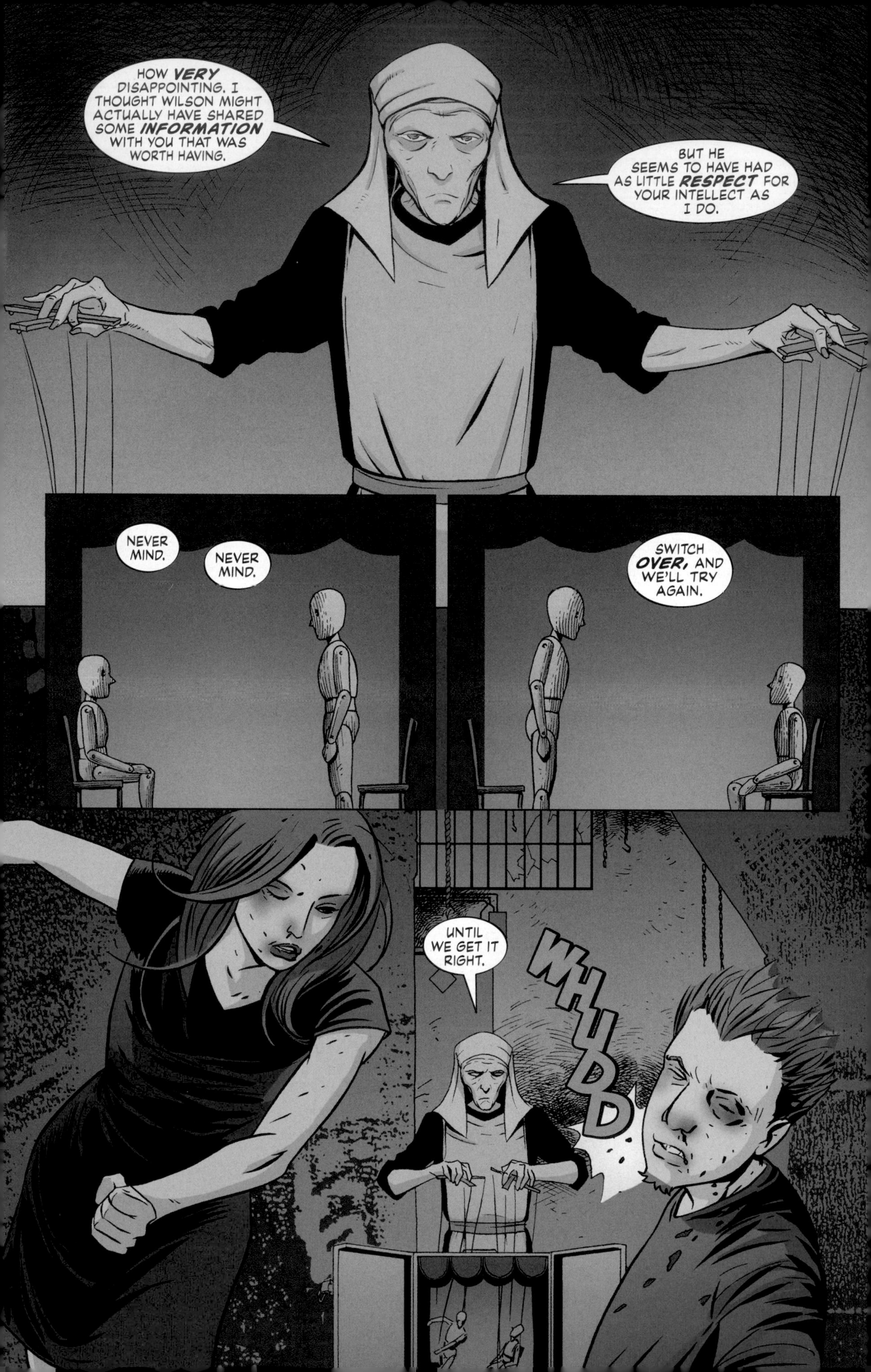
HOW VERY DISAPPOINTING. I THOUGHT WILSON MIGHT ACTUALLY HAVE SHARED SOME INFORMATION WITH YOU THAT WAS WORTH HAVING.
BUT HE SEEMS TO HAVE HAD AS LITTLE RESPECT FOR YOUR INTELLECT AS I DO.
NEVER MIND.
NEVER MIND.
SWITCH OVER, AND WE'LL TRY AGAIN.
UNTIL WE GET IT RIGHT.
WHUDD

# Mutiny on the High Seas

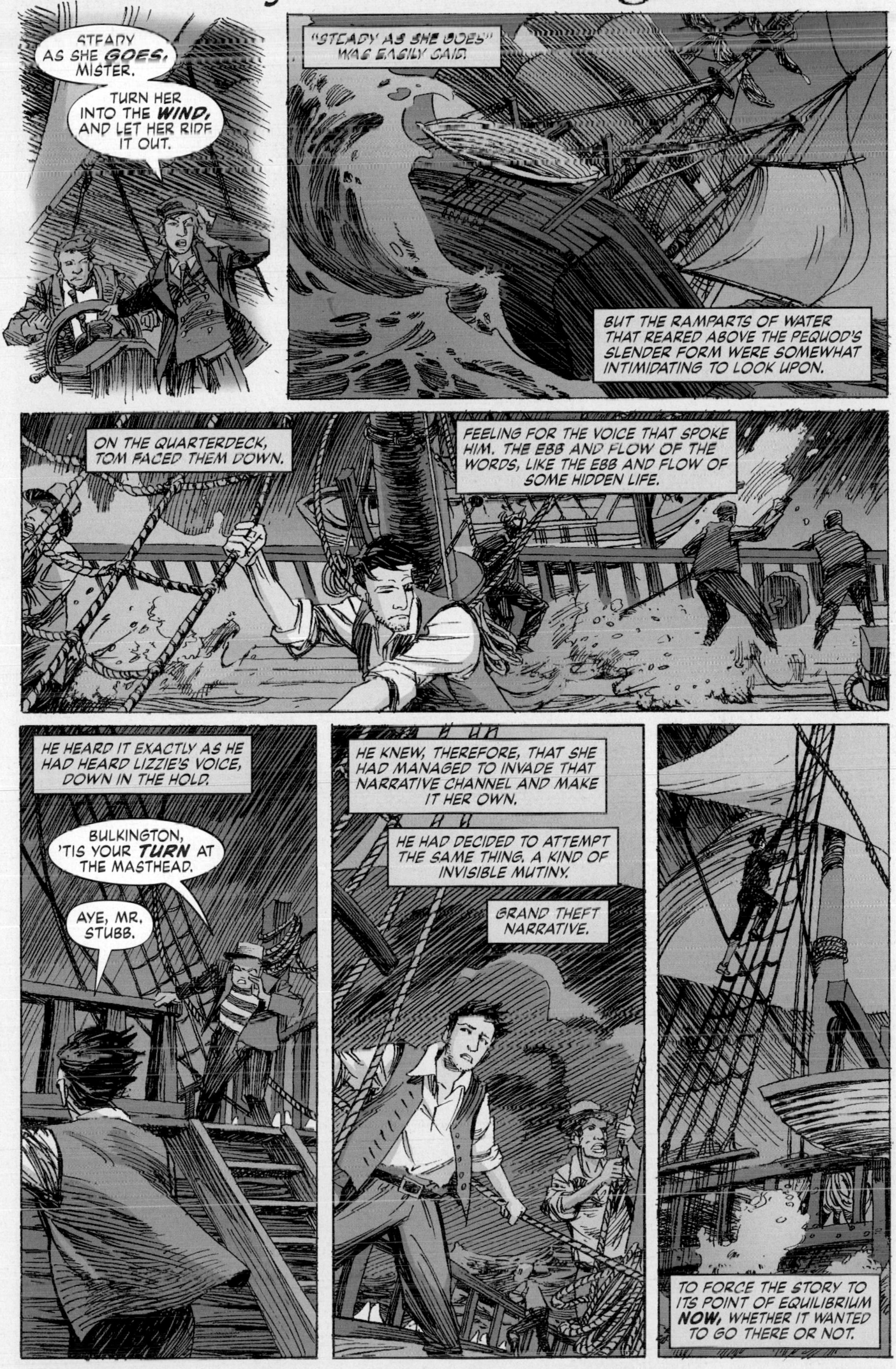
STEADY AS SHE GOES, MISTER.
TURN HER INTO THE WIND, AND LET HER RIDE IT OUT.
"STEADY AS SHE GOES" WAS EASILY SAID.
BUT THE RAMPARTS OF WATER THAT REARED ABOVE THE PEQUOD'S SLENDER FORM WERE SOMEWHAT INTIMIDATING TO LOOK UPON.
ON THE QUARTERDECK, TOM FACED THEM DOWN.
FEELING FOR THE VOICE THAT SPOKE HIM. THE EBB AND FLOW OF THE WORDS, LIKE THE EBB AND FLOW OF SOME HIDDEN LIFE.
HE HEARD IT EXACTLY AS HE HAD HEARD LIZZIE'S VOICE, DOWN IN THE HOLD.
BULKINGTON, 'TIS YOUR TURN AT THE MASTHEAD.
AYE, MR. STUBB.
HE KNEW, THEREFORE, THAT SHE HAD MANAGED TO INVADE THAT NARRATIVE CHANNEL AND MAKE IT HER OWN.
HE HAD DECIDED TO ATTEMPT THE SAME THING. A KIND OF INVISIBLE MUTINY.
GRAND THEFT NARRATIVE.
TO FORCE THE STORY TO ITS POINT OF EQUILIBRIUM NOW, WHETHER IT WANTED TO GO THERE OR NOT.

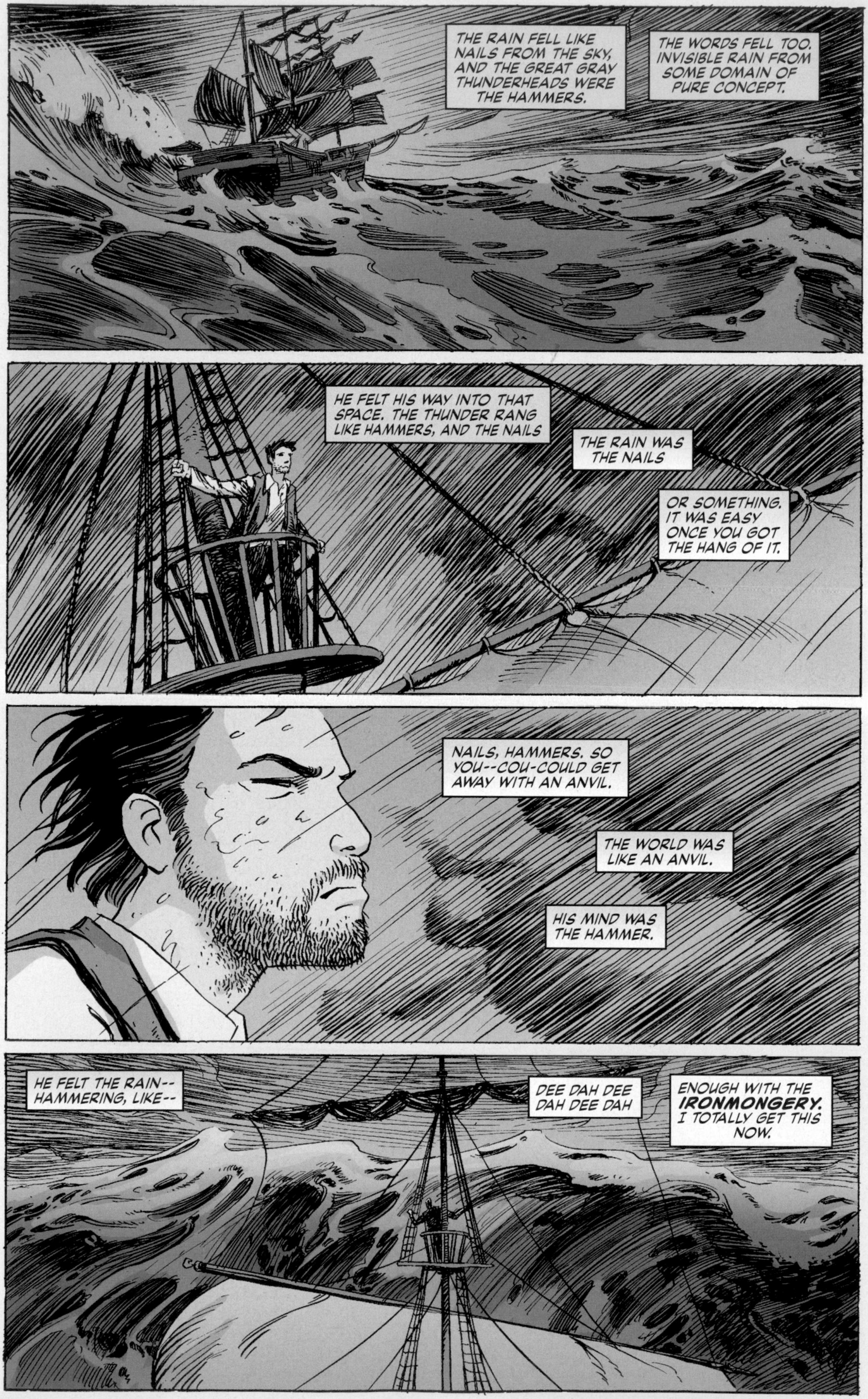
THE RAIN FELL LIKE NAILS FROM THE SKY, AND THE GREAT GRAY THUNDERHEADS WERE THE HAMMERS.
THE WORDS FELL TOO. INVISIBLE RAIN FROM SOME DOMAIN OF PURE CONCEPT.
HE FELT HIS WAY INTO THAT SPACE. THE THUNDER RANG LIKE HAMMERS, AND THE NAILS
THE RAIN WAS THE NAILS
OR SOMETHING. IT WAS EASY ONCE YOU GOT THE HANG OF IT.
NAILS, HAMMERS. SO YOU--COU-COULD GET AWAY WITH AN ANVIL.
THE WORLD WAS LIKE AN ANVIL.
HIS MIND WAS THE HAMMER.
HE FELT THE RAIN-- HAMMERING, LIKE--
DEE DAH DEE DAH DEE DAH
ENOUGH WITH THE **IRONMONGERY.** I TOTALLY GET THIS NOW.

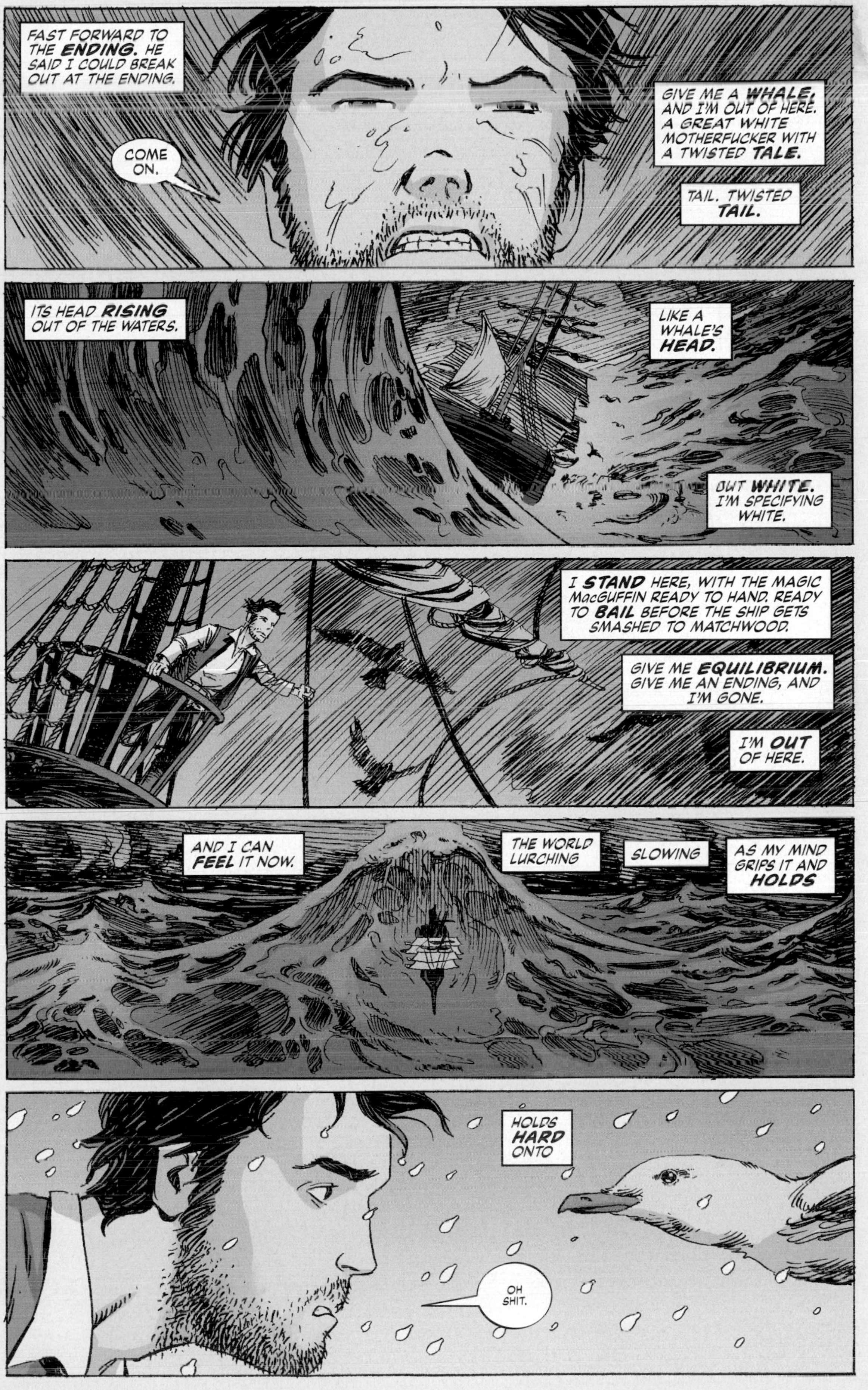
FAST FORWARD TO THE ENDING. HE SAID I COULD BREAK OUT AT THE ENDING.
COME ON.
GIVE ME A WHALE, AND I'M OUT OF HERE. A GREAT WHITE MOTHERFUCKER WITH A TWISTED TALE.
TAIL. TWISTED TAIL.
ITS HEAD RISING OUT OF THE WATERS.
LIKE A WHALE'S HEAD.
BUT WHITE. I'M SPECIFYING WHITE.
I STAND HERE, WITH THE MAGIC MacGUFFIN READY TO HAND. READY TO BAIL BEFORE THE SHIP GETS SMASHED TO MATCHWOOD.
GIVE ME EQUILIBRIUM. GIVE ME AN ENDING, AND I'M GONE.
I'M OUT OF HERE.
AND I CAN FEEL IT NOW.
THE WORLD LURCHING
SLOWING
AS MY MIND GRIPS IT AND HOLDS
HOLDS HARD ONTO
OH SHIT.

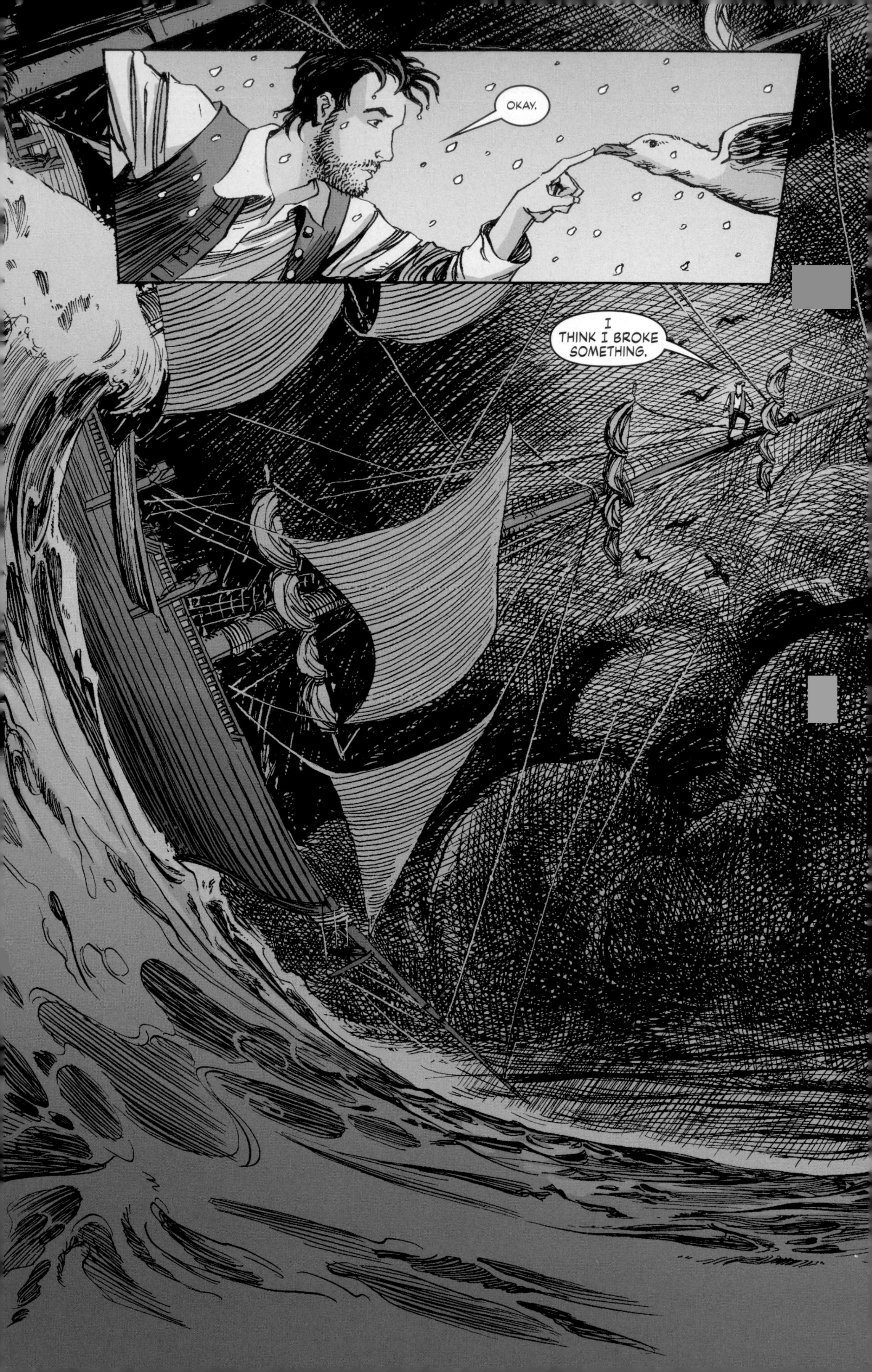
OKAY.
I THINK I BROKE SOMETHING.

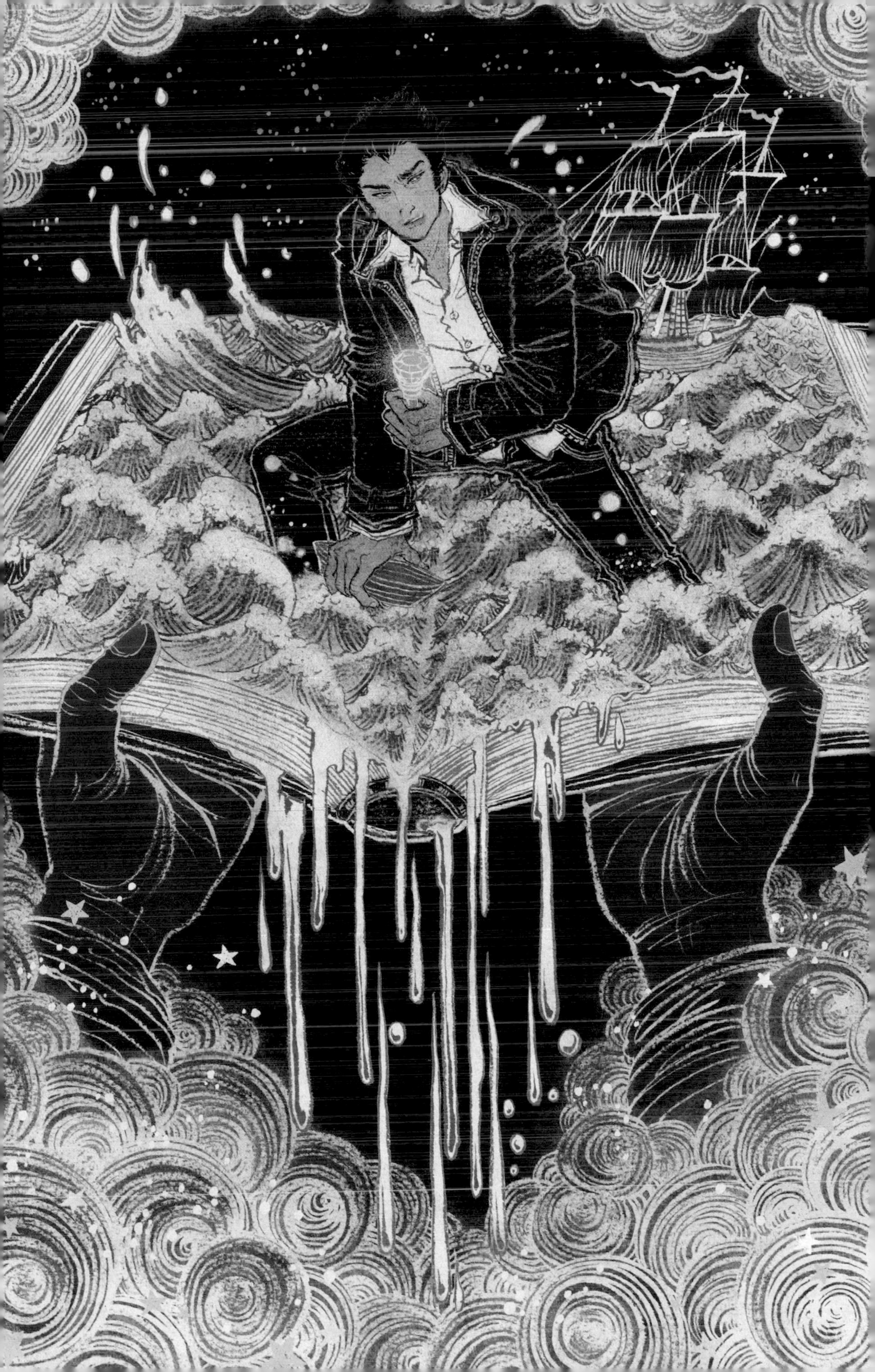

# A Life on the Ocean Wave, A Home on the Rolling Deep

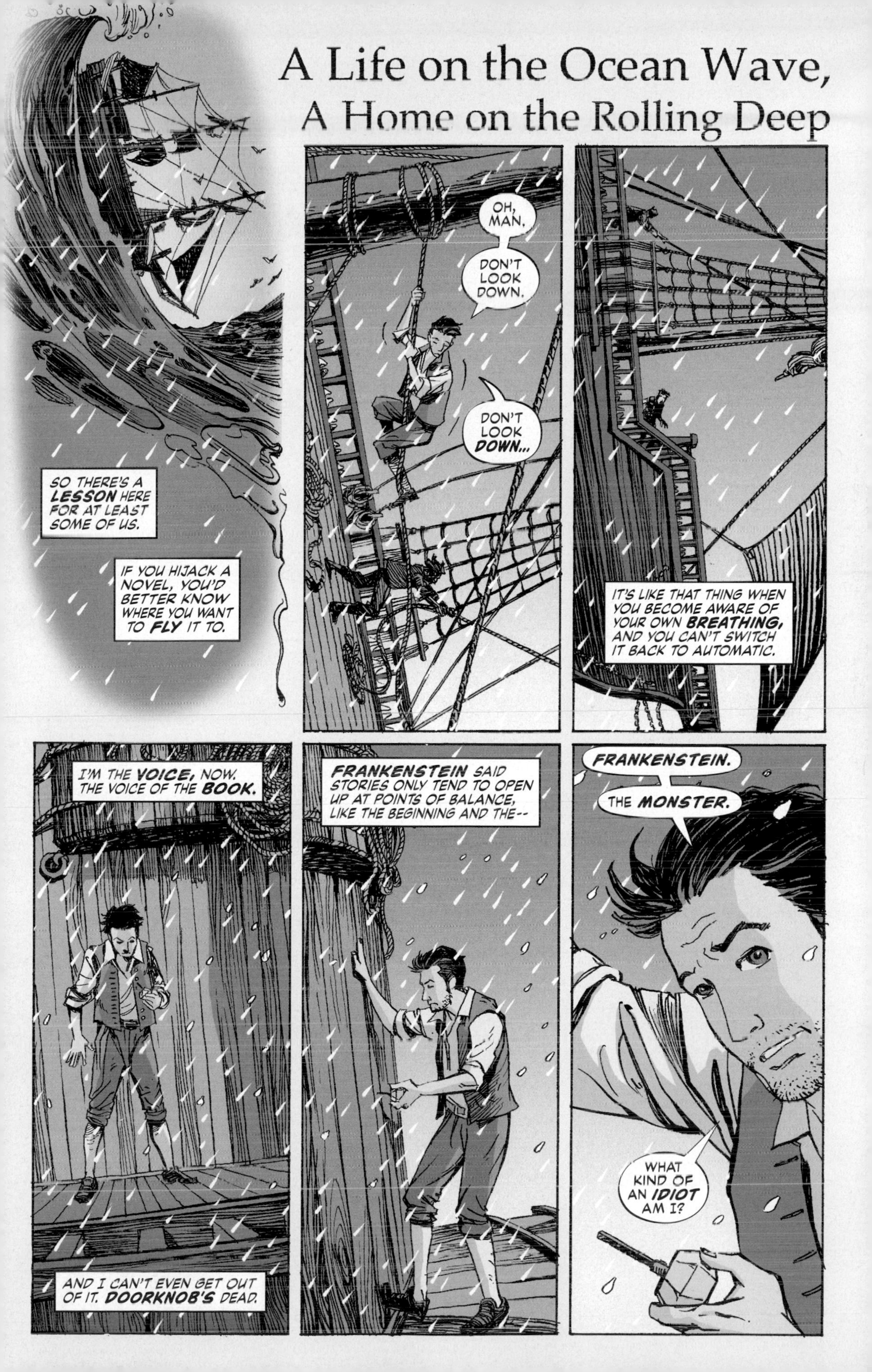
SO THERE'S A LESSON HERE FOR AT LEAST SOME OF US.
IF YOU HIJACK A NOVEL, YOU'D BETTER KNOW WHERE YOU WANT TO FLY IT TO.
OH, MAN.
DON'T LOOK DOWN.
DON'T LOOK DOWN...
IT'S LIKE THAT THING WHEN YOU BECOME AWARE OF YOUR OWN BREATHING, AND YOU CAN'T SWITCH IT BACK TO AUTOMATIC.
I'M THE VOICE, NOW. THE VOICE OF THE BOOK.
AND I CAN'T EVEN GET OUT OF IT. DOORKNOB'S DEAD.
FRANKENSTEIN SAID STORIES ONLY TEND TO OPEN UP AT POINTS OF BALANCE, LIKE THE BEGINNING AND THE--
FRANKENSTEIN.
THE MONSTER.
WHAT KIND OF AN IDIOT AM I?

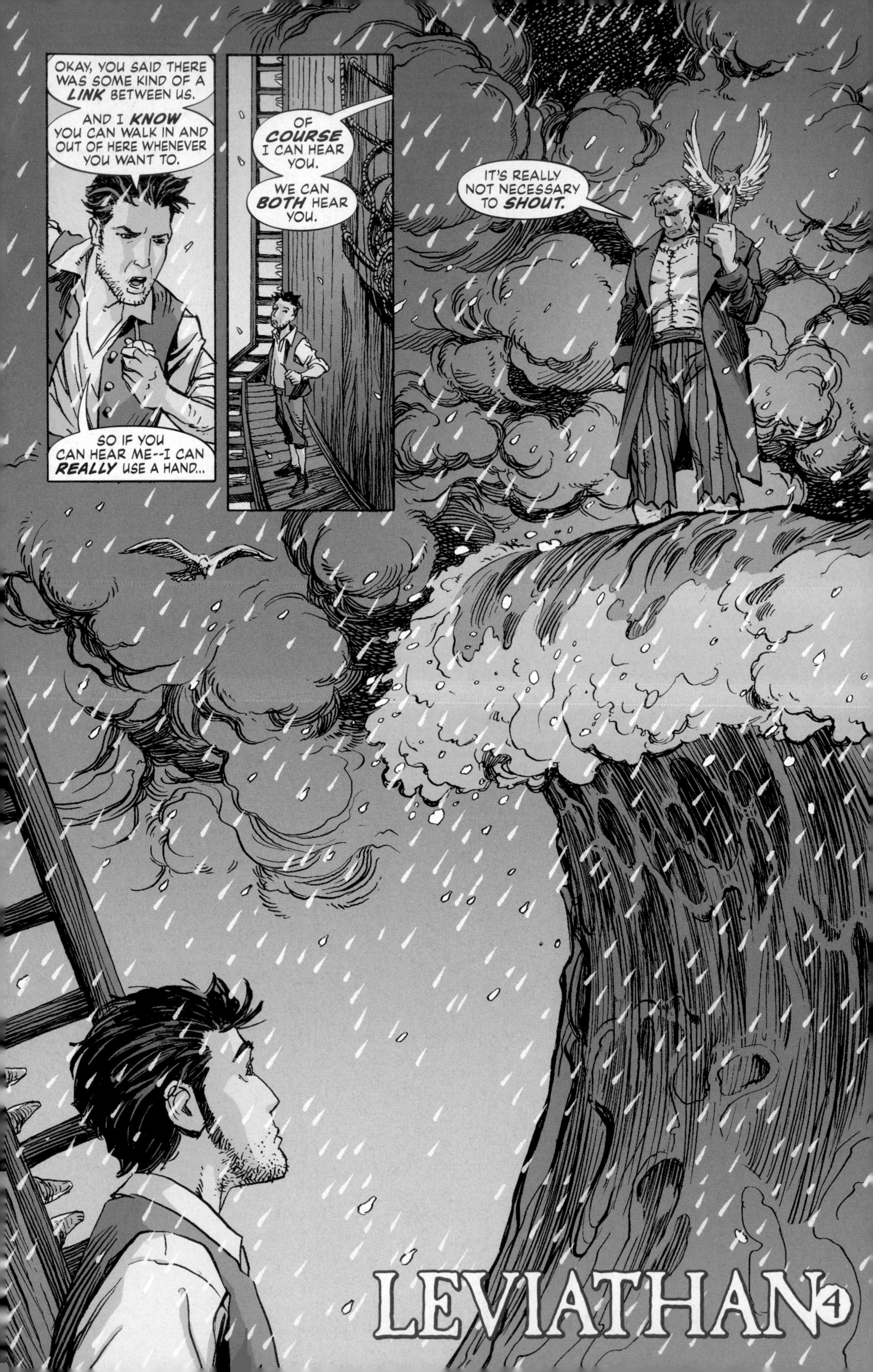

OKAY, YOU SAID THERE WAS SOME KIND OF A LINK BETWEEN US.
AND I KNOW YOU CAN WALK IN AND OUT OF HERE WHENEVER YOU WANT TO.
SO IF YOU CAN HEAR ME--I CAN REALLY USE A HAND...
OF COURSE I CAN HEAR YOU.
WE CAN BOTH HEAR YOU.
IT'S REALLY NOT NECESSARY TO SHOUT.
LEVIATHAN 4

# Angels and Trumpets

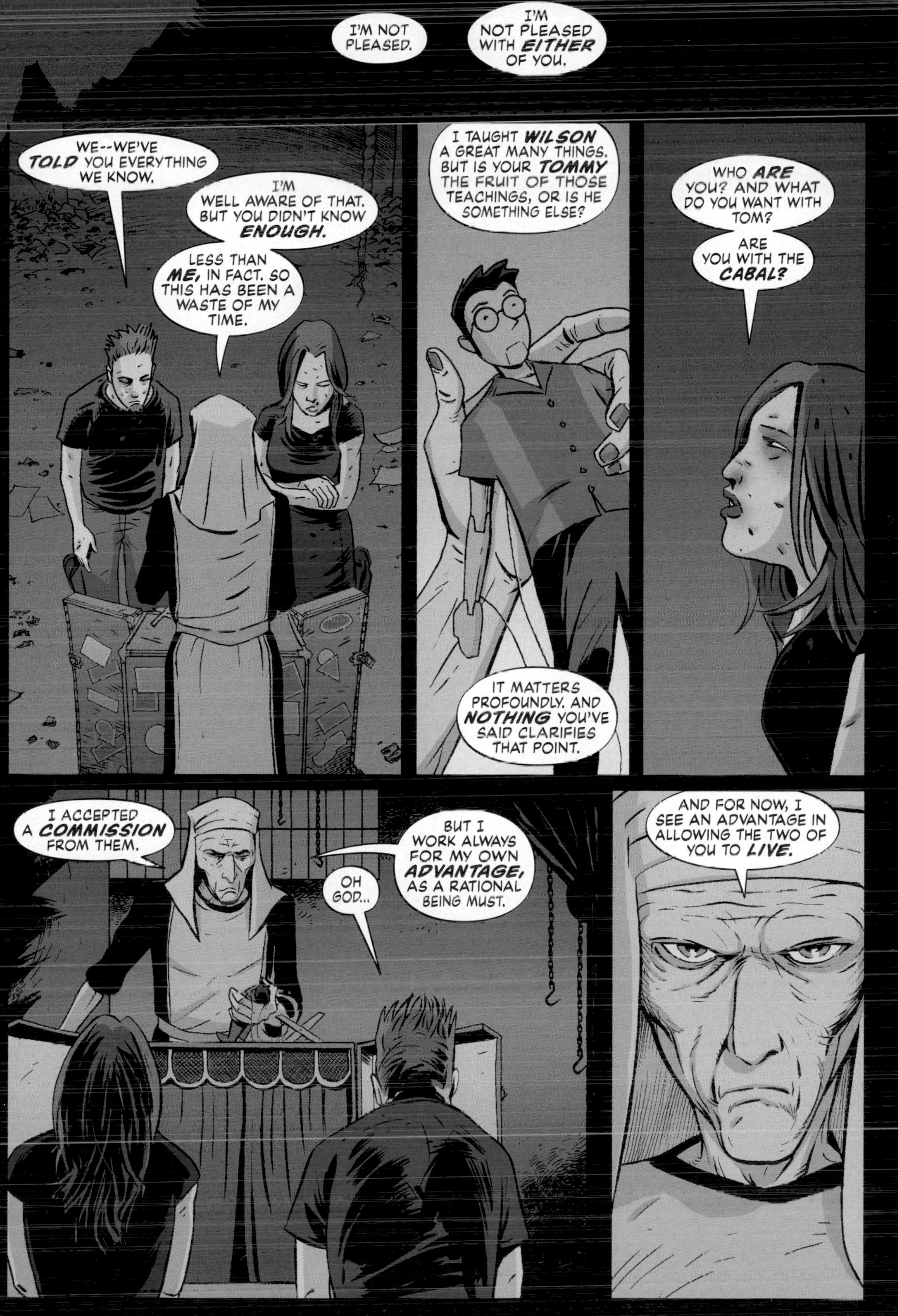
I'M NOT PLEASED.
I'M NOT PLEASED WITH EITHER OF YOU.
WE--WE'VE TOLD YOU EVERYTHING WE KNOW.
I'M WELL AWARE OF THAT. BUT YOU DIDN'T KNOW ENOUGH.
LESS THAN ME, IN FACT. SO THIS HAS BEEN A WASTE OF MY TIME.
I TAUGHT WILSON A GREAT MANY THINGS. BUT IS YOUR TOMMY THE FRUIT OF THOSE TEACHINGS, OR IS HE SOMETHING ELSE?
IT MATTERS PROFOUNDLY. AND NOTHING YOU'VE SAID CLARIFIES THAT POINT.
WHO ARE YOU? AND WHAT DO YOU WANT WITH TOM?
ARE YOU WITH THE CABAL?
I ACCEPTED A COMMISSION FROM THEM.
BUT I WORK ALWAYS FOR MY OWN ADVANTAGE, AS A RATIONAL BEING MUST.
OH GOD...
AND FOR NOW, I SEE AN ADVANTAGE IN ALLOWING THE TWO OF YOU TO LIVE.

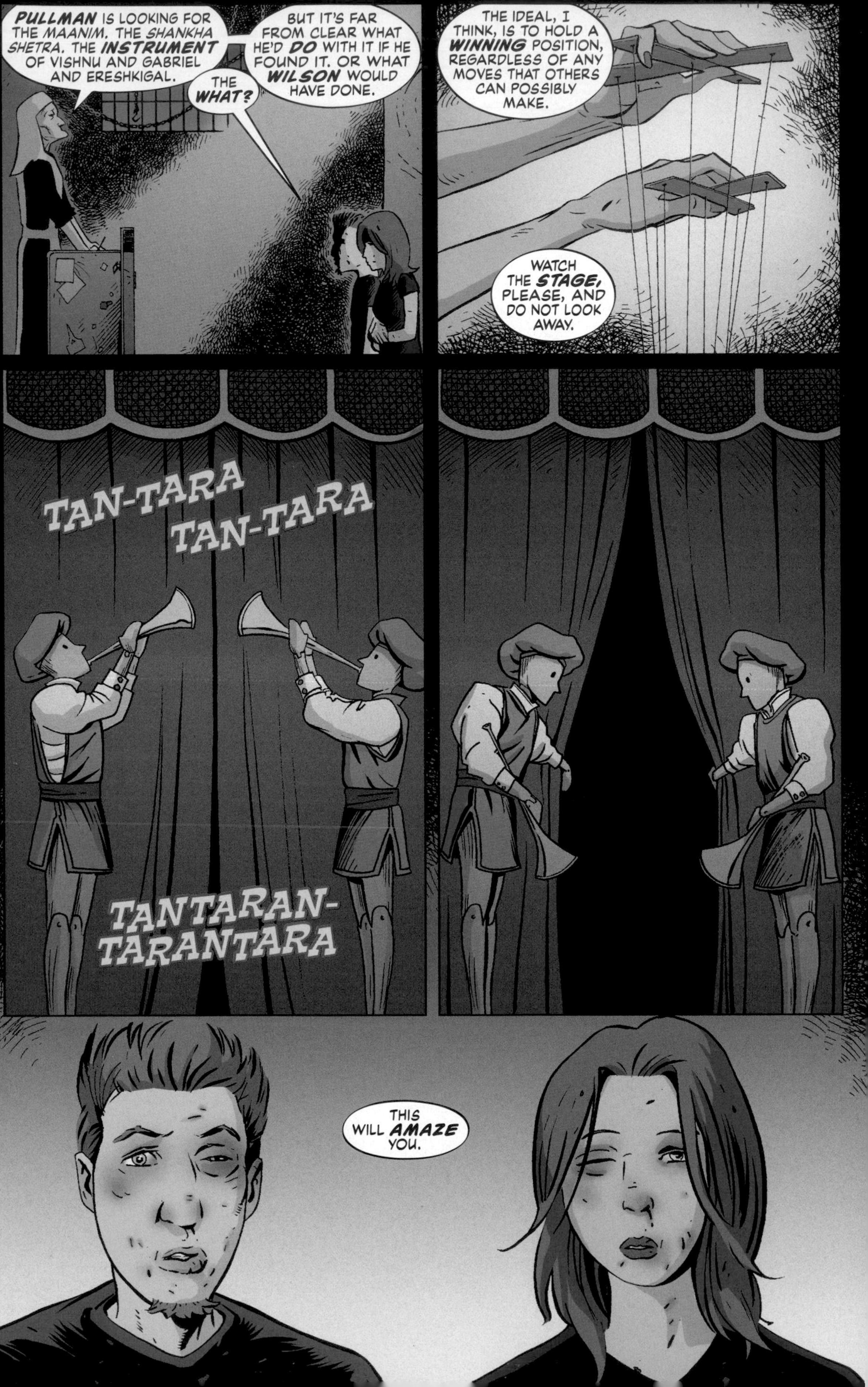
PULLMAN IS LOOKING FOR THE MAANIM. THE SHANKHA SHETRA. THE INSTRUMENT OF VISHNU AND GABRIEL AND ERESHKIGAL.
THE WHAT?
BUT IT'S FAR FROM CLEAR WHAT HE'D DO WITH IT IF HE FOUND IT. OR WHAT WILSON WOULD HAVE DONE.
THE IDEAL, I THINK, IS TO HOLD A WINNING POSITION, REGARDLESS OF ANY MOVES THAT OTHERS CAN POSSIBLY MAKE.
WATCH THE STAGE, PLEASE, AND DO NOT LOOK AWAY.
TAN-TARA TAN-TARA
TANTARAN-TARANTARA
THIS WILL AMAZE YOU.

# The Back Stairs

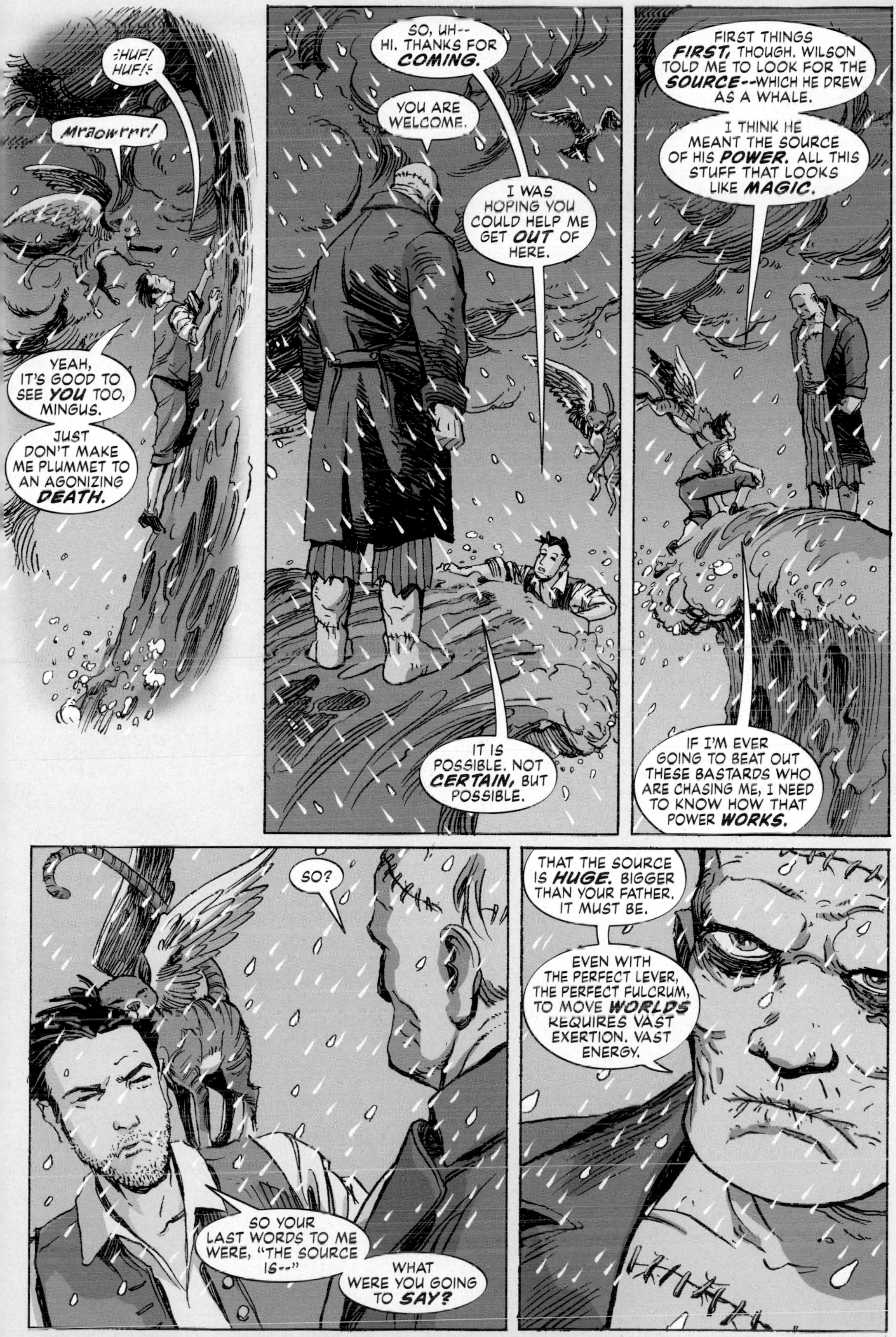

HUF! HUF!
Mraowrrr!
YEAH, IT'S GOOD TO SEE YOU TOO, MINGUS.
JUST DON'T MAKE ME PLUMMET TO AN AGONIZING DEATH.
SO, UH-- HI. THANKS FOR COMING.
YOU ARE WELCOME.
I WAS HOPING YOU COULD HELP ME GET OUT OF HERE.
IT IS POSSIBLE. NOT CERTAIN, BUT POSSIBLE.
FIRST THINGS FIRST, THOUGH. WILSON TOLD ME TO LOOK FOR THE SOURCE--WHICH HE DREW AS A WHALE.
I THINK HE MEANT THE SOURCE OF HIS POWER. ALL THIS STUFF THAT LOOKS LIKE MAGIC.
IF I'M EVER GOING TO BEAT OUT THESE BASTARDS WHO ARE CHASING ME, I NEED TO KNOW HOW THAT POWER WORKS.
SO?
SO YOUR LAST WORDS TO ME WERE, "THE SOURCE IS--"
WHAT WERE YOU GOING TO SAY?
THAT THE SOURCE IS HUGE. BIGGER THAN YOUR FATHER. IT MUST BE.
EVEN WITH THE PERFECT LEVER, THE PERFECT FULCRUM, TO MOVE WORLDS REQUIRES VAST EXERTION. VAST ENERGY.

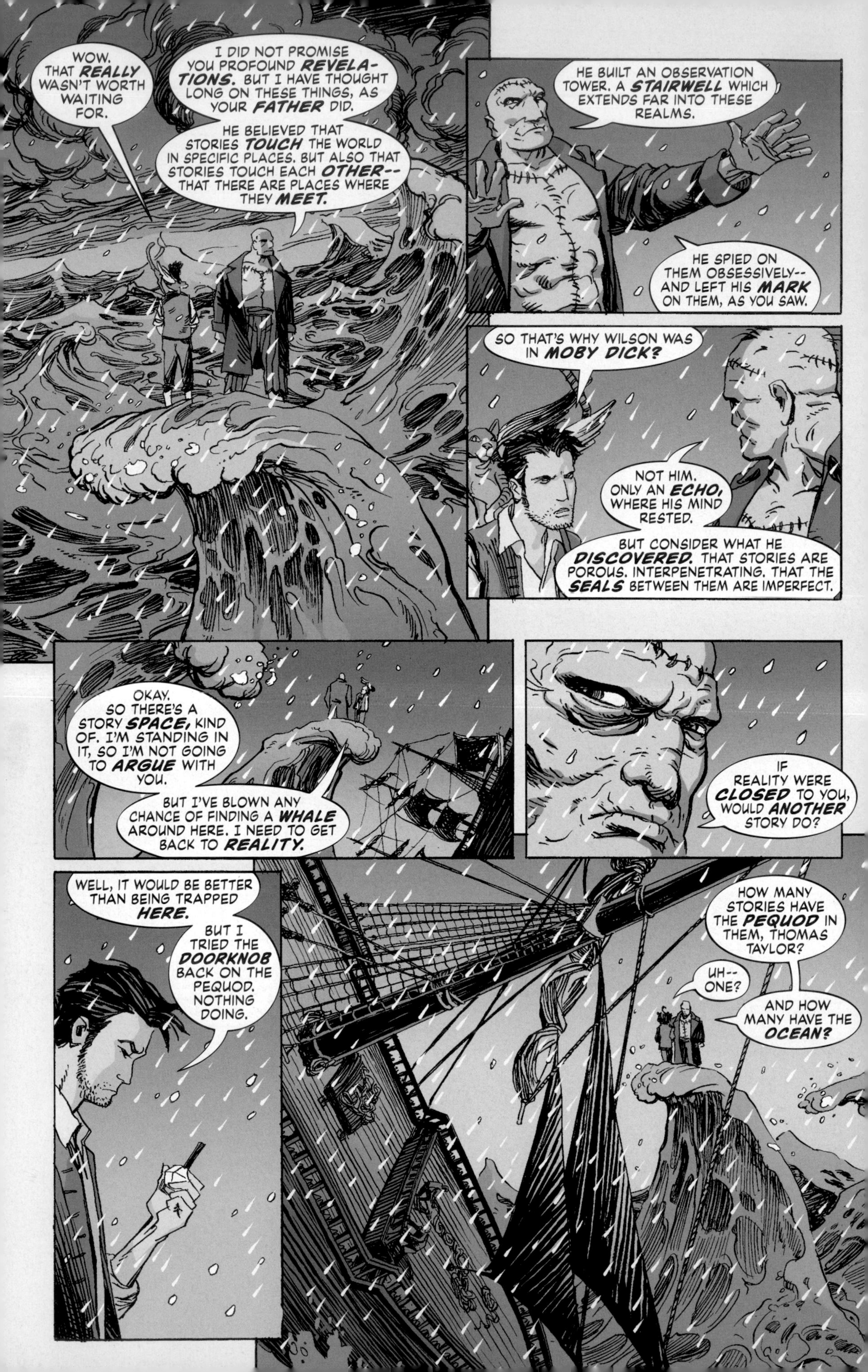
WOW. THAT REALLY WASN'T WORTH WAITING FOR.
I DID NOT PROMISE YOU PROFOUND REVELATIONS. BUT I HAVE THOUGHT LONG ON THESE THINGS, AS YOUR FATHER DID.
HE BELIEVED THAT STORIES TOUCH THE WORLD IN SPECIFIC PLACES. BUT ALSO THAT STORIES TOUCH EACH OTHER-- THAT THERE ARE PLACES WHERE THEY MEET.
HE BUILT AN OBSERVATION TOWER. A STAIRWELL WHICH EXTENDS FAR INTO THESE REALMS.
HE SPIED ON THEM OBSESSIVELY-- AND LEFT HIS MARK ON THEM, AS YOU SAW.
SO THAT'S WHY WILSON WAS IN MOBY DICK?
NOT HIM. ONLY AN ECHO, WHERE HIS MIND RESTED.
BUT CONSIDER WHAT HE DISCOVERED. THAT STORIES ARE POROUS. INTERPENETRATING. THAT THE SEALS BETWEEN THEM ARE IMPERFECT.
OKAY. SO THERE'S A STORY SPACE, KIND OF. I'M STANDING IN IT, SO I'M NOT GOING TO ARGUE WITH YOU.
BUT I'VE BLOWN ANY CHANCE OF FINDING A WHALE AROUND HERE. I NEED TO GET BACK TO REALITY.
IF REALITY WERE CLOSED TO YOU, WOULD ANOTHER STORY DO?
WELL, IT WOULD BE BETTER THAN BEING TRAPPED HERE.
BUT I TRIED THE DOORKNOB BACK ON THE PEQUOD. NOTHING DOING.
HOW MANY STORIES HAVE THE PEQUOD IN THEM, THOMAS TAYLOR?
UH-- ONE?
AND HOW MANY HAVE THE OCEAN?

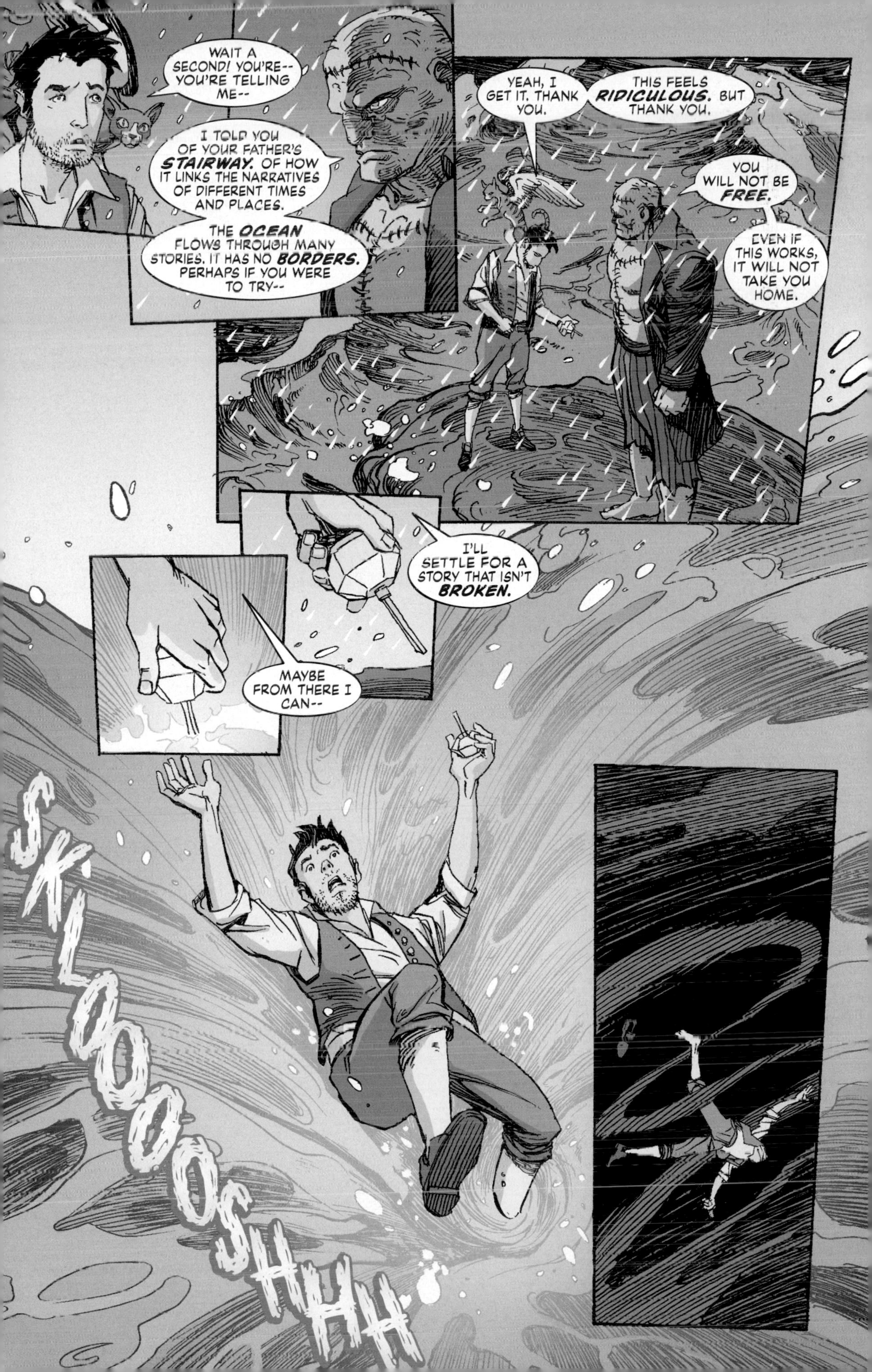
WAIT A SECOND! YOU'RE-- YOU'RE TELLING ME--
I TOLD YOU OF YOUR FATHER'S STAIRWAY. OF HOW IT LINKS THE NARRATIVES OF DIFFERENT TIMES AND PLACES.
THE OCEAN FLOWS THROUGH MANY STORIES. IT HAS NO BORDERS. PERHAPS IF YOU WERE TO TRY--
YEAH, I GET IT. THANK YOU.
THIS FEELS RIDICULOUS. BUT THANK YOU.
YOU WILL NOT BE FREE.
EVEN IF THIS WORKS, IT WILL NOT TAKE YOU HOME.
I'LL SETTLE FOR A STORY THAT ISN'T BROKEN.
MAYBE FROM THERE I CAN--
SKLOOOOSHHH

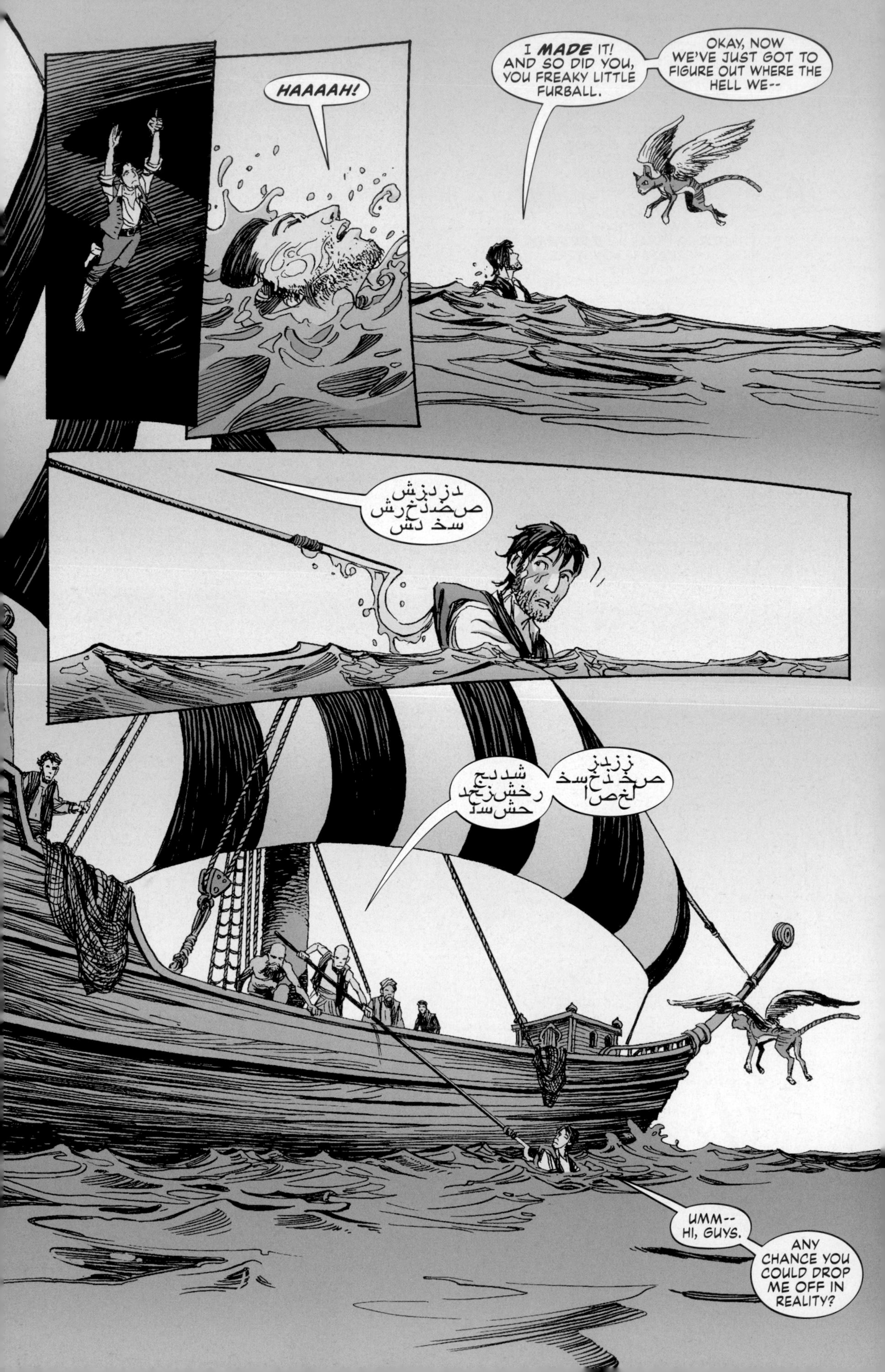

HAAAAH!
I MADE IT! AND SO DID YOU, YOU FREAKY LITTLE FURBALL.
OKAY, NOW WE'VE JUST GOT TO FIGURE OUT WHERE THE HELL WE--
دزدزش صضدخرش سخ دش
شددج رخشزجد حش سد
زززدز صخ دخ سخ لخ صا
UMM-- HI, GUYS.
ANY CHANCE YOU COULD DROP ME OFF IN REALITY?

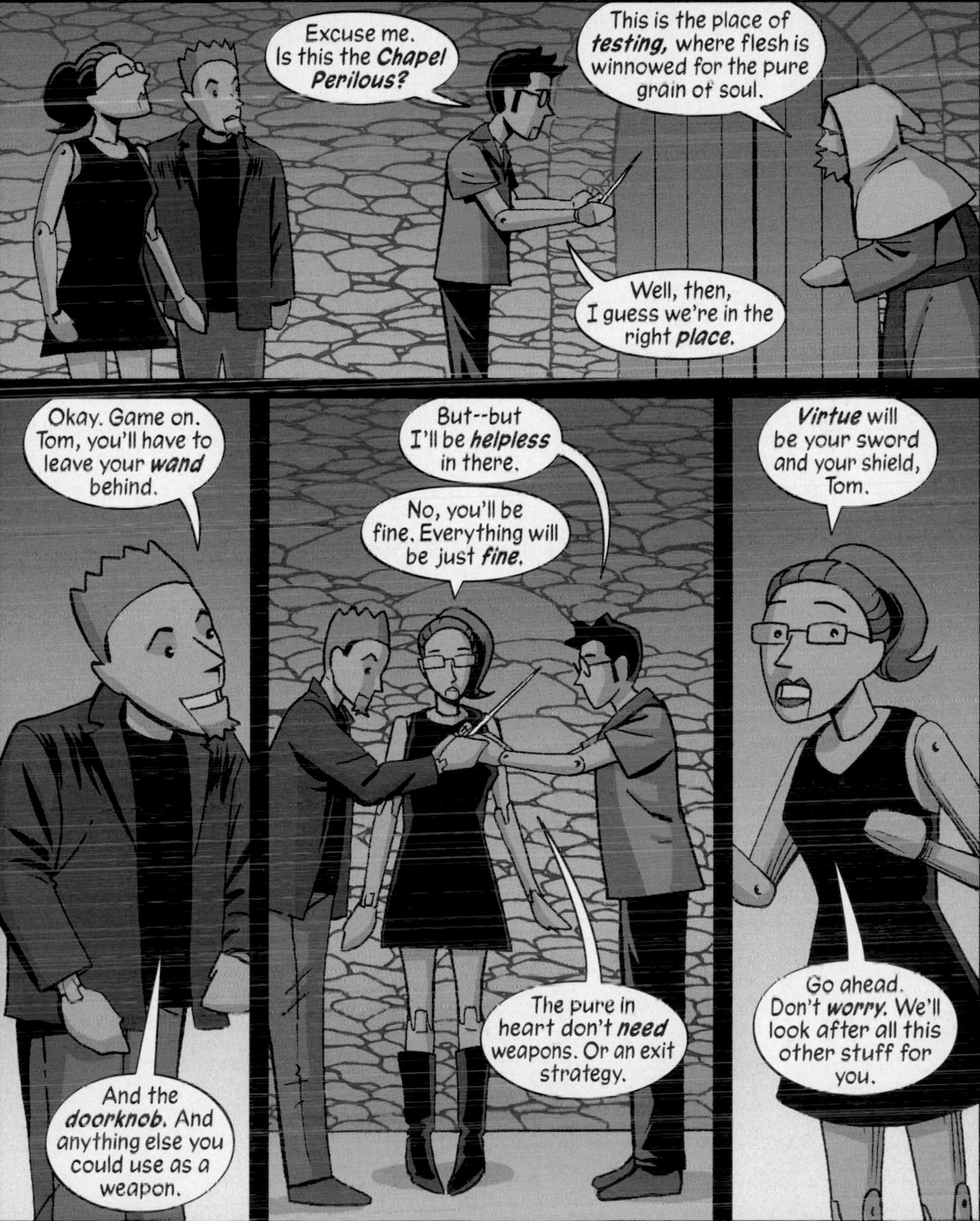
Excuse me. Is this the Chapel Perilous?
This is the place of testing, where flesh is winnowed for the pure grain of soul.
Well, then, I guess we're in the right place.
Okay. Game on. Tom, you'll have to leave your wand behind.
And the doorknob. And anything else you could use as a weapon.
But--but I'll be helpless in there.
No, you'll be fine. Everything will be just fine.
The pure in heart don't need weapons. Or an exit strategy.
Virtue will be your sword and your shield, Tom.
Go ahead. Don't worry. We'll look after all this other stuff for you.

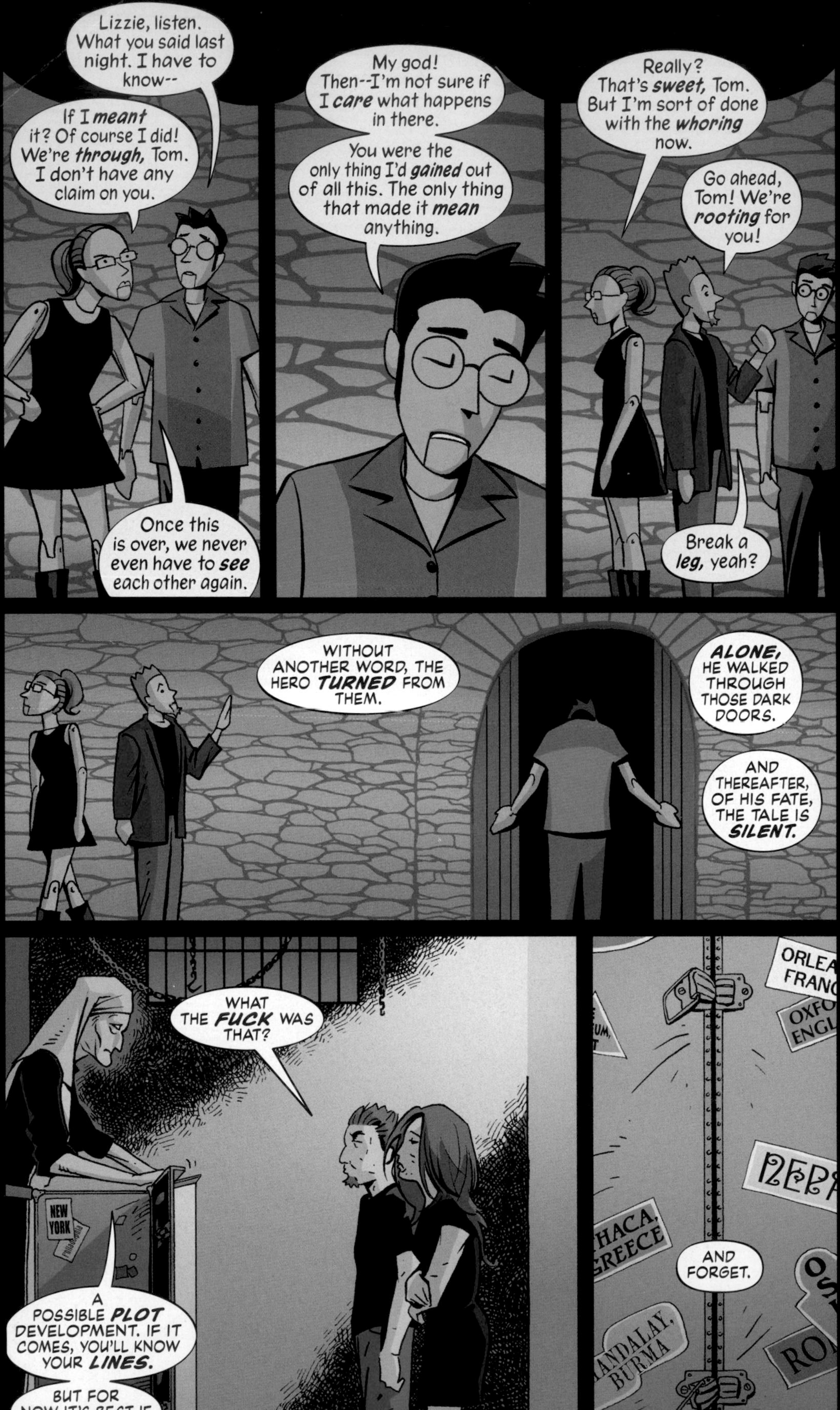
Lizzie, listen. What you said last night. I have to know--
If I *meant* it? Of course I did! We're *through,* Tom. I don't have any claim on you.
Once this is over, we never even have to *see* each other again.
My god! Then--I'm not sure if I *care* what happens in there.
You were the only thing I'd *gained* out of all this. The only thing that made it *mean* anything.
Really? That's *sweet,* Tom. But I'm sort of done with the *whoring* now.
Go ahead, Tom! We're *rooting* for you!
Break a *leg,* yeah?
WITHOUT ANOTHER WORD, THE HERO *TURNED* FROM THEM.
*ALONE,* HE WALKED THROUGH THOSE DARK DOORS.
AND THEREAFTER, OF HIS FATE, THE TALE IS *SILENT.*
WHAT THE *FUCK* WAS THAT?
NEW YORK
A POSSIBLE *PLOT* DEVELOPMENT. IF IT COMES, YOU'LL KNOW YOUR *LINES.*
BUT FOR NOW IT'S BEST IF YOU *SLEEP.*
ITHACA, GREECE
MANDALAY, BURMA
AND FORGET.

# More Tragic Failures to Communicate

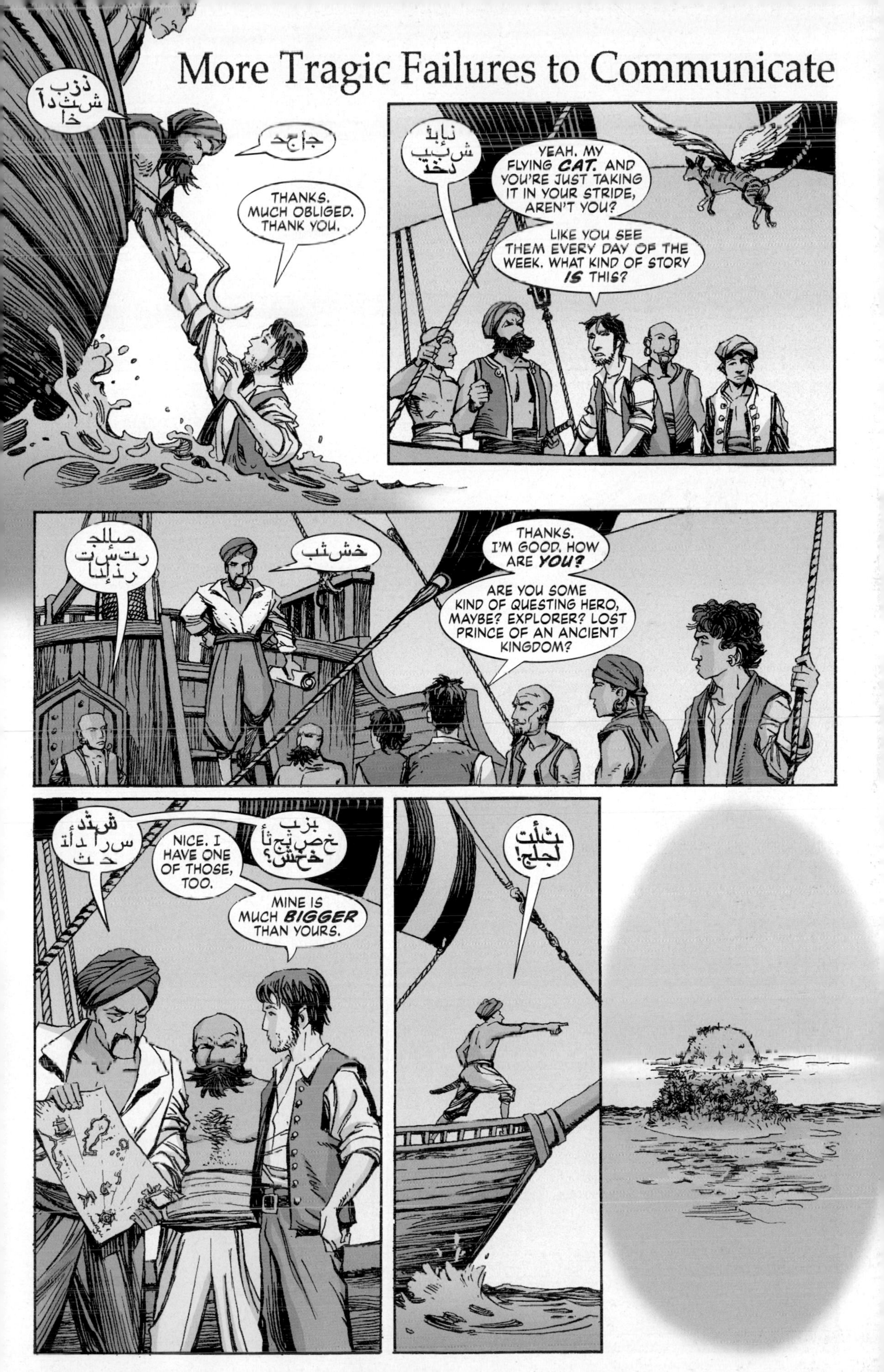
THANKS. MUCH OBLIGED. THANK YOU.
YEAH. MY FLYING CAT. AND YOU'RE JUST TAKING IT IN YOUR STRIDE, AREN'T YOU?
LIKE YOU SEE THEM EVERY DAY OF THE WEEK. WHAT KIND OF STORY IS THIS?
THANKS. I'M GOOD. HOW ARE YOU?
ARE YOU SOME KIND OF QUESTING HERO, MAYBE? EXPLORER? LOST PRINCE OF AN ANCIENT KINGDOM?
NICE. I HAVE ONE OF THOSE, TOO.
MINE IS MUCH BIGGER THAN YOURS.

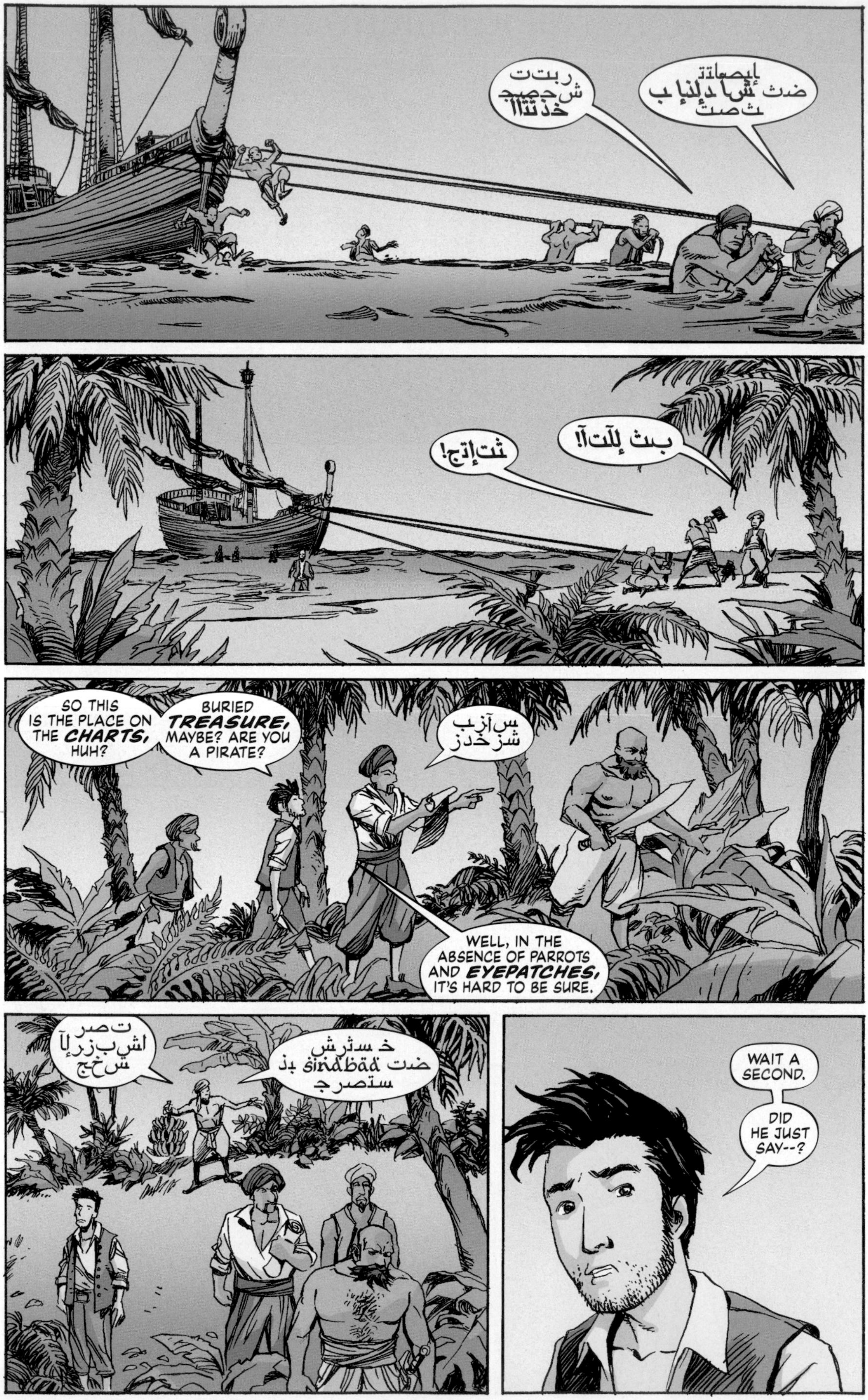
ايصاتت ضث شا دلنإ ب ثصت
ربتت ش حجيج خذ تتاا
بث إلّتآ!
ثتإتج!
SO THIS IS THE PLACE ON THE *CHARTS*, HUH?
BURIED *TREASURE*, MAYBE? ARE YOU A PIRATE?
س آزب شزخدز
WELL, IN THE ABSENCE OF PARROTS AND *EYEPATCHES*, IT'S HARD TO BE SURE.
تصر اشي ب زرإآ س خج
خ سثرش ضت sindbad بذ ستصرج
WAIT A SECOND.
DID HE JUST SAY--?

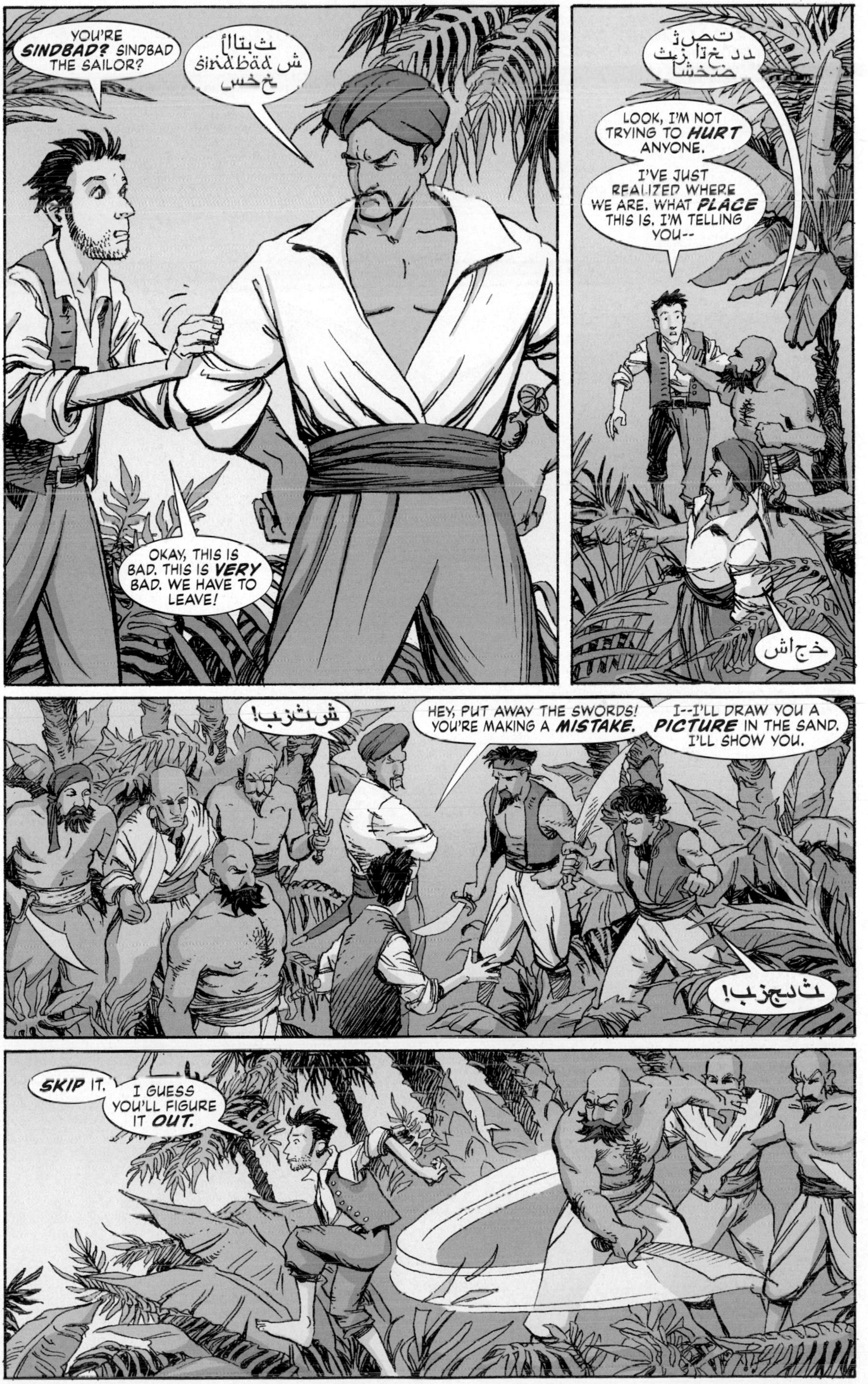
YOU'RE SINDBAD? SINDBAD THE SAILOR?
ثبتاأ sindbad ش خخس
OKAY, THIS IS BAD. THIS IS VERY BAD. WE HAVE TO LEAVE!
تصث دد خ تا زبث ضخشا
LOOK, I'M NOT TRYING TO HURT ANYONE.
I'VE JUST REALIZED WHERE WE ARE. WHAT PLACE THIS IS. I'M TELLING YOU--
خج اش
شثزب!
HEY, PUT AWAY THE SWORDS! YOU'RE MAKING A MISTAKE.
I--I'LL DRAW YOU A PICTURE IN THE SAND. I'LL SHOW YOU.
ثدجزب!
SKIP IT.
I GUESS YOU'LL FIGURE IT OUT.

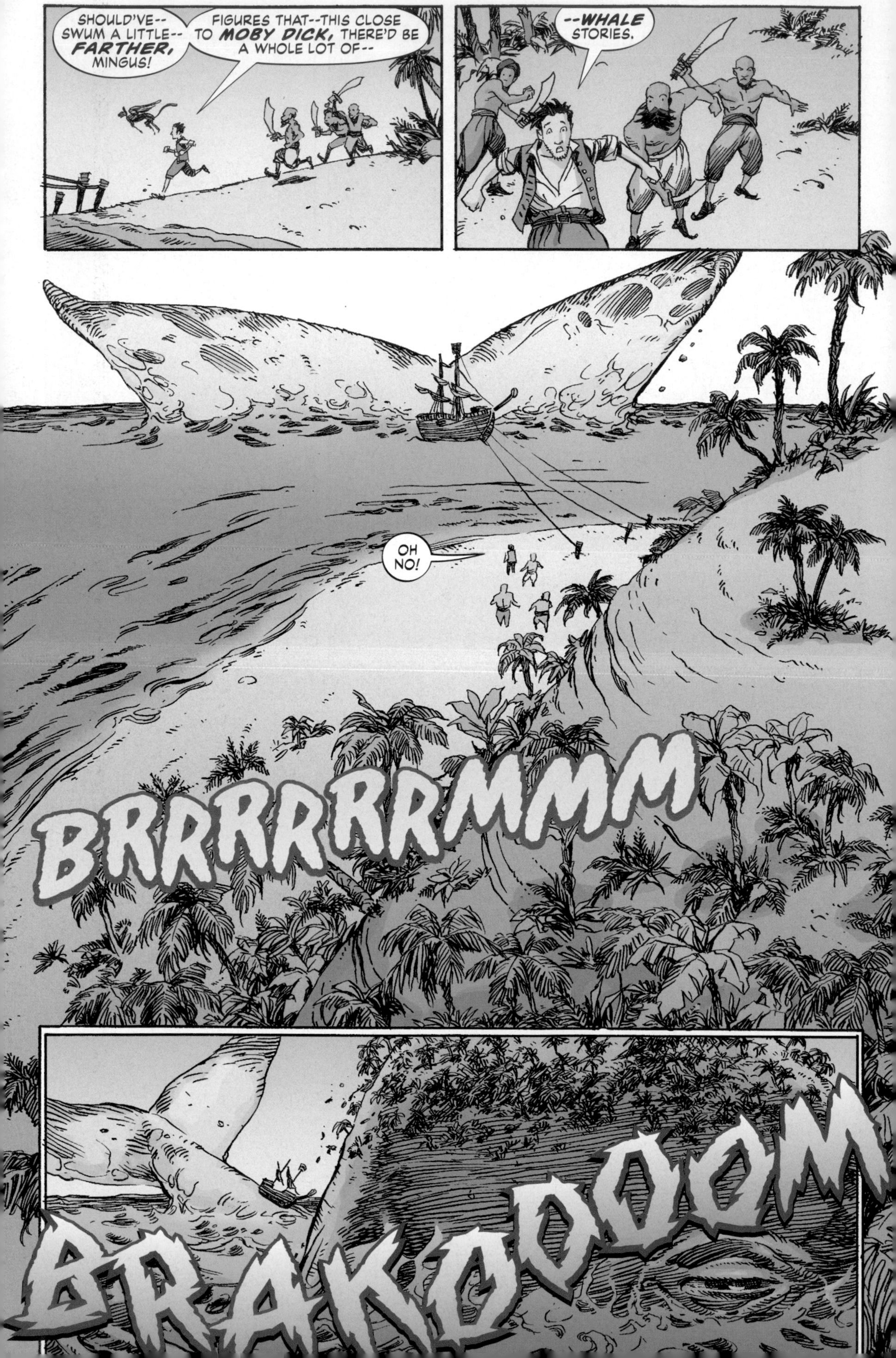
SHOULD'VE-- SWUM A LITTLE-- FARTHER, MINGUS!
FIGURES THAT--THIS CLOSE TO MOBY DICK, THERE'D BE A WHOLE LOT OF--
--WHALE STORIES.
OH NO!
BRRRRRRMMM
BRAKOOOOM

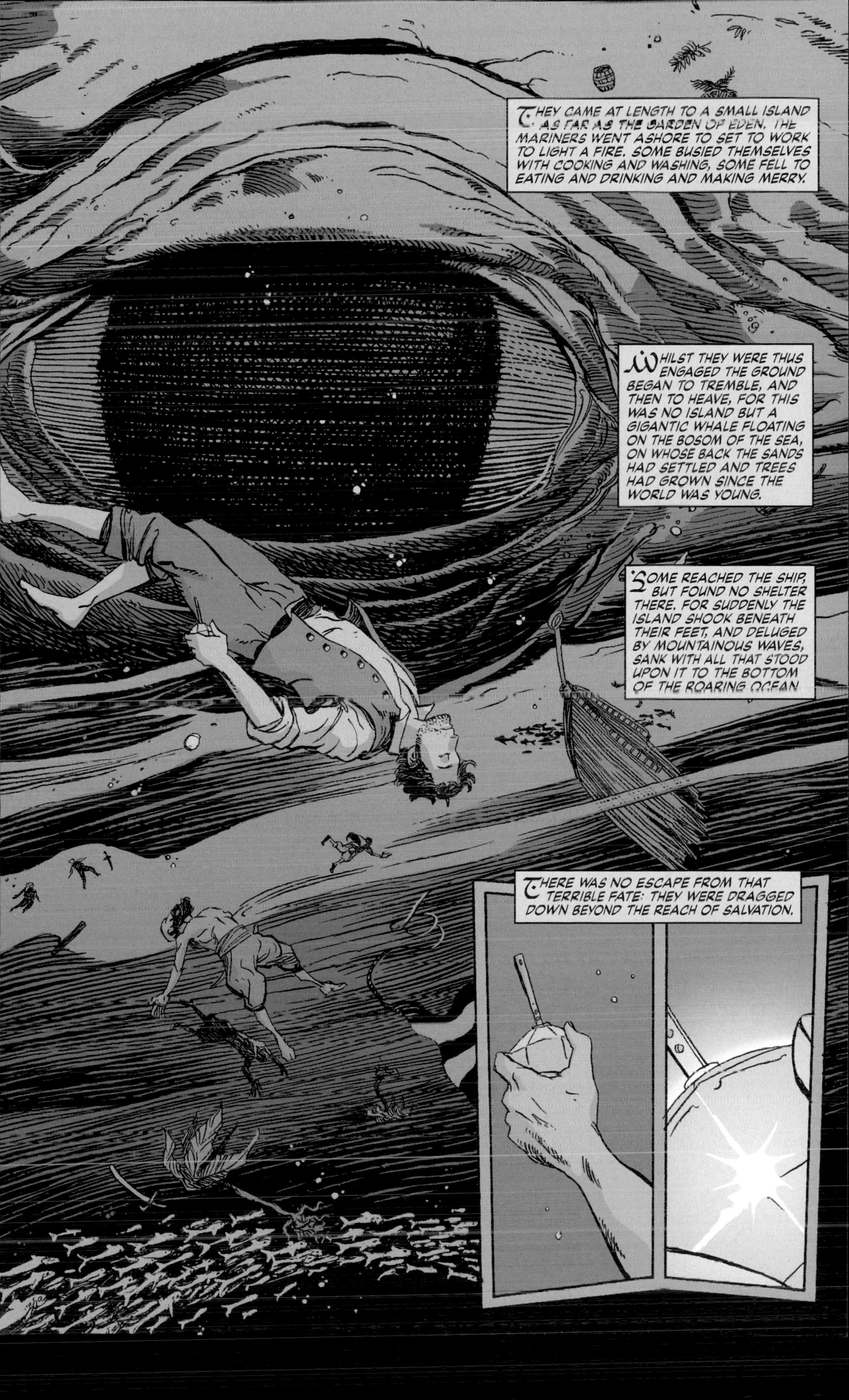
THEY CAME AT LENGTH TO A SMALL ISLAND AS FAR AS THE GARDEN OF EDEN. THE MARINERS WENT ASHORE TO SET TO WORK TO LIGHT A FIRE. SOME BUSIED THEMSELVES WITH COOKING AND WASHING, SOME FELL TO EATING AND DRINKING AND MAKING MERRY.
WHILST THEY WERE THUS ENGAGED THE GROUND BEGAN TO TREMBLE, AND THEN TO HEAVE, FOR THIS WAS NO ISLAND BUT A GIGANTIC WHALE FLOATING ON THE BOSOM OF THE SEA, ON WHOSE BACK THE SANDS HAD SETTLED AND TREES HAD GROWN SINCE THE WORLD WAS YOUNG.
SOME REACHED THE SHIP, BUT FOUND NO SHELTER THERE. FOR SUDDENLY THE ISLAND SHOOK BENEATH THEIR FEET, AND DELUGED BY MOUNTAINOUS WAVES, SANK WITH ALL THAT STOOD UPON IT TO THE BOTTOM OF THE ROARING OCEAN.
THERE WAS NO ESCAPE FROM THAT TERRIBLE FATE: THEY WERE DRAGGED DOWN BEYOND THE REACH OF SALVATION.

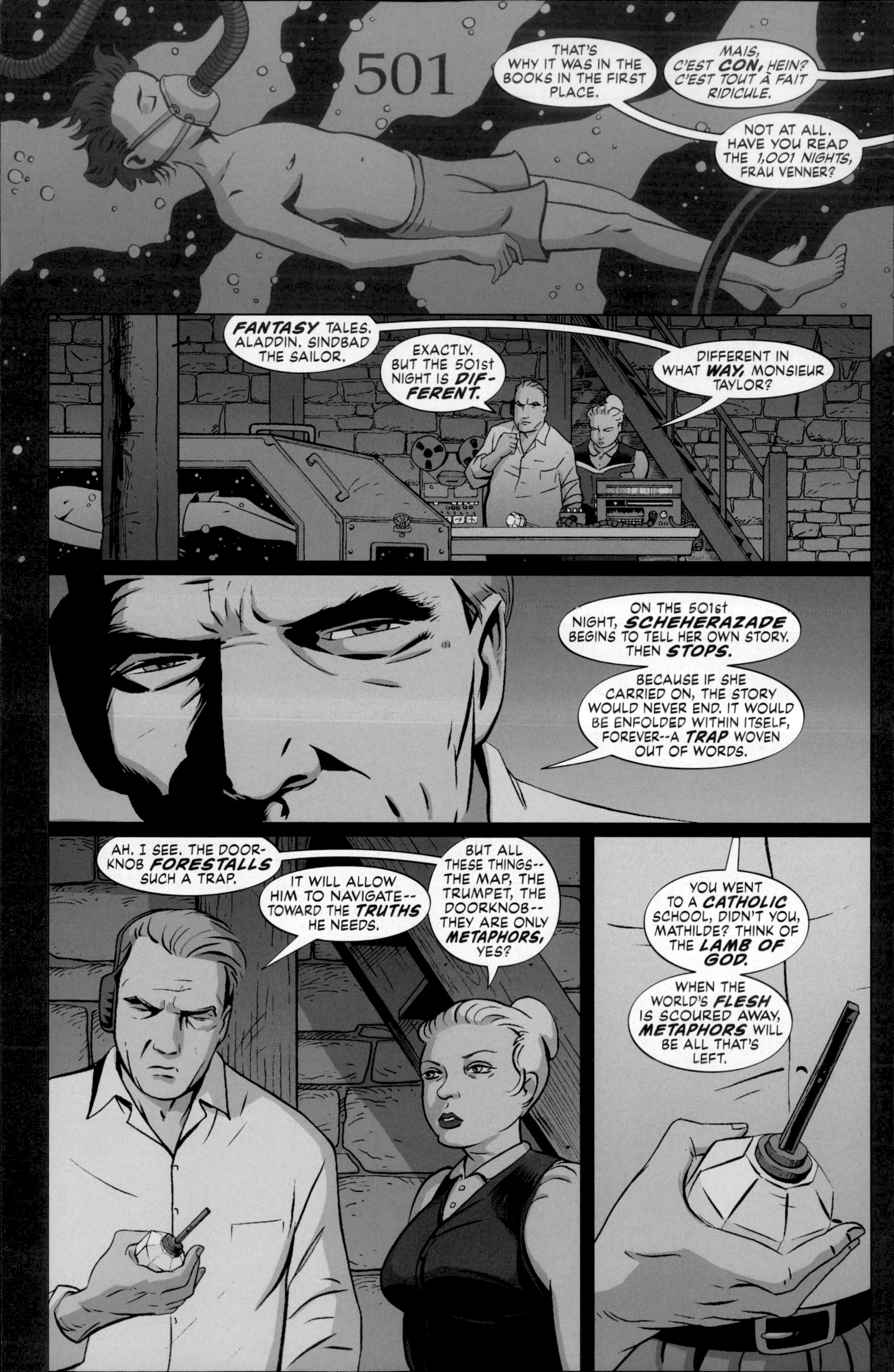
501
THAT'S WHY IT WAS IN THE BOOKS IN THE FIRST PLACE.
MAIS, C'EST CON, HEIN? C'EST TOUT À FAIT RIDICULE.
NOT AT ALL. HAVE YOU READ THE 1,001 NIGHTS, FRAU VENNER?
FANTASY TALES. ALADDIN. SINDBAD THE SAILOR.
EXACTLY. BUT THE 501st NIGHT IS DIF-FERENT.
DIFFERENT IN WHAT WAY, MONSIEUR TAYLOR?
ON THE 501st NIGHT, SCHEHERAZADE BEGINS TO TELL HER OWN STORY. THEN STOPS.
BECAUSE IF SHE CARRIED ON, THE STORY WOULD NEVER END. IT WOULD BE ENFOLDED WITHIN ITSELF, FOREVER--A TRAP WOVEN OUT OF WORDS.
AH. I SEE. THE DOOR-KNOB FORESTALLS SUCH A TRAP.
IT WILL ALLOW HIM TO NAVIGATE--TOWARD THE TRUTHS HE NEEDS.
BUT ALL THESE THINGS--THE MAP, THE TRUMPET, THE DOORKNOB--THEY ARE ONLY METAPHORS, YES?
YOU WENT TO A CATHOLIC SCHOOL, DIDN'T YOU, MATHILDE? THINK OF THE LAMB OF GOD.
WHEN THE WORLD'S FLESH IS SCOURED AWAY, METAPHORS WILL BE ALL THAT'S LEFT.

# Munchhausen's Syndrome

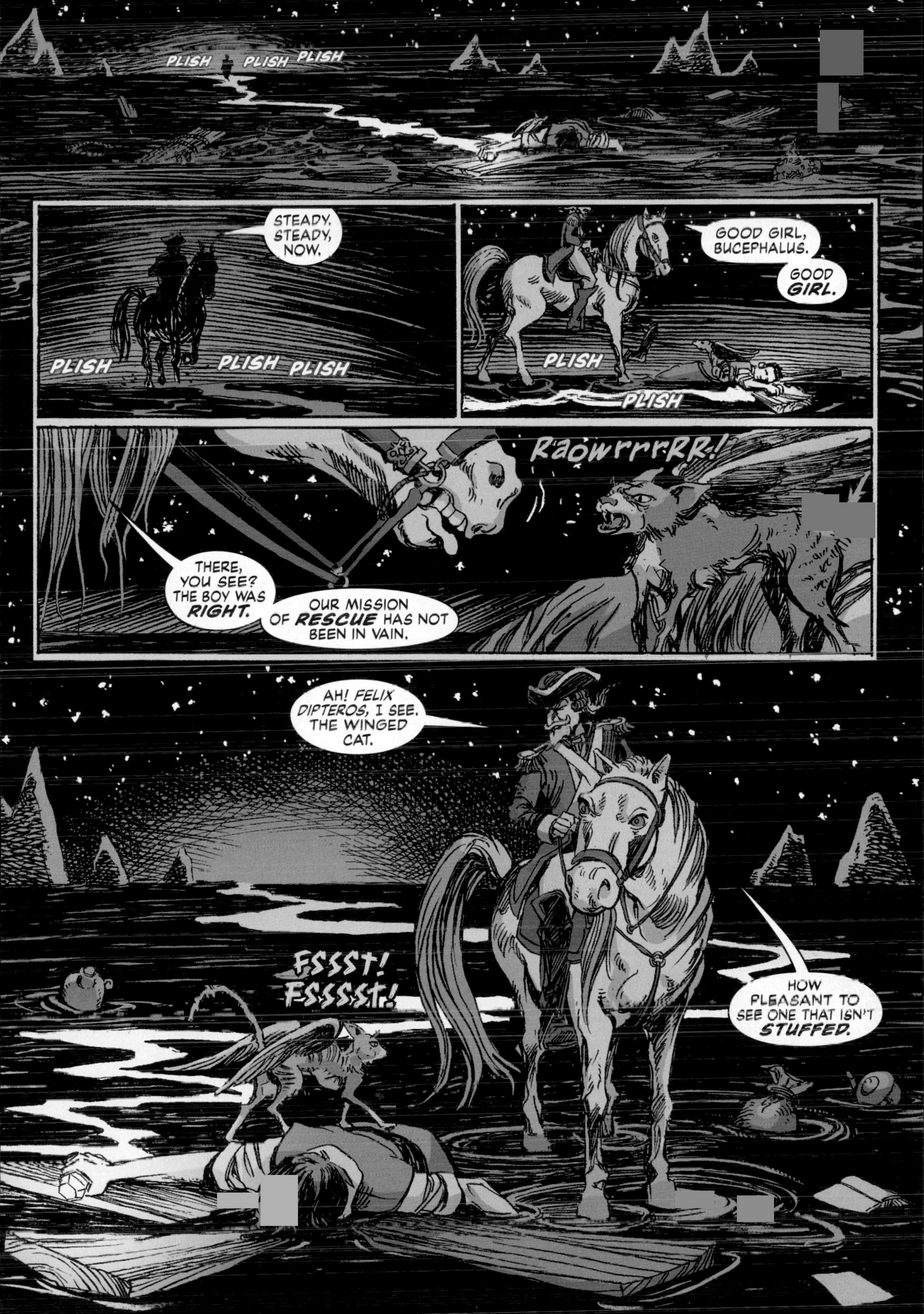
PLISH PLISH PLISH
STEADY. STEADY, NOW.
PLISH PLISH PLISH
GOOD GIRL, BUCEPHALUS.
GOOD GIRL.
PLISH
PLISH
RAOWRRRRR!
THERE, YOU SEE? THE BOY WAS RIGHT.
OUR MISSION OF RESCUE HAS NOT BEEN IN VAIN.
AH! FELIX DIPTEROS, I SEE. THE WINGED CAT.
FSSST! FSSSST!
HOW PLEASANT TO SEE ONE THAT ISN'T STUFFED.

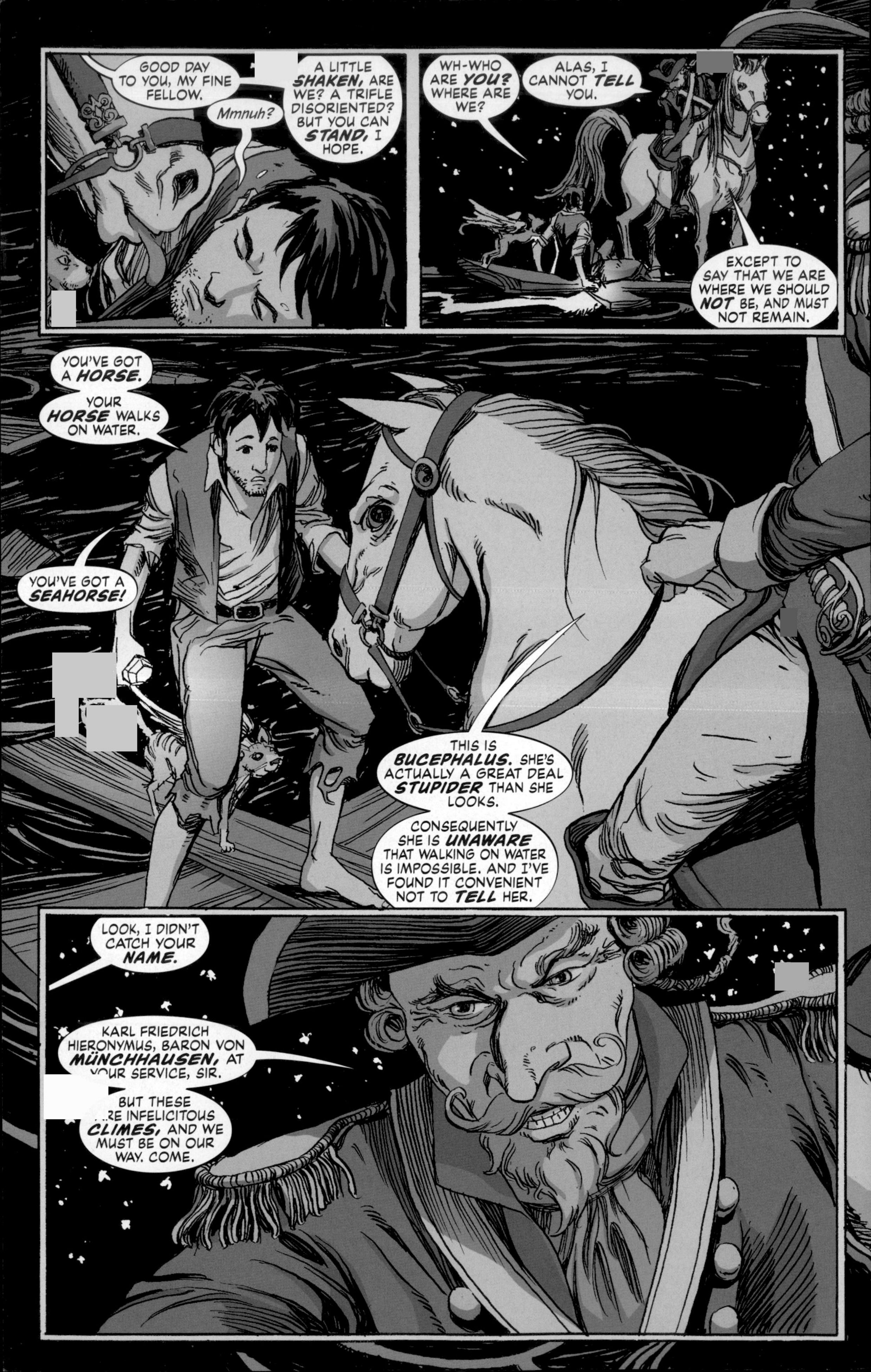
GOOD DAY TO YOU, MY FINE FELLOW.
Mmnuh?
A LITTLE SHAKEN, ARE WE? A TRIFLE DISORIENTED? BUT YOU CAN STAND, I HOPE.
WH-WHO ARE YOU? WHERE ARE WE?
ALAS, I CANNOT TELL YOU.
EXCEPT TO SAY THAT WE ARE WHERE WE SHOULD NOT BE, AND MUST NOT REMAIN.
YOU'VE GOT A HORSE.
YOUR HORSE WALKS ON WATER.
YOU'VE GOT A SEAHORSE!
THIS IS BUCEPHALUS. SHE'S ACTUALLY A GREAT DEAL STUPIDER THAN SHE LOOKS.
CONSEQUENTLY SHE IS UNAWARE THAT WALKING ON WATER IS IMPOSSIBLE. AND I'VE FOUND IT CONVENIENT NOT TO TELL HER.
LOOK, I DIDN'T CATCH YOUR NAME.
KARL FRIEDRICH HIERONYMUS, BARON VON MÜNCHHAUSEN, AT YOUR SERVICE, SIR.
BUT THESE RE INFELICITOUS CLIMES, AND WE MUST BE ON OUR WAY. COME.

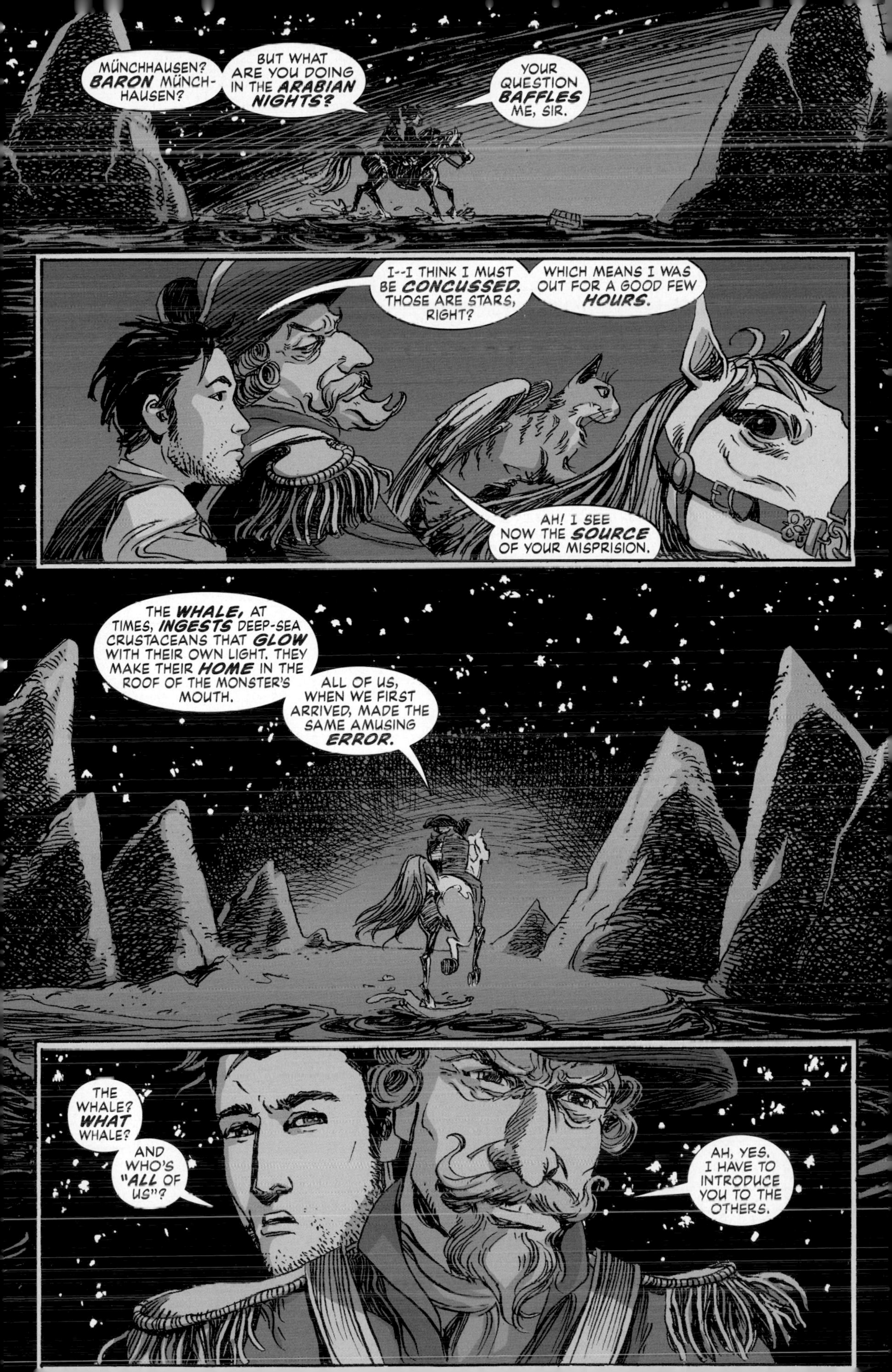
MÜNCHHAUSEN? BARON MÜNCH-HAUSEN?
BUT WHAT ARE YOU DOING IN THE ARABIAN NIGHTS?
YOUR QUESTION BAFFLES ME, SIR.
I--I THINK I MUST BE CONCUSSED. THOSE ARE STARS, RIGHT?
WHICH MEANS I WAS OUT FOR A GOOD FEW HOURS.
AH! I SEE NOW THE SOURCE OF YOUR MISPRISION.
THE WHALE, AT TIMES, INGESTS DEEP-SEA CRUSTACEANS THAT GLOW WITH THEIR OWN LIGHT. THEY MAKE THEIR HOME IN THE ROOF OF THE MONSTER'S MOUTH.
ALL OF US, WHEN WE FIRST ARRIVED, MADE THE SAME AMUSING ERROR.
THE WHALE? WHAT WHALE?
AND WHO'S "ALL OF US"?
AH, YES. I HAVE TO INTRODUCE YOU TO THE OTHERS.

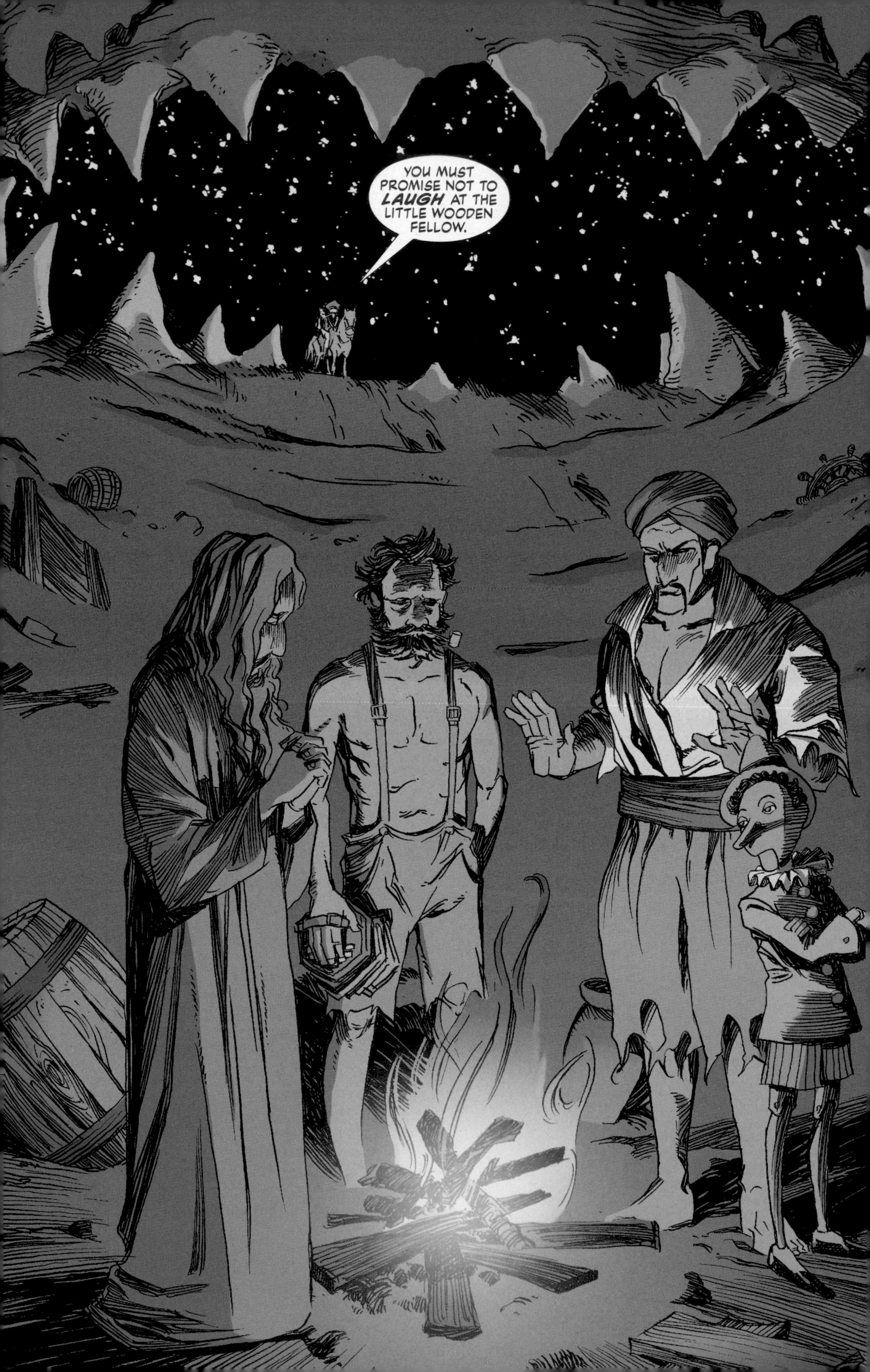
YOU MUST PROMISE NOT TO LAUGH AT THE LITTLE WOODEN FELLOW.

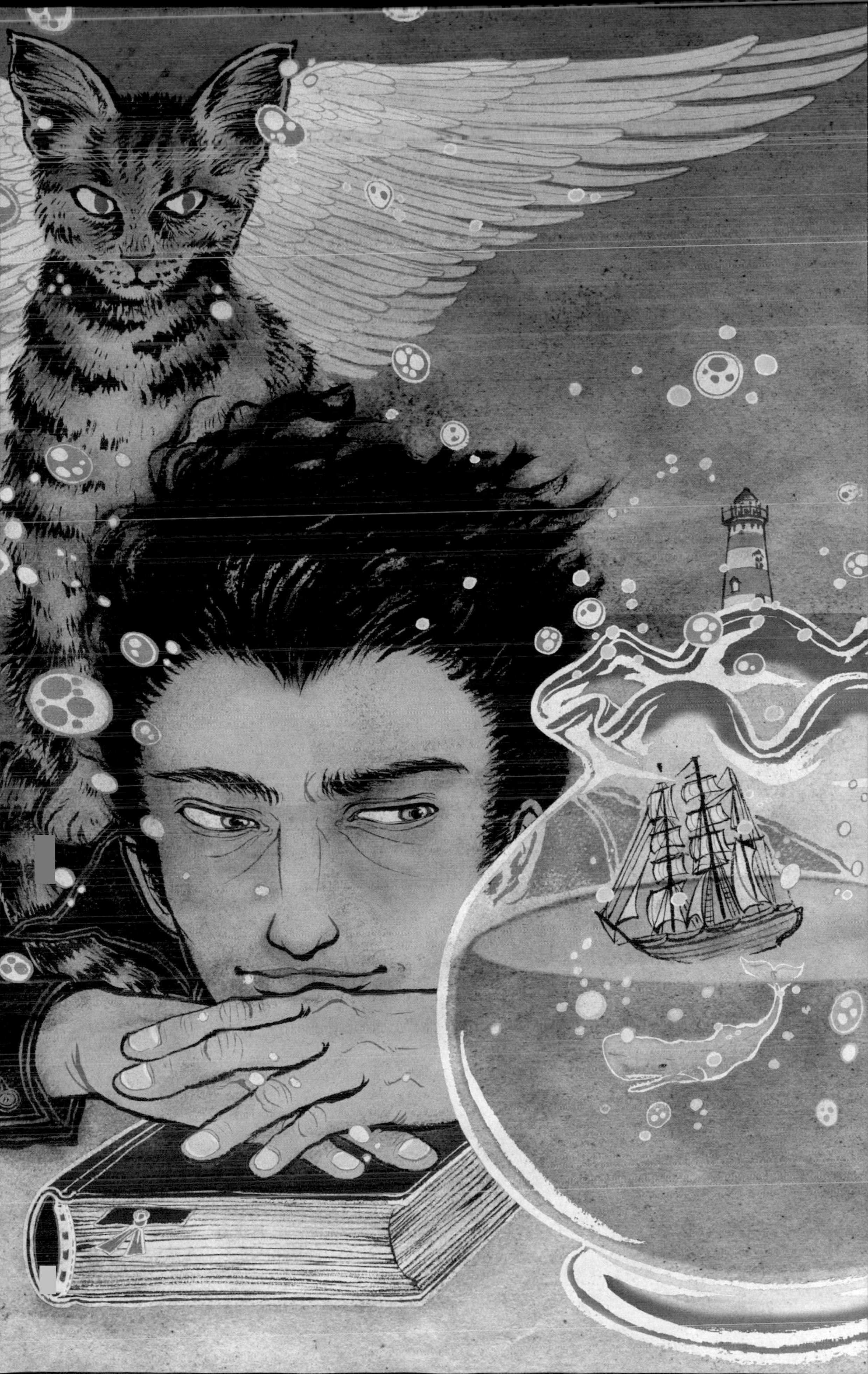

# Negotiating with a Loaded Gun

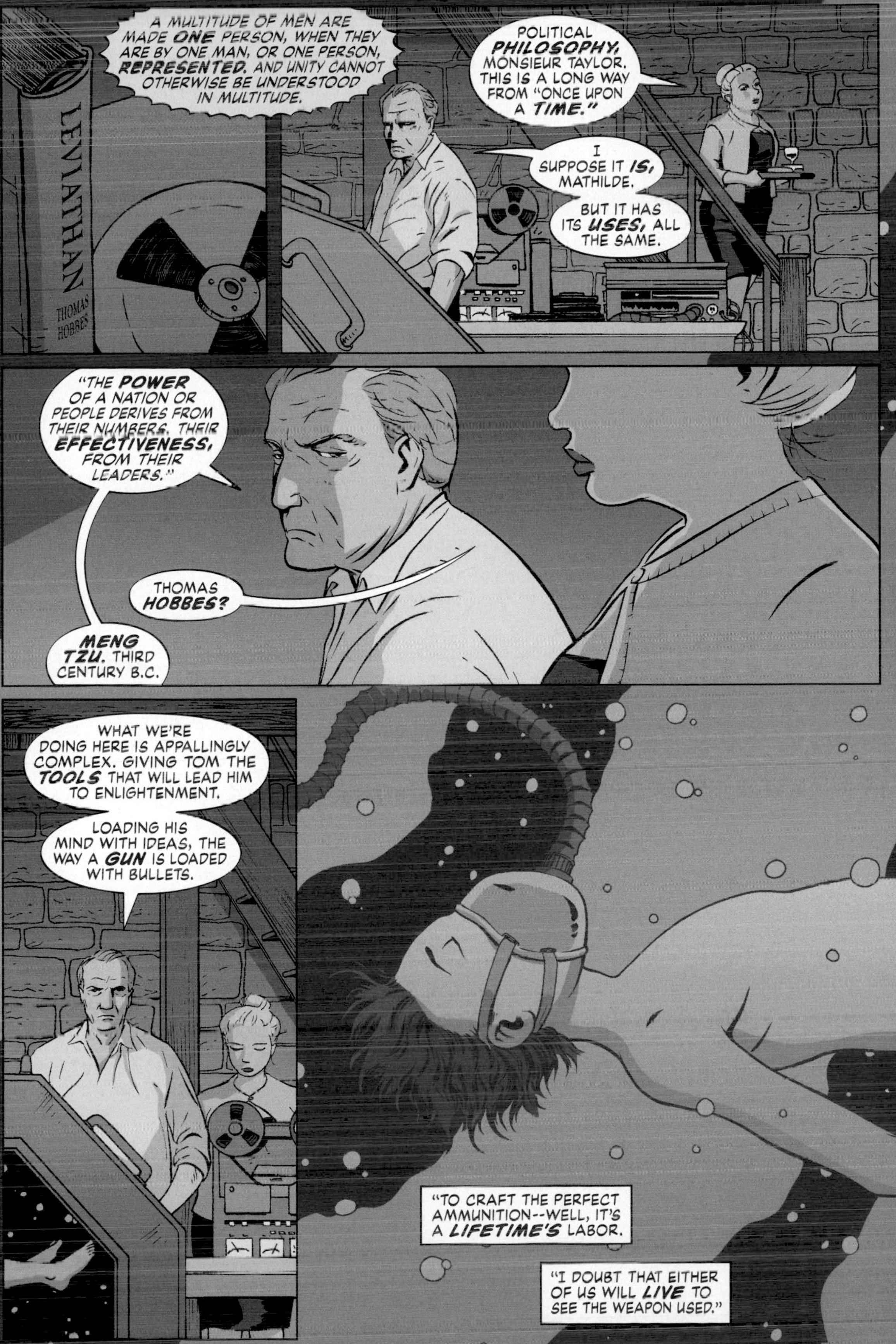

A MULTITUDE OF MEN ARE MADE ONE PERSON, WHEN THEY ARE BY ONE MAN, OR ONE PERSON, REPRESENTED. AND UNITY CANNOT OTHERWISE BE UNDERSTOOD IN MULTITUDE.
LEVIATHAN
THOMAS HOBBES
POLITICAL PHILOSOPHY, MONSIEUR TAYLOR. THIS IS A LONG WAY FROM "ONCE UPON A TIME."
I SUPPOSE IT IS, MATHILDE.
BUT IT HAS ITS USES, ALL THE SAME.
"THE POWER OF A NATION OR PEOPLE DERIVES FROM THEIR NUMBERS. THEIR EFFECTIVENESS, FROM THEIR LEADERS."
THOMAS HOBBES?
MENG TZU. THIRD CENTURY B.C.
WHAT WE'RE DOING HERE IS APPALLINGLY COMPLEX. GIVING TOM THE TOOLS THAT WILL LEAD HIM TO ENLIGHTENMENT.
LOADING HIS MIND WITH IDEAS, THE WAY A GUN IS LOADED WITH BULLETS.
"TO CRAFT THE PERFECT AMMUNITION--WELL, IT'S A LIFETIME'S LABOR.
"I DOUBT THAT EITHER OF US WILL LIVE TO SEE THE WEAPON USED."

# In the Belly of the Beast

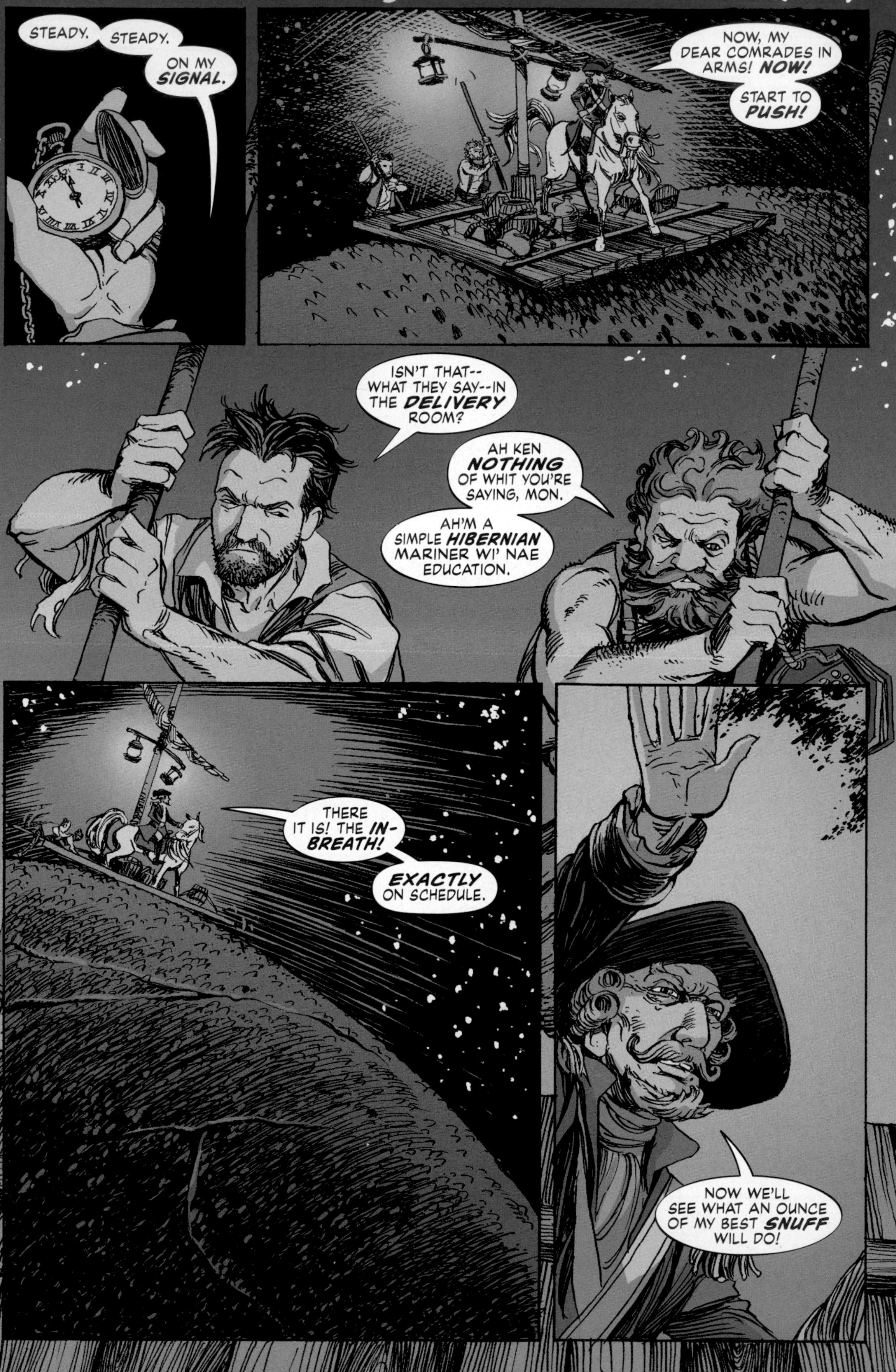

STEADY.
STEADY.
ON MY SIGNAL.
NOW, MY DEAR COMRADES IN ARMS! NOW!
START TO PUSH!
ISN'T THAT-- WHAT THEY SAY--IN THE DELIVERY ROOM?
AH KEN NOTHING OF WHIT YOU'RE SAYING, MON.
AH'M A SIMPLE HIBERNIAN MARINER WI' NAE EDUCATION.
THERE IT IS! THE IN-BREATH!
EXACTLY ON SCHEDULE.
NOW WE'LL SEE WHAT AN OUNCE OF MY BEST SNUFF WILL DO!

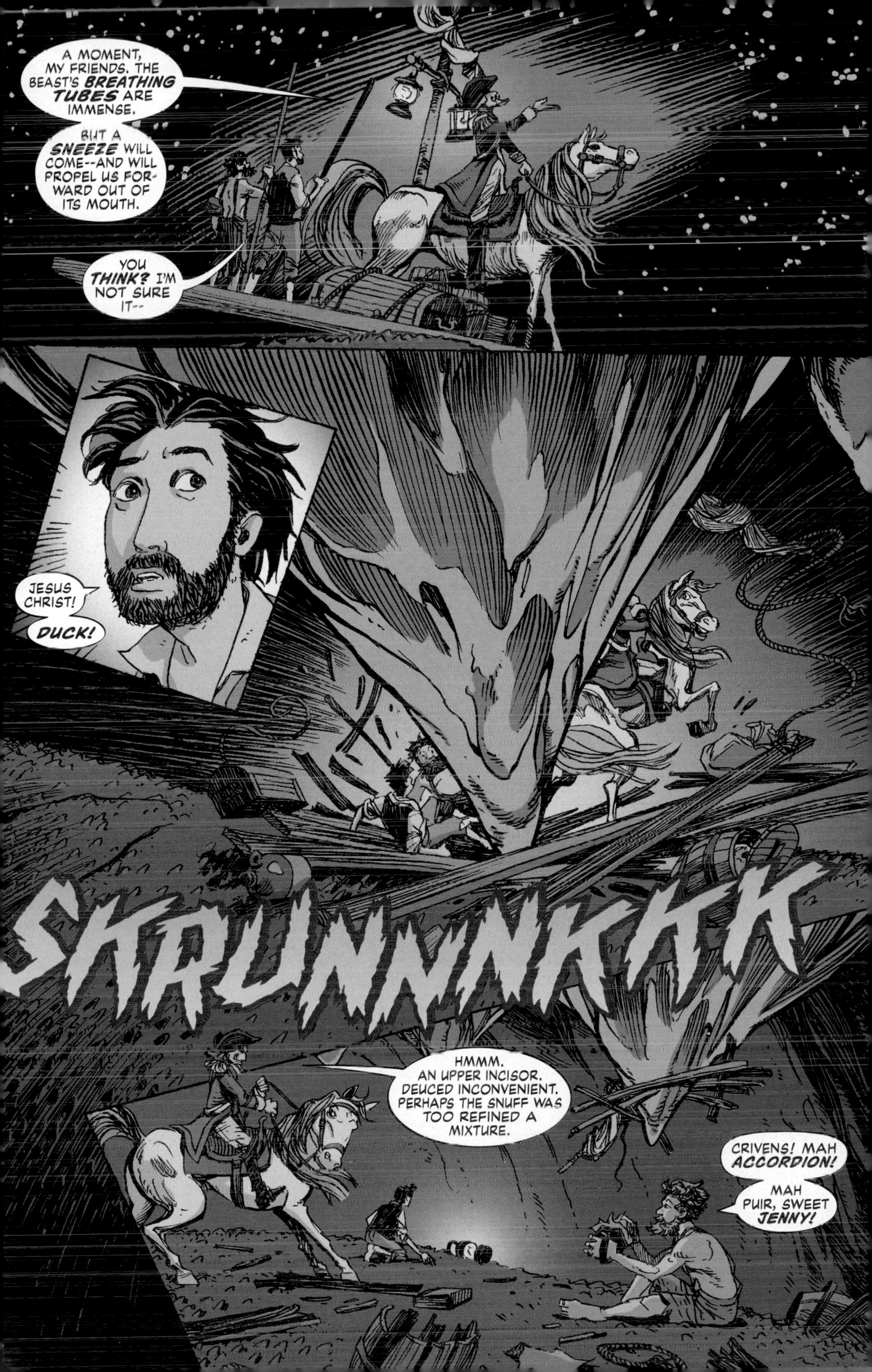
A MOMENT, MY FRIENDS. THE BEAST'S BREATHING TUBES ARE IMMENSE.
BUT A SNEEZE WILL COME--AND WILL PROPEL US FORWARD OUT OF ITS MOUTH.
YOU THINK? I'M NOT SURE IT--
JESUS CHRIST!
DUCK!
SHRUNNNKAK
HMMM. AN UPPER INCISOR. DEUCED INCONVENIENT. PERHAPS THE SNUFF WAS TOO REFINED A MIXTURE.
CRIVENS! MAH ACCORDION!
MAH PUIR, SWEET JENNY!

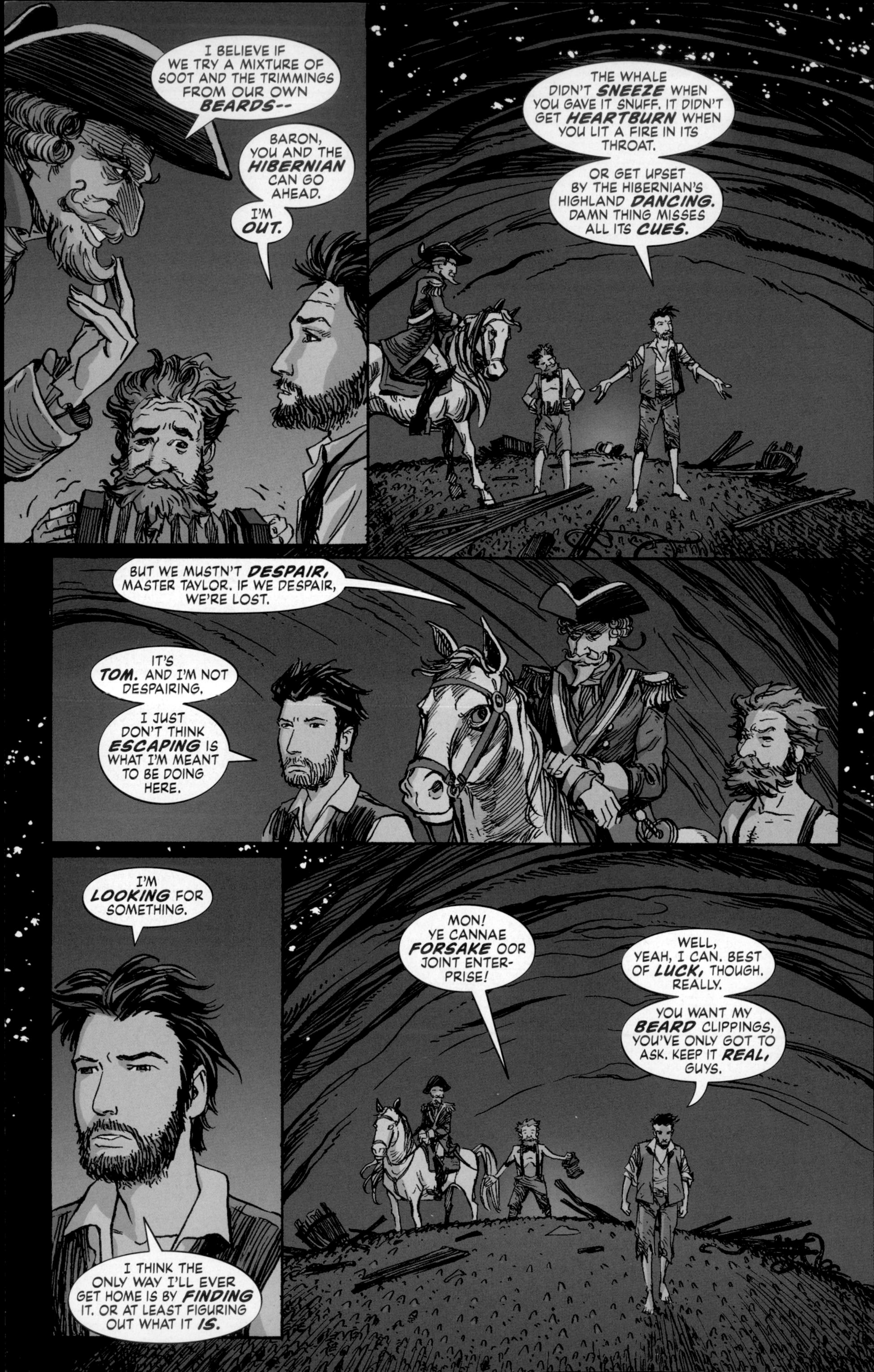
I BELIEVE IF WE TRY A MIXTURE OF SOOT AND THE TRIMMINGS FROM OUR OWN BEARDS--
BARON, YOU AND THE HIBERNIAN CAN GO AHEAD.
I'M OUT.
THE WHALE DIDN'T SNEEZE WHEN YOU GAVE IT SNUFF. IT DIDN'T GET HEARTBURN WHEN YOU LIT A FIRE IN ITS THROAT.
OR GET UPSET BY THE HIBERNIAN'S HIGHLAND DANCING. DAMN THING MISSES ALL ITS CUES.
BUT WE MUSTN'T DESPAIR, MASTER TAYLOR. IF WE DESPAIR, WE'RE LOST.
IT'S TOM. AND I'M NOT DESPAIRING.
I JUST DON'T THINK ESCAPING IS WHAT I'M MEANT TO BE DOING HERE.
I'M LOOKING FOR SOMETHING.
I THINK THE ONLY WAY I'LL EVER GET HOME IS BY FINDING IT. OR AT LEAST FIGURING OUT WHAT IT IS.
MON! YE CANNAE FORSAKE OOR JOINT ENTER-PRISE!
WELL, YEAH, I CAN. BEST OF LUCK, THOUGH. REALLY.
YOU WANT MY BEARD CLIPPINGS, YOU'VE ONLY GOT TO ASK. KEEP IT REAL, GUYS.

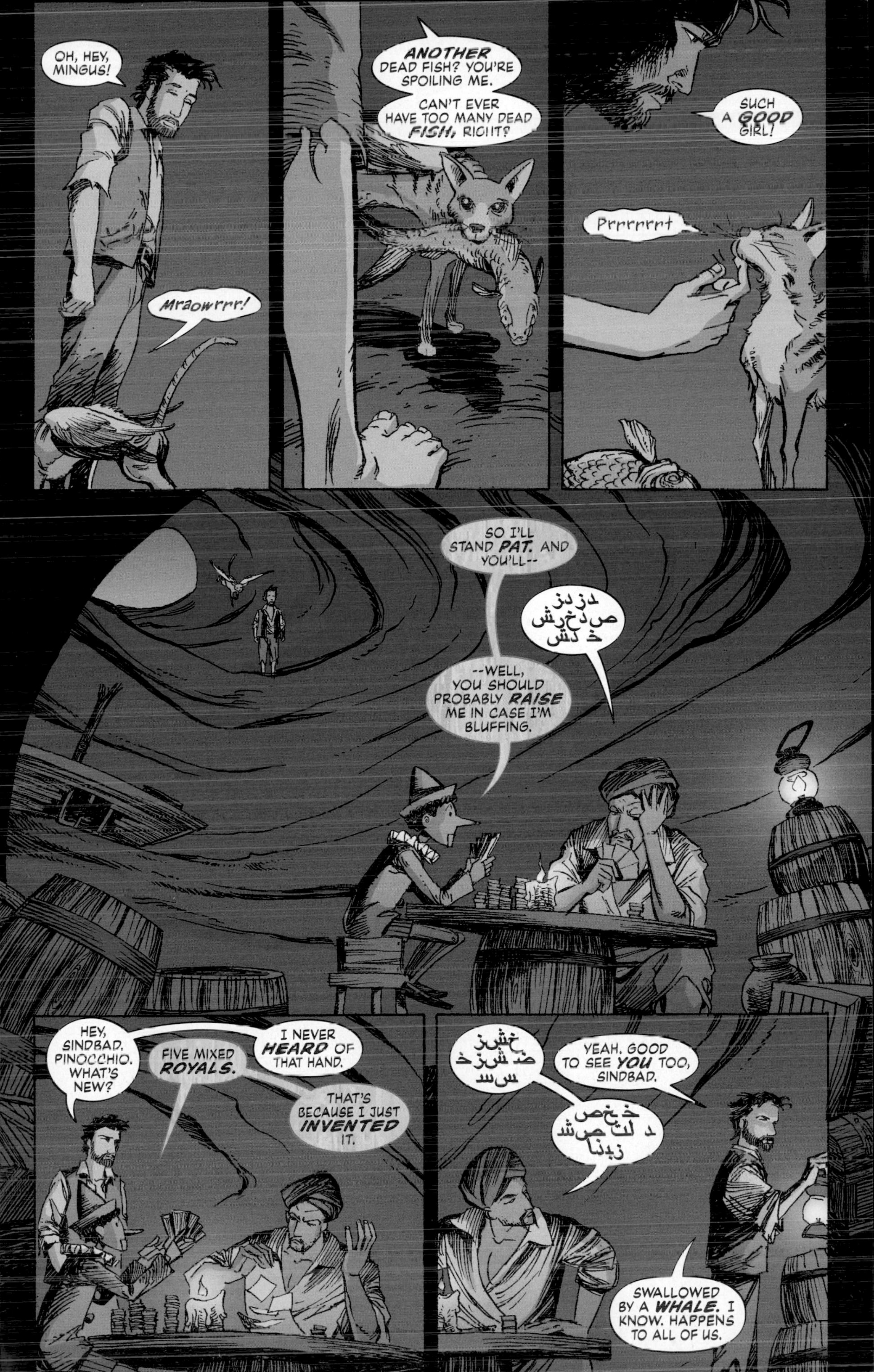
OH, HEY, MINGUS!
Mraowrrr!
ANOTHER DEAD FISH? YOU'RE SPOILING ME.
CAN'T EVER HAVE TOO MANY DEAD FISH, RIGHT?
SUCH A GOOD GIRL!
Prrrrrrt
SO I'LL STAND PAT. AND YOU'LL--
--WELL, YOU SHOULD PROBABLY RAISE ME IN CASE I'M BLUFFING.
HEY, SINDBAD. PINOCCHIO. WHAT'S NEW?
FIVE MIXED ROYALS.
I NEVER HEARD OF THAT HAND.
THAT'S BECAUSE I JUST INVENTED IT.
YEAH. GOOD TO SEE YOU TOO, SINDBAD.
SWALLOWED BY A WHALE. I KNOW. HAPPENS TO ALL OF US.

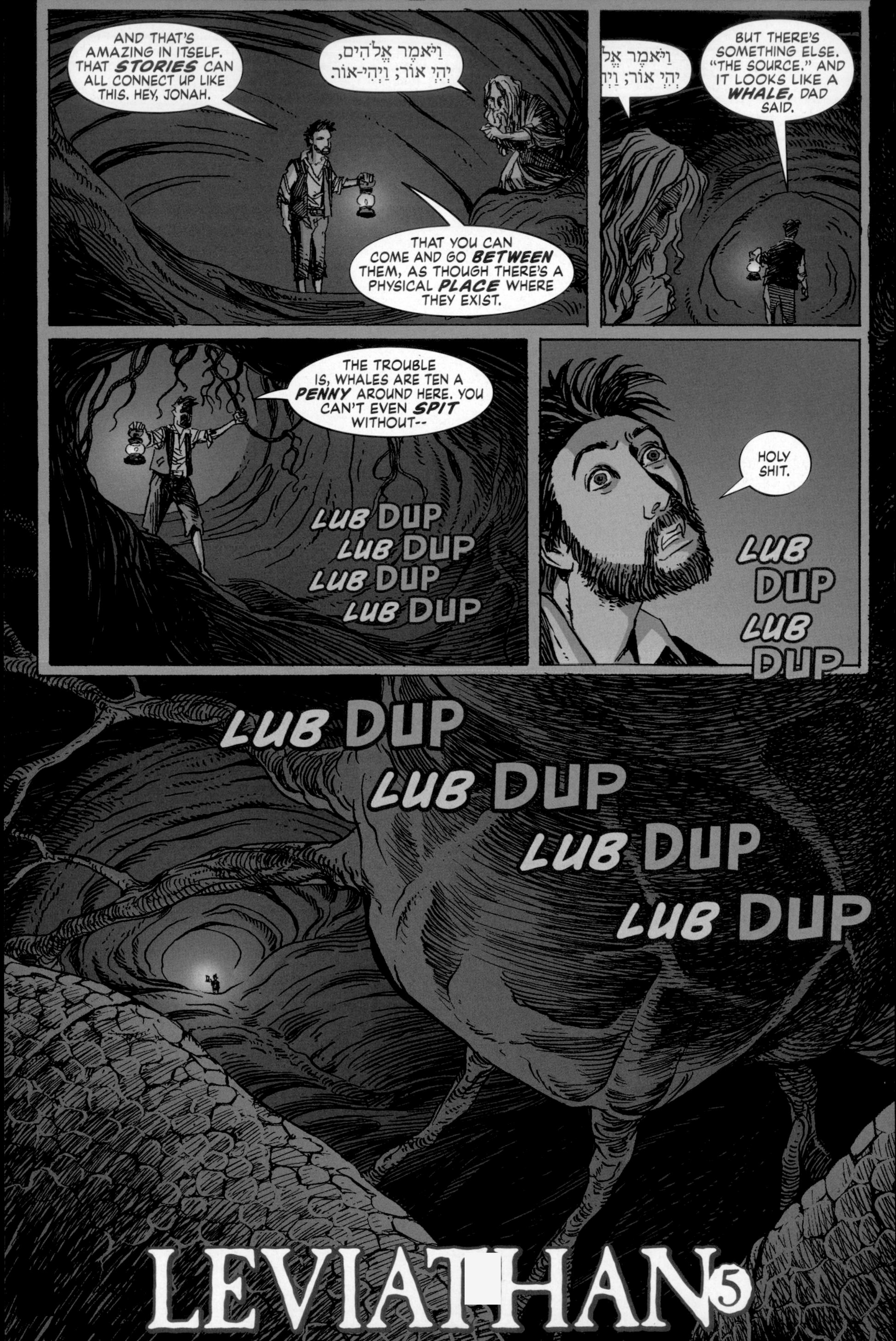
AND THAT'S AMAZING IN ITSELF. THAT STORIES CAN ALL CONNECT UP LIKE THIS. HEY, JONAH.
וַיֹּאמֶר אֱלֹהִים, יְהִי אוֹר; וַיְהִי-אוֹר.
THAT YOU CAN COME AND GO BETWEEN THEM, AS THOUGH THERE'S A PHYSICAL PLACE WHERE THEY EXIST.
וַיֹּאמֶר
יְהִי אוֹר;
BUT THERE'S SOMETHING ELSE. "THE SOURCE." AND IT LOOKS LIKE A WHALE, DAD SAID.
THE TROUBLE IS, WHALES ARE TEN A PENNY AROUND HERE. YOU CAN'T EVEN SPIT WITHOUT--
LUB DUP
LUB DUP
LUB DUP
LUB DUP
HOLY SHIT.
LUB DUP
LUB DUP
LUB DUP
LUB DUP
LUB DUP
LUB DUP
LEVIATHAN 5

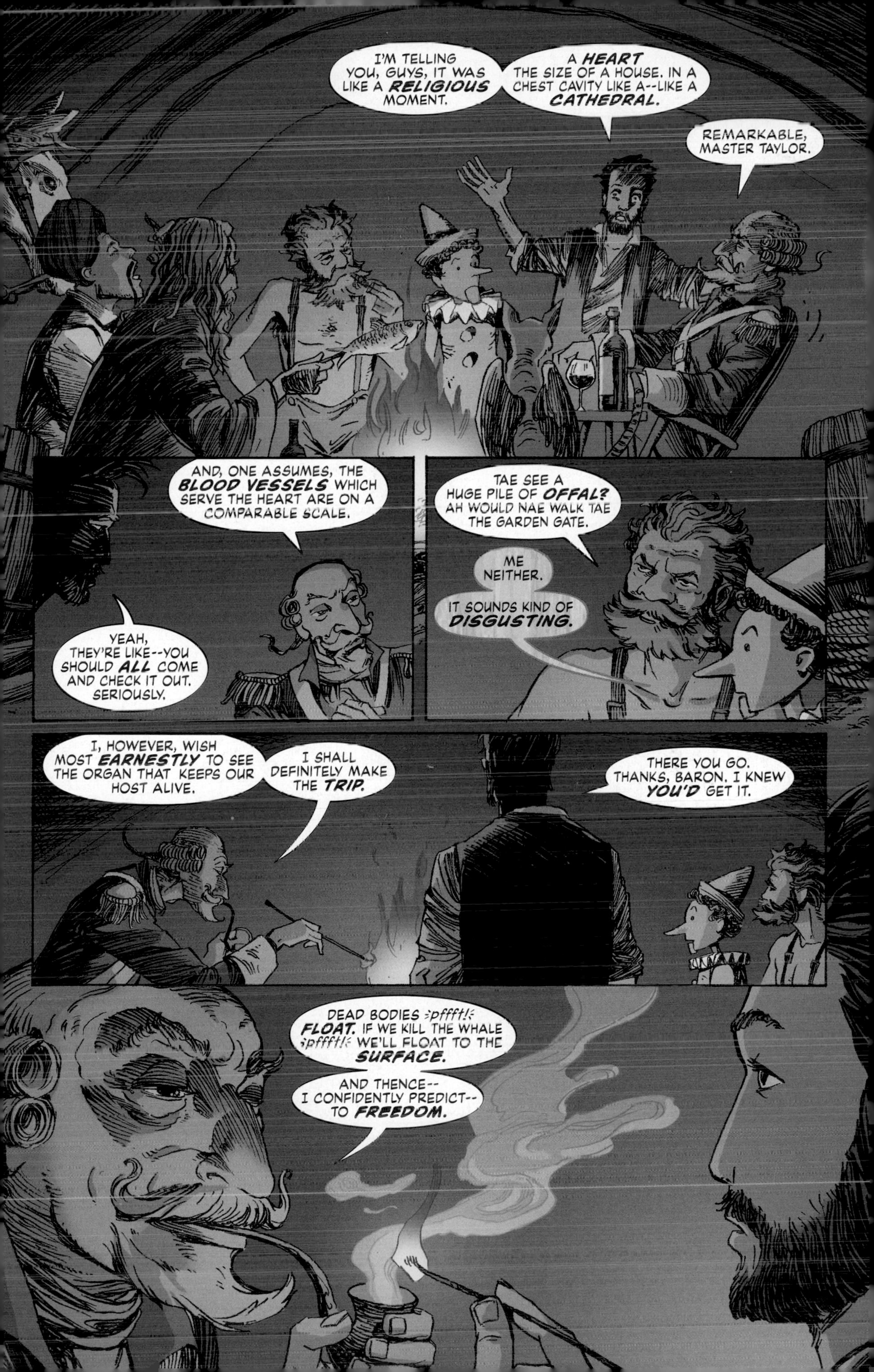

I'M TELLING YOU, GUYS, IT WAS LIKE A **RELIGIOUS** MOMENT.
A **HEART** THE SIZE OF A HOUSE. IN A CHEST CAVITY LIKE A--LIKE A **CATHEDRAL.**
REMARKABLE, MASTER TAYLOR.
AND, ONE ASSUMES, THE **BLOOD VESSELS** WHICH SERVE THE HEART ARE ON A COMPARABLE SCALE.
YEAH, THEY'RE LIKE--YOU SHOULD **ALL** COME AND CHECK IT OUT. SERIOUSLY.
TAE SEE A HUGE PILE OF **OFFAL?** AH WOULD NAE WALK TAE THE GARDEN GATE.
ME NEITHER.
IT SOUNDS KIND OF **DISGUSTING.**
I, HOWEVER, WISH MOST **EARNESTLY** TO SEE THE ORGAN THAT KEEPS OUR HOST ALIVE.
I SHALL DEFINITELY MAKE THE **TRIP.**
THERE YOU GO. THANKS, BARON. I KNEW **YOU'D** GET IT.
DEAD BODIES *pffft!* **FLOAT.** IF WE KILL THE WHALE *pffft!* WE'LL FLOAT TO THE **SURFACE.**
AND THENCE-- I CONFIDENTLY PREDICT-- TO **FREEDOM.**

# The Power of a Nation

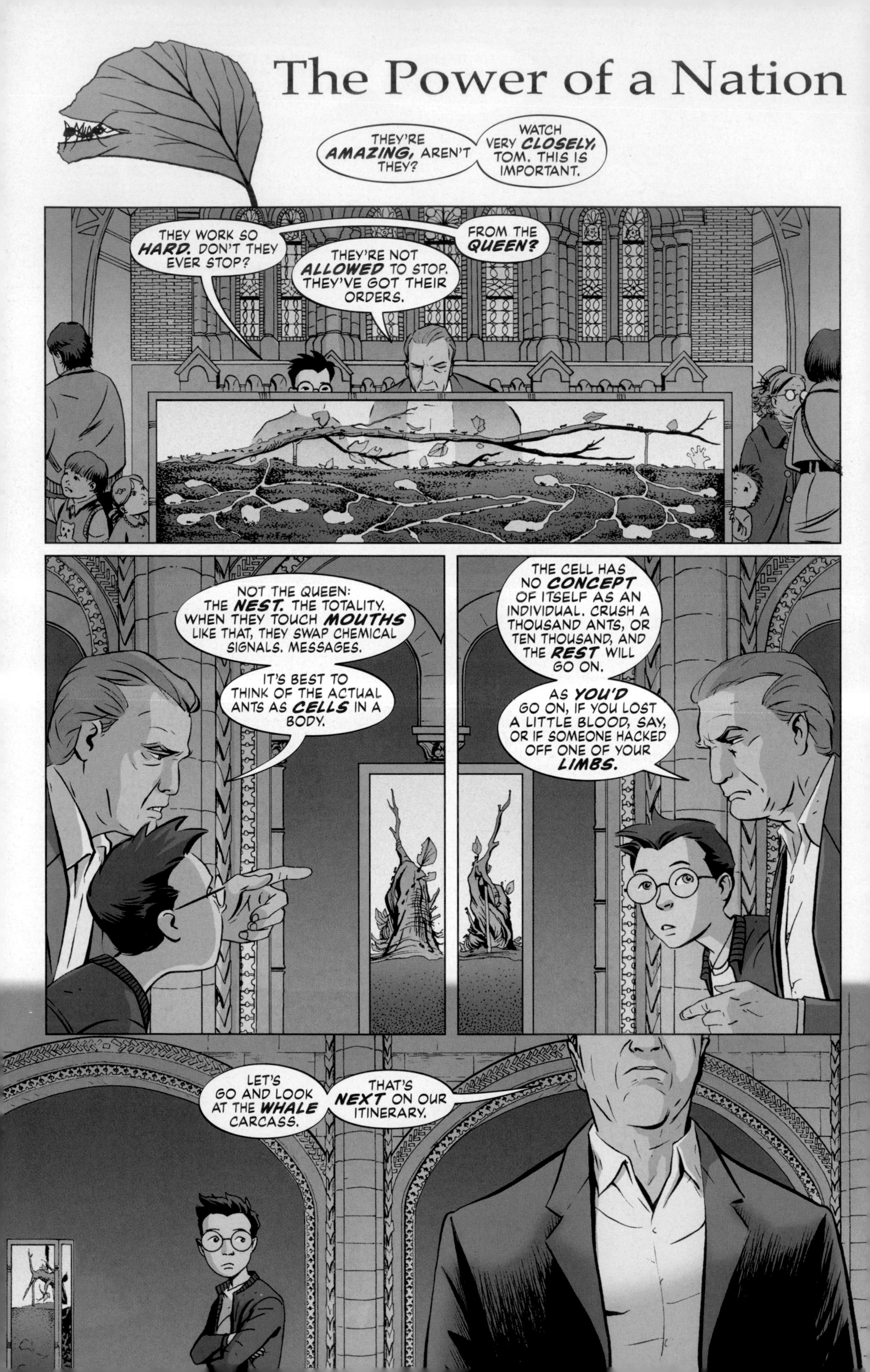

THEY'RE AMAZING, AREN'T THEY?
WATCH VERY CLOSELY, TOM. THIS IS IMPORTANT.
THEY WORK SO HARD. DON'T THEY EVER STOP?
THEY'RE NOT ALLOWED TO STOP. THEY'VE GOT THEIR ORDERS.
FROM THE QUEEN?
NOT THE QUEEN: THE NEST. THE TOTALITY. WHEN THEY TOUCH MOUTHS LIKE THAT, THEY SWAP CHEMICAL SIGNALS. MESSAGES.
IT'S BEST TO THINK OF THE ACTUAL ANTS AS CELLS IN A BODY.
THE CELL HAS NO CONCEPT OF ITSELF AS AN INDIVIDUAL. CRUSH A THOUSAND ANTS, OR TEN THOUSAND, AND THE REST WILL GO ON.
AS YOU'D GO ON, IF YOU LOST A LITTLE BLOOD, SAY, OR IF SOMEONE HACKED OFF ONE OF YOUR LIMBS.
LET'S GO AND LOOK AT THE WHALE CARCASS.
THAT'S NEXT ON OUR ITINERARY.

# The Frontispiece

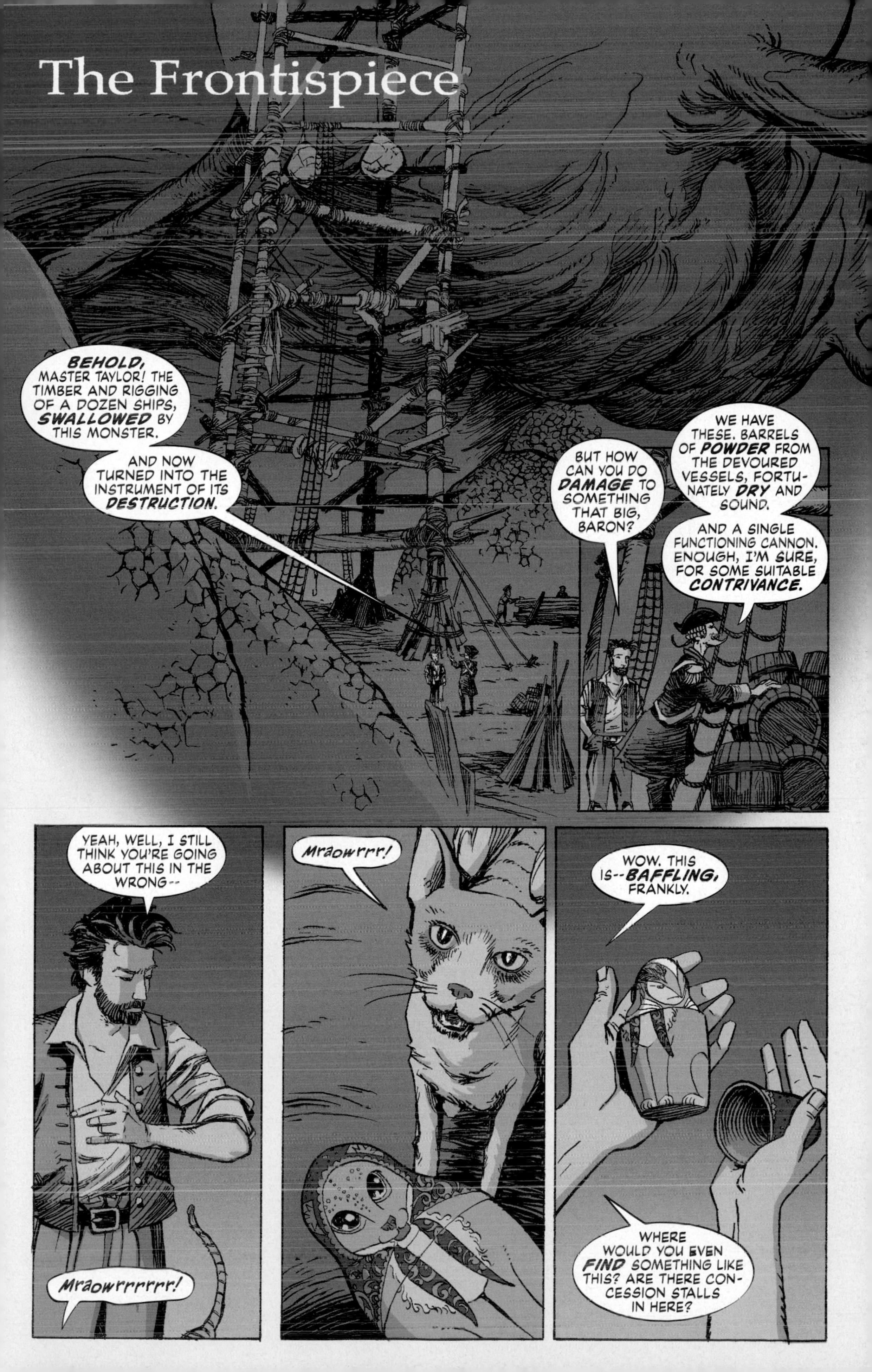
BEHOLD, MASTER TAYLOR! THE TIMBER AND RIGGING OF A DOZEN SHIPS, SWALLOWED BY THIS MONSTER.
AND NOW TURNED INTO THE INSTRUMENT OF ITS DESTRUCTION.
BUT HOW CAN YOU DO DAMAGE TO SOMETHING THAT BIG, BARON?
WE HAVE THESE. BARRELS OF POWDER FROM THE DEVOURED VESSELS, FORTU-NATELY DRY AND SOUND.
AND A SINGLE FUNCTIONING CANNON. ENOUGH, I'M SURE, FOR SOME SUITABLE CONTRIVANCE.
YEAH, WELL, I STILL THINK YOU'RE GOING ABOUT THIS IN THE WRONG--
Mraowrrrrr!
Mraowrrr!
WOW. THIS IS--BAFFLING, FRANKLY.
WHERE WOULD YOU EVEN FIND SOMETHING LIKE THIS? ARE THERE CON-CESSION STALLS IN HERE?

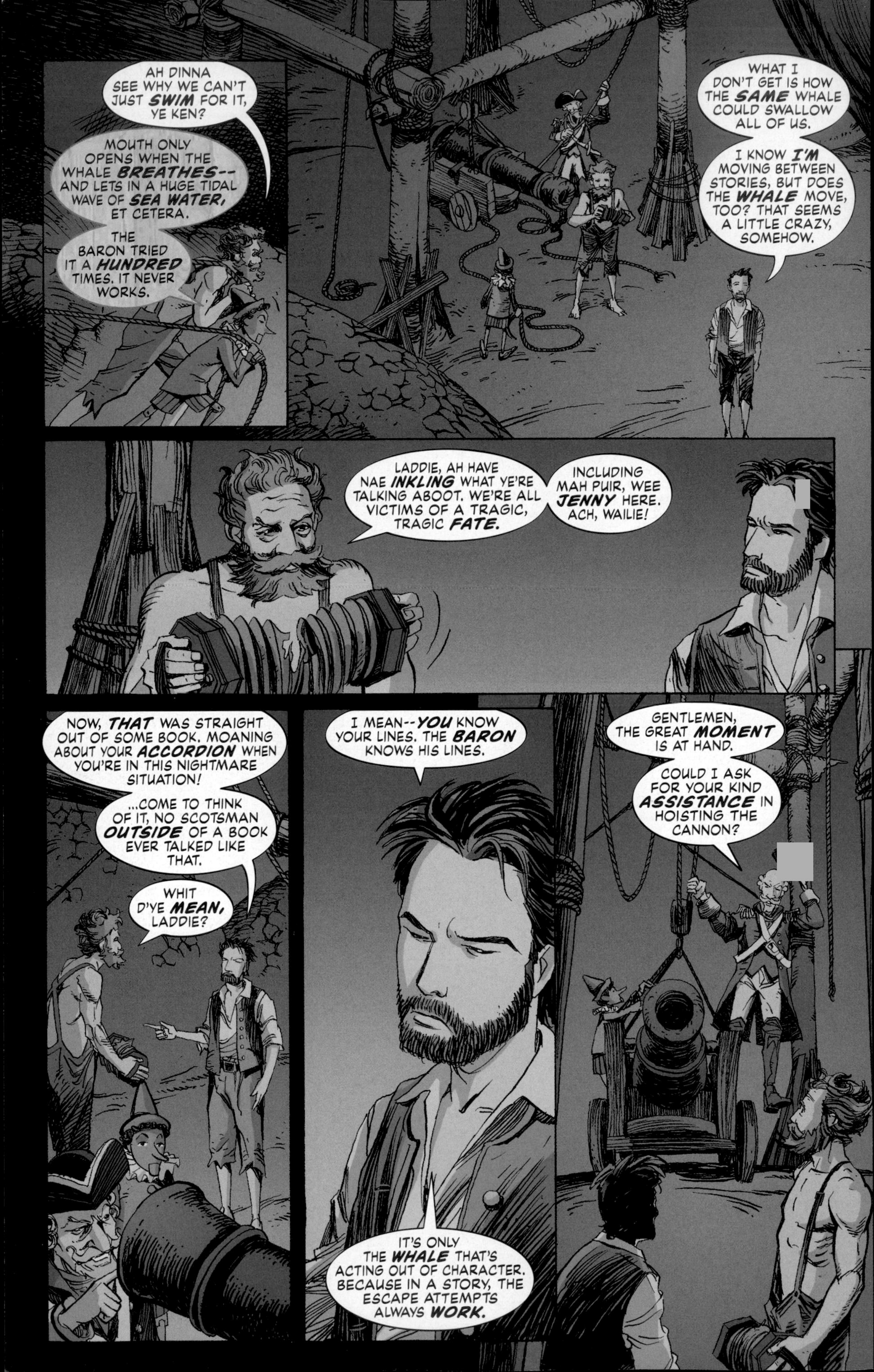
AH DINNA SEE WHY WE CAN'T JUST SWIM FOR IT, YE KEN?
MOUTH ONLY OPENS WHEN THE WHALE BREATHES--AND LETS IN A HUGE TIDAL WAVE OF SEA WATER, ET CETERA.
THE BARON TRIED IT A HUNDRED TIMES. IT NEVER WORKS.
WHAT I DON'T GET IS HOW THE SAME WHALE COULD SWALLOW ALL OF US.
I KNOW I'M MOVING BETWEEN STORIES, BUT DOES THE WHALE MOVE, TOO? THAT SEEMS A LITTLE CRAZY, SOMEHOW.
LADDIE, AH HAVE NAE INKLING WHAT YE'RE TALKING ABOOT. WE'RE ALL VICTIMS OF A TRAGIC, TRAGIC FATE.
INCLUDING MAH PUIR, WEE JENNY HERE. ACH, WAILIE!
NOW, THAT WAS STRAIGHT OUT OF SOME BOOK. MOANING ABOUT YOUR ACCORDION WHEN YOU'RE IN THIS NIGHTMARE SITUATION!
...COME TO THINK OF IT, NO SCOTSMAN OUTSIDE OF A BOOK EVER TALKED LIKE THAT.
WHIT D'YE MEAN, LADDIE?
I MEAN--YOU KNOW YOUR LINES. THE BARON KNOWS HIS LINES.
IT'S ONLY THE WHALE THAT'S ACTING OUT OF CHARACTER. BECAUSE IN A STORY, THE ESCAPE ATTEMPTS ALWAYS WORK.
GENTLEMEN, THE GREAT MOMENT IS AT HAND.
COULD I ASK FOR YOUR KIND ASSISTANCE IN HOISTING THE CANNON?

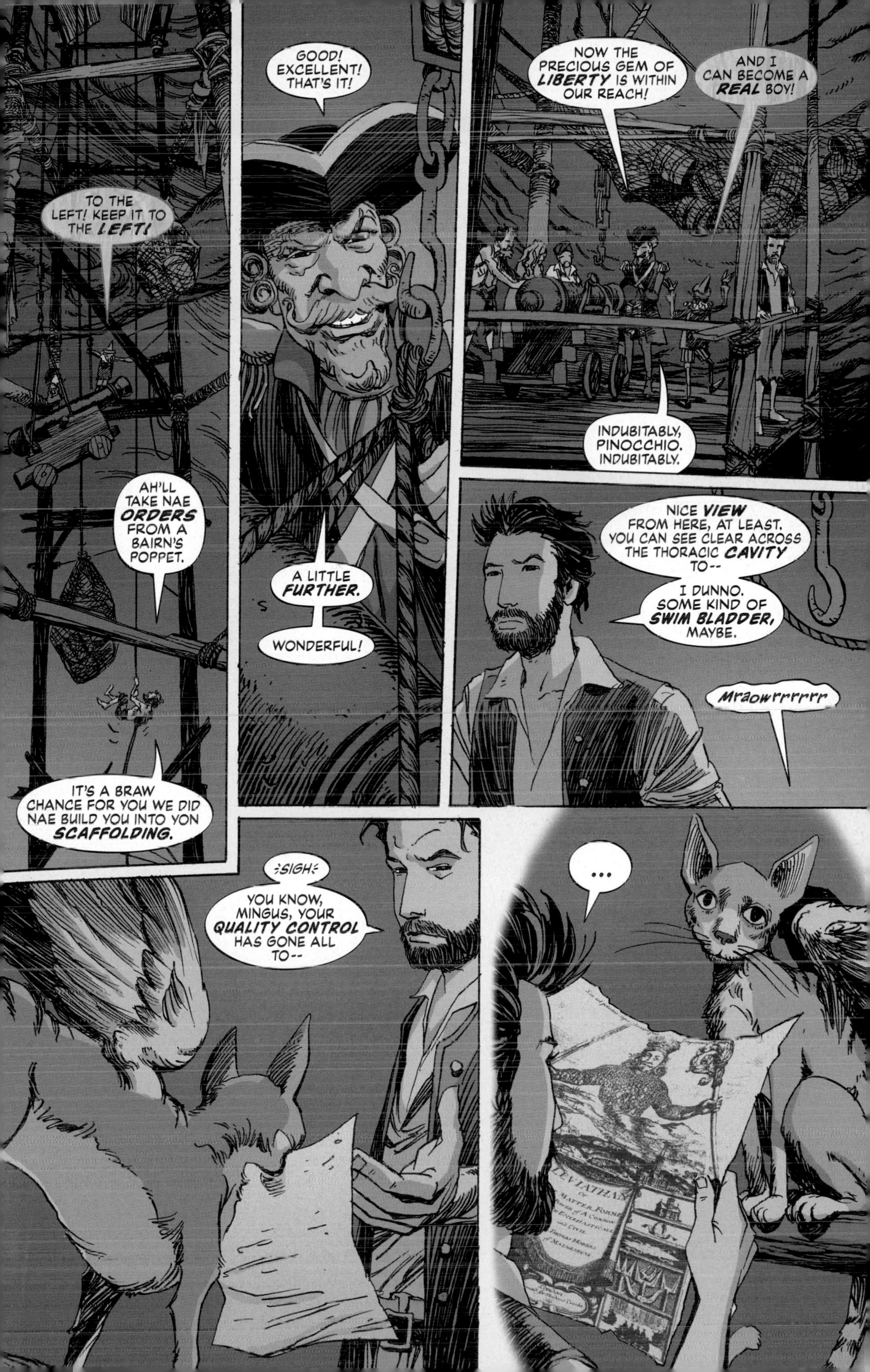
TO THE LEFT! KEEP IT TO THE LEFT!
AH'LL TAKE NAE ORDERS FROM A BAIRN'S POPPET.
IT'S A BRAW CHANCE FOR YOU WE DID NAE BUILD YOU INTO YON SCAFFOLDING.
GOOD! EXCELLENT! THAT'S IT!
A LITTLE FURTHER.
WONDERFUL!
NOW THE PRECIOUS GEM OF LIBERTY IS WITHIN OUR REACH!
AND I CAN BECOME A REAL BOY!
INDUBITABLY, PINOCCHIO. INDUBITABLY.
NICE VIEW FROM HERE, AT LEAST. YOU CAN SEE CLEAR ACROSS THE THORACIC CAVITY TO--
I DUNNO. SOME KIND OF SWIM BLADDER, MAYBE.
Mraowrrrrrr
SIGH
YOU KNOW, MINGUS, YOUR QUALITY CONTROL HAS GONE ALL TO--
...
LEVIATHAN

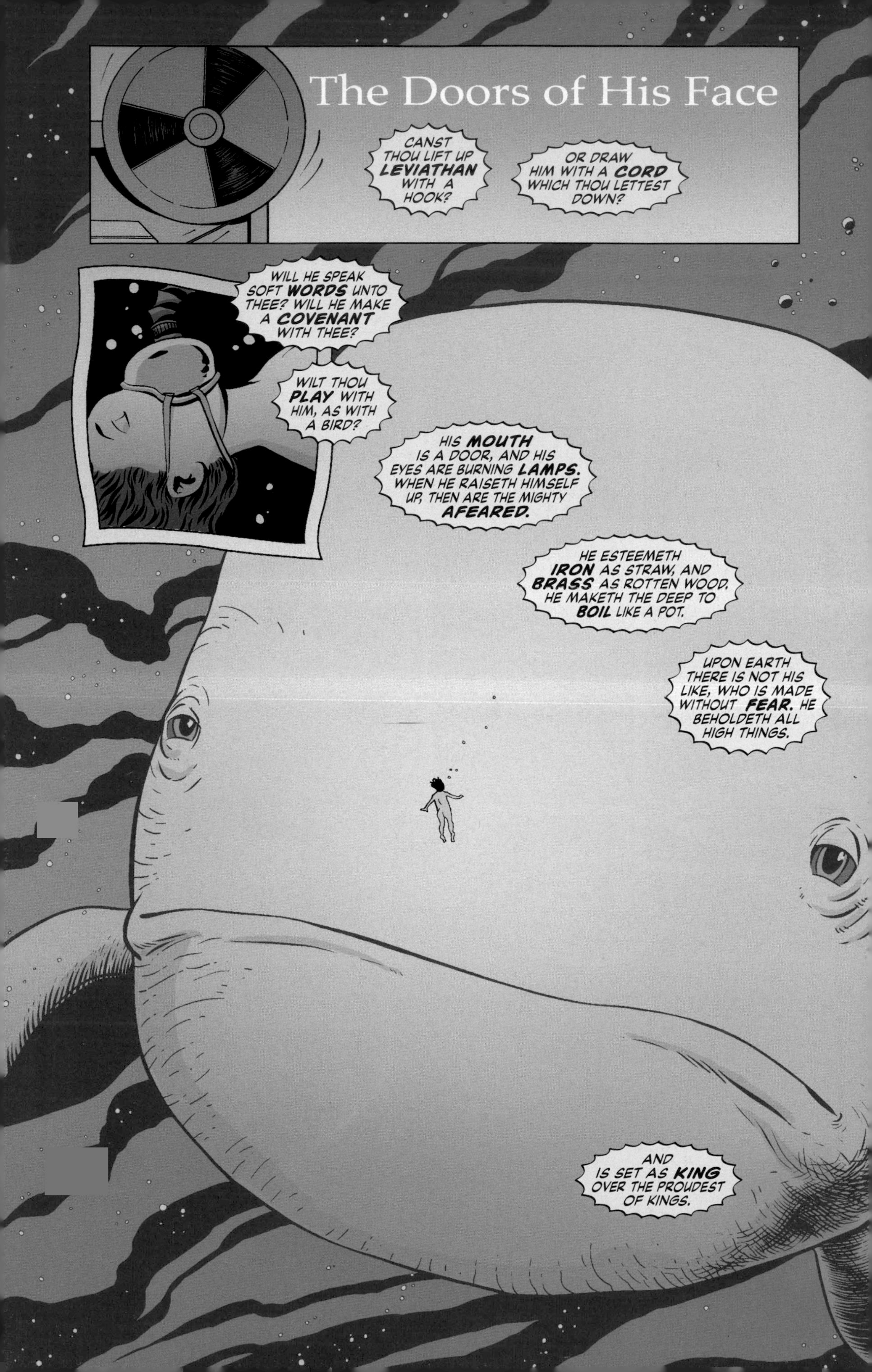
The Doors of His Face
CANST THOU LIFT UP LEVIATHAN WITH A HOOK?
OR DRAW HIM WITH A CORD WHICH THOU LETTEST DOWN?
WILL HE SPEAK SOFT WORDS UNTO THEE? WILL HE MAKE A COVENANT WITH THEE?
WILT THOU PLAY WITH HIM, AS WITH A BIRD?
HIS MOUTH IS A DOOR, AND HIS EYES ARE BURNING LAMPS. WHEN HE RAISETH HIMSELF UP, THEN ARE THE MIGHTY AFEARED.
HE ESTEEMETH IRON AS STRAW, AND BRASS AS ROTTEN WOOD. HE MAKETH THE DEEP TO BOIL LIKE A POT.
UPON EARTH THERE IS NOT HIS LIKE, WHO IS MADE WITHOUT FEAR. HE BEHOLDETH ALL HIGH THINGS.
AND IS SET AS KING OVER THE PROUDEST OF KINGS.

# Leviathan

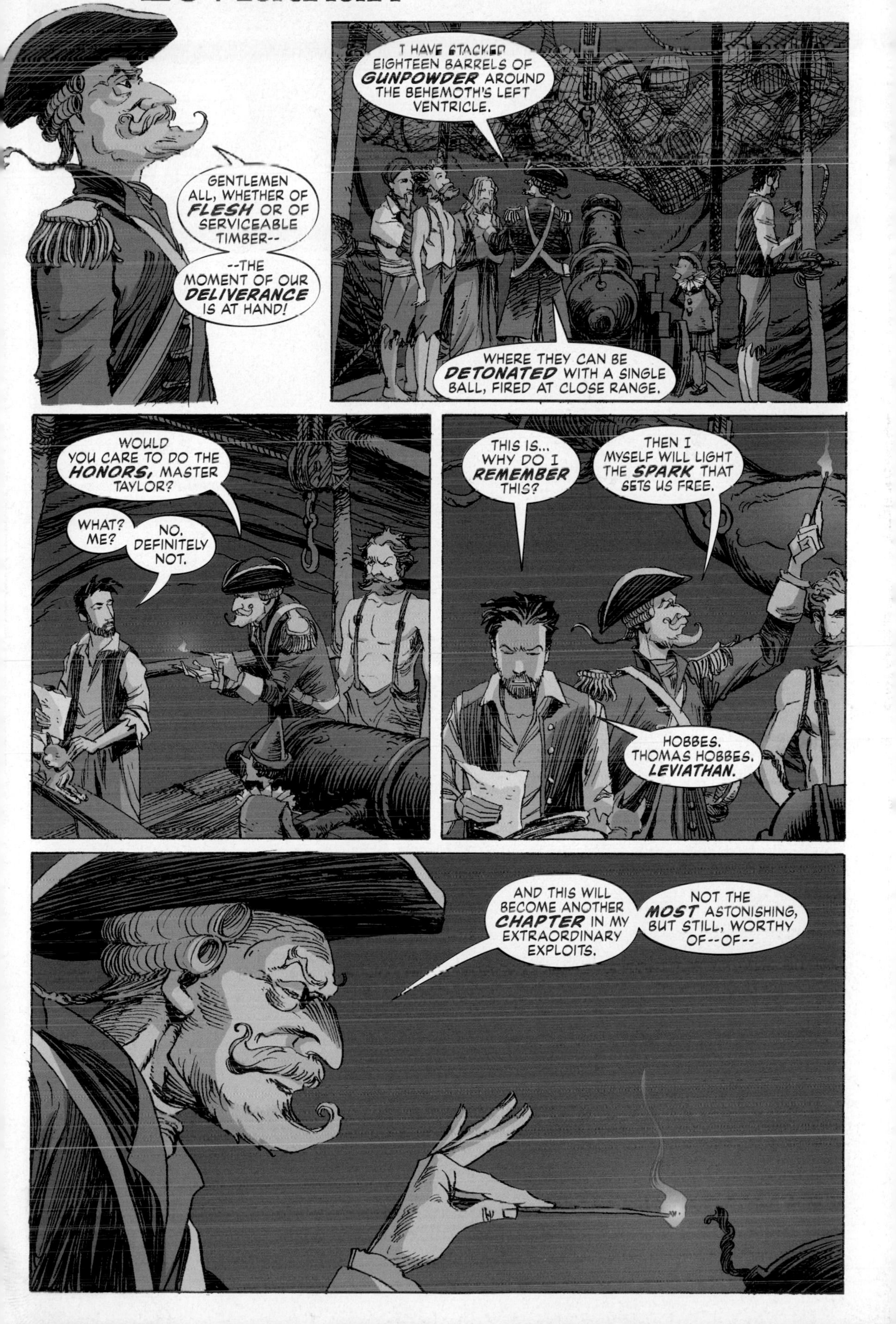
GENTLEMEN ALL, WHETHER OF FLESH OR OF SERVICEABLE TIMBER--
--THE MOMENT OF OUR DELIVERANCE IS AT HAND!
I HAVE STACKED EIGHTEEN BARRELS OF GUNPOWDER AROUND THE BEHEMOTH'S LEFT VENTRICLE.
WHERE THEY CAN BE DETONATED WITH A SINGLE BALL, FIRED AT CLOSE RANGE.
WOULD YOU CARE TO DO THE HONORS, MASTER TAYLOR?
WHAT? ME?
NO. DEFINITELY NOT.
THIS IS... WHY DO I REMEMBER THIS?
THEN I MYSELF WILL LIGHT THE SPARK THAT SETS US FREE.
HOBBES. THOMAS HOBBES. LEVIATHAN.
AND THIS WILL BECOME ANOTHER CHAPTER IN MY EXTRAORDINARY EXPLOITS.
NOT THE MOST ASTONISHING, BUT STILL, WORTHY OF--OF--

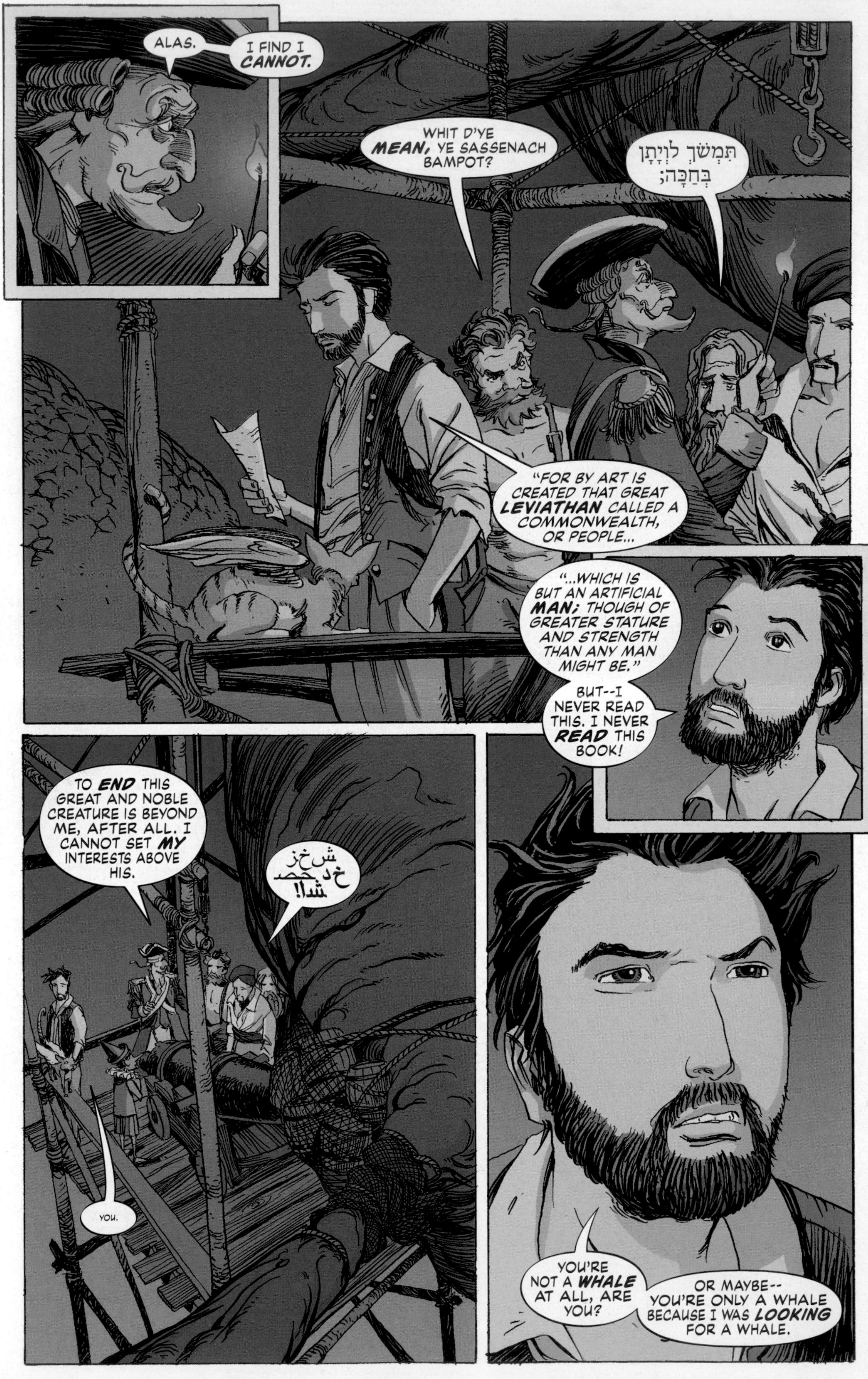
ALAS.
I FIND I CANNOT.
WHIT D'YE MEAN, YE SASSENACH BAMPOT?
תִּמְשֹׁךְ לִוְיָתָן בְּחַכָּה;
"FOR BY ART IS CREATED THAT GREAT LEVIATHAN CALLED A COMMONWEALTH, OR PEOPLE...
"...WHICH IS BUT AN ARTIFICIAL MAN; THOUGH OF GREATER STATURE AND STRENGTH THAN ANY MAN MIGHT BE."
BUT--I NEVER READ THIS. I NEVER READ THIS BOOK!
TO END THIS GREAT AND NOBLE CREATURE IS BEYOND ME, AFTER ALL. I CANNOT SET MY INTERESTS ABOVE HIS.
شخز خد حجص شدا!
YOU.
YOU'RE NOT A WHALE AT ALL, ARE YOU?
OR MAYBE-- YOU'RE ONLY A WHALE BECAUSE I WAS LOOKING FOR A WHALE.

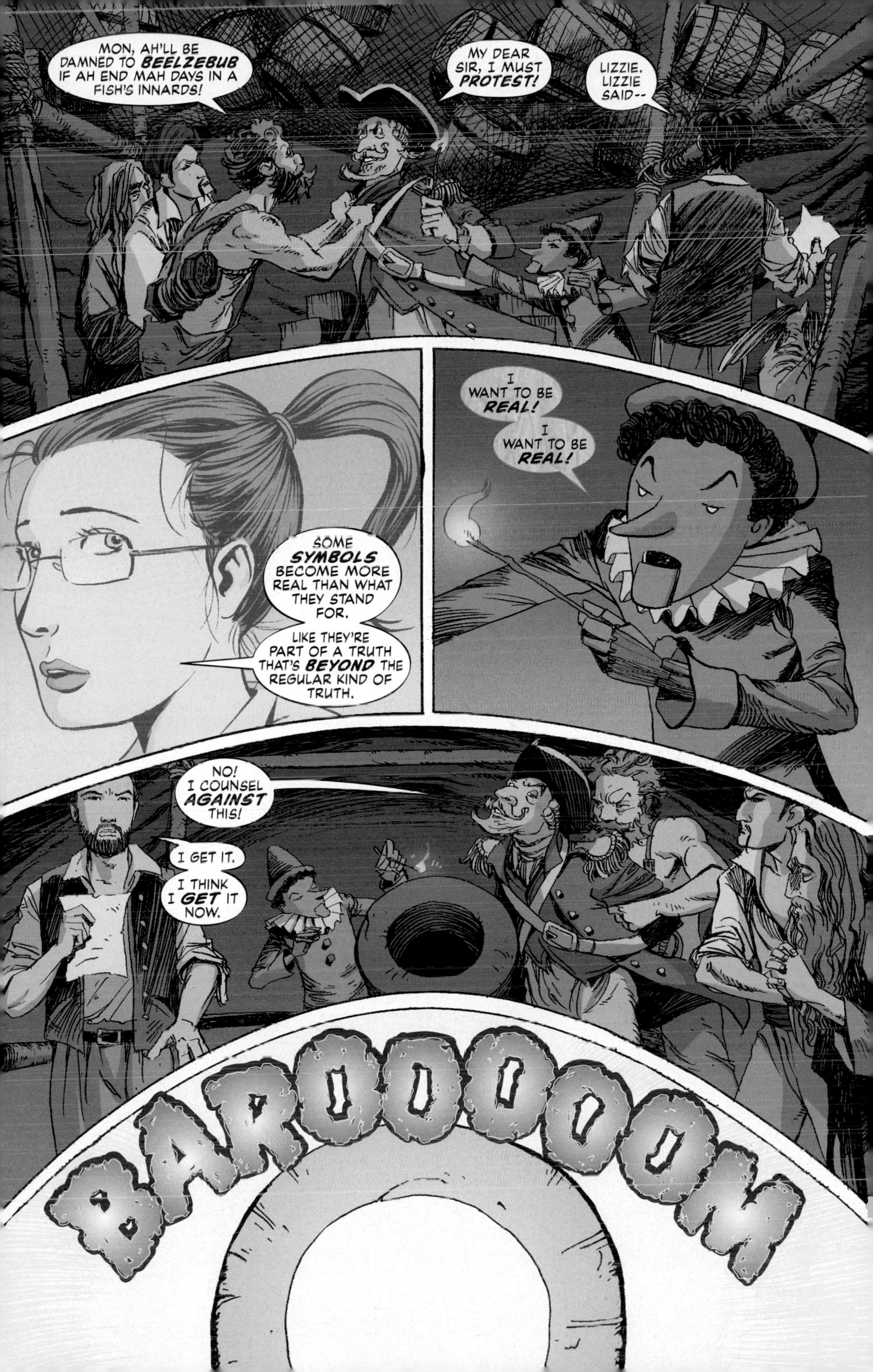
MON, AH'LL BE DAMNED TO BEELZEBUB IF AH END MAH DAYS IN A FISH'S INNARDS!
MY DEAR SIR, I MUST PROTEST!
LIZZIE. LIZZIE SAID--
SOME SYMBOLS BECOME MORE REAL THAN WHAT THEY STAND FOR.
LIKE THEY'RE PART OF A TRUTH THAT'S BEYOND THE REGULAR KIND OF TRUTH.
I WANT TO BE REAL!
I WANT TO BE REAL!
NO! I COUNSEL AGAINST THIS!
I GET IT.
I THINK I GET IT NOW.
BAROOOOOM

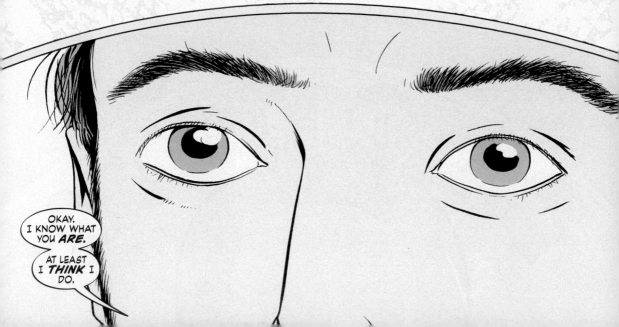

OKAY. I KNOW WHAT YOU *ARE.*

AT LEAST I *THINK* I DO.

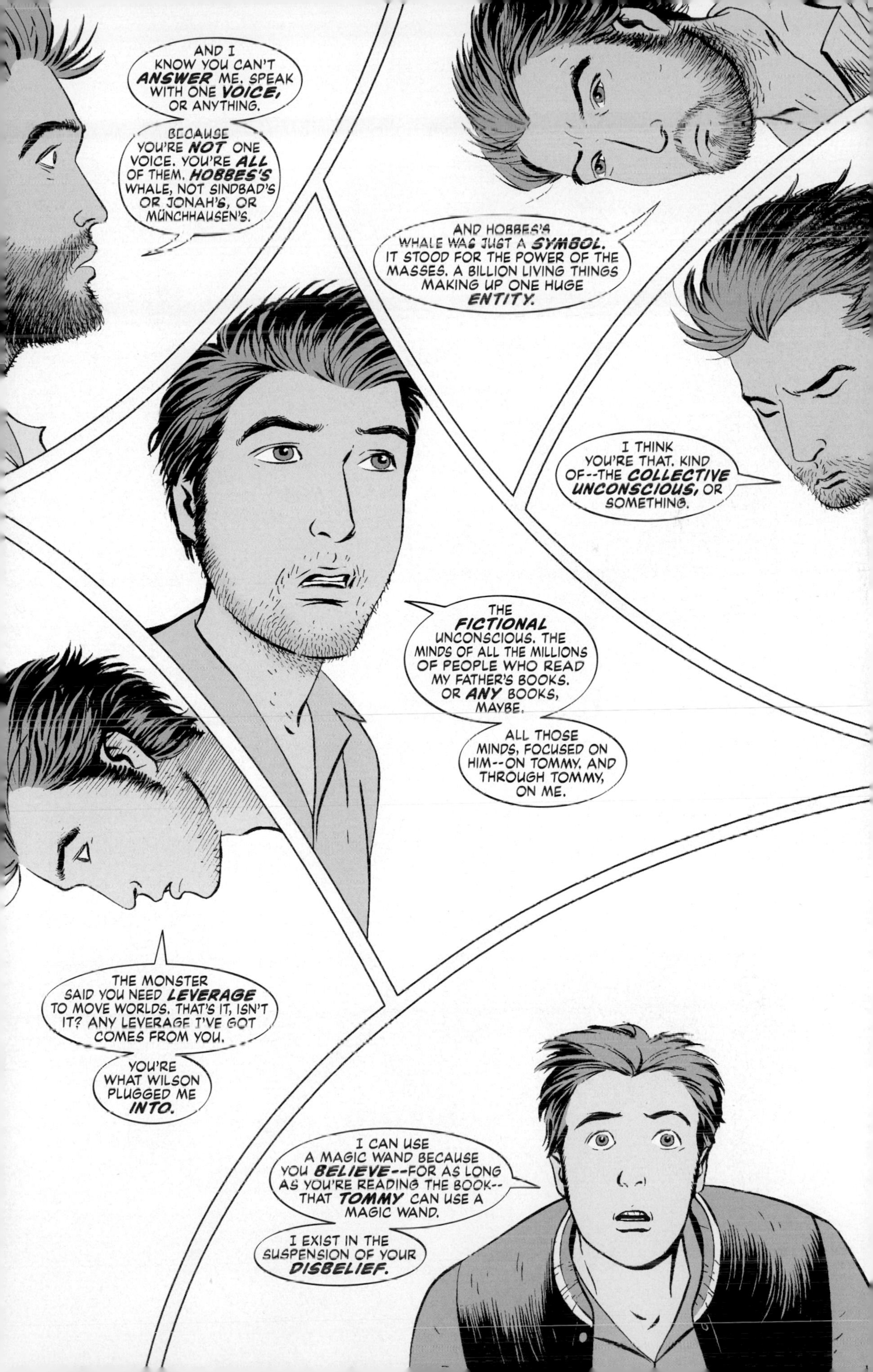
AND I KNOW YOU CAN'T ANSWER ME. SPEAK WITH ONE VOICE, OR ANYTHING.
BECAUSE YOU'RE NOT ONE VOICE. YOU'RE ALL OF THEM. HOBBES'S WHALE, NOT SINDBAD'S OR JONAH'S, OR MÜNCHHAUSEN'S.
AND HOBBES'S WHALE WAS JUST A SYMBOL. IT STOOD FOR THE POWER OF THE MASSES. A BILLION LIVING THINGS MAKING UP ONE HUGE ENTITY.
I THINK YOU'RE THAT. KIND OF--THE COLLECTIVE UNCONSCIOUS, OR SOMETHING.
THE FICTIONAL UNCONSCIOUS. THE MINDS OF ALL THE MILLIONS OF PEOPLE WHO READ MY FATHER'S BOOKS. OR ANY BOOKS, MAYBE.
ALL THOSE MINDS, FOCUSED ON HIM--ON TOMMY. AND THROUGH TOMMY, ON ME.
THE MONSTER SAID YOU NEED LEVERAGE TO MOVE WORLDS. THAT'S IT, ISN'T IT? ANY LEVERAGE I'VE GOT COMES FROM YOU.
YOU'RE WHAT WILSON PLUGGED ME INTO.
I CAN USE A MAGIC WAND BECAUSE YOU BELIEVE--FOR AS LONG AS YOU'RE READING THE BOOK--THAT TOMMY CAN USE A MAGIC WAND.
I EXIST IN THE SUSPENSION OF YOUR DISBELIEF.

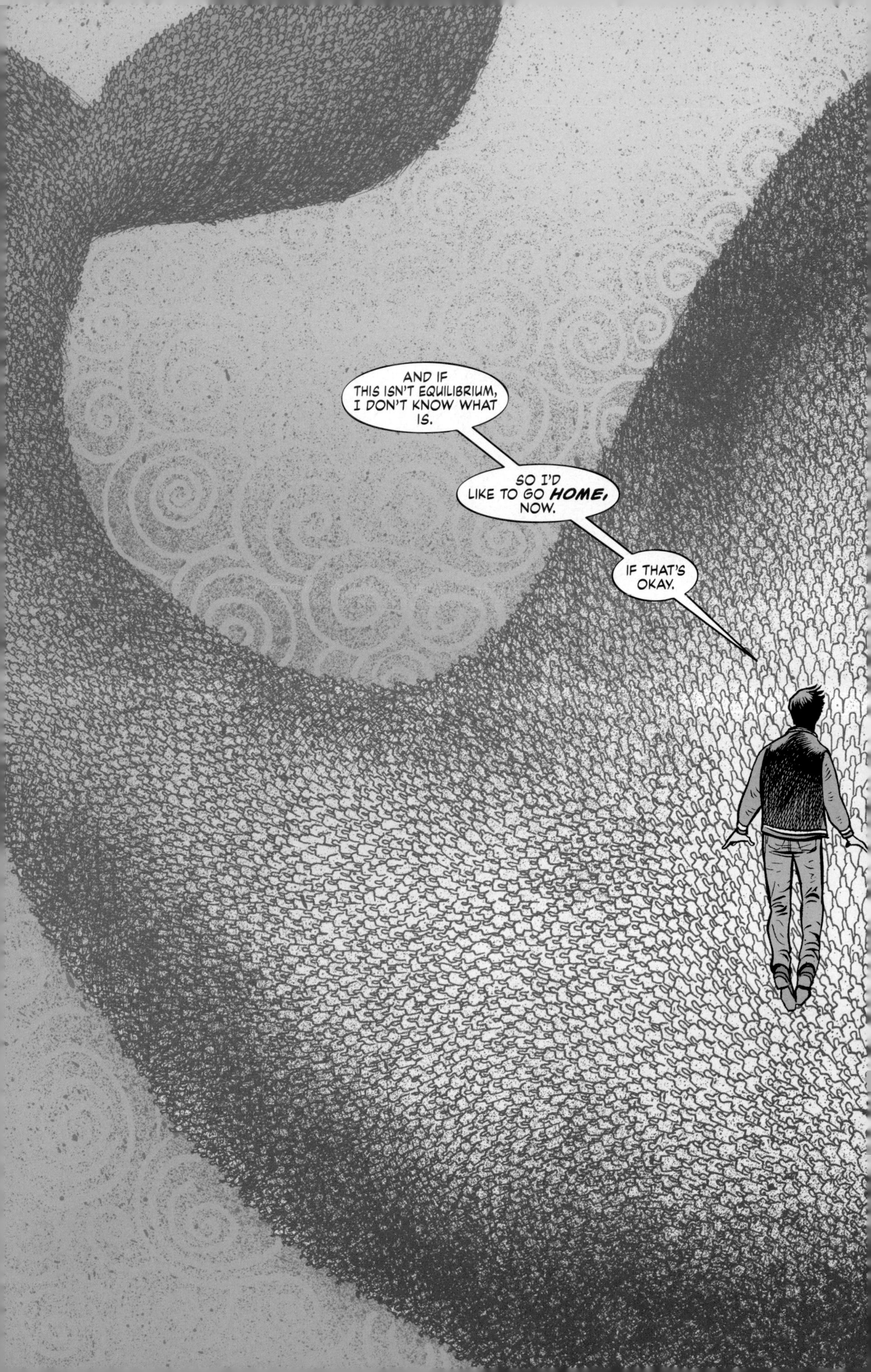
AND IF THIS ISN'T EQUILIBRIUM, I DON'T KNOW WHAT IS.
SO I'D LIKE TO GO HOME, NOW.
IF THAT'S OKAY.

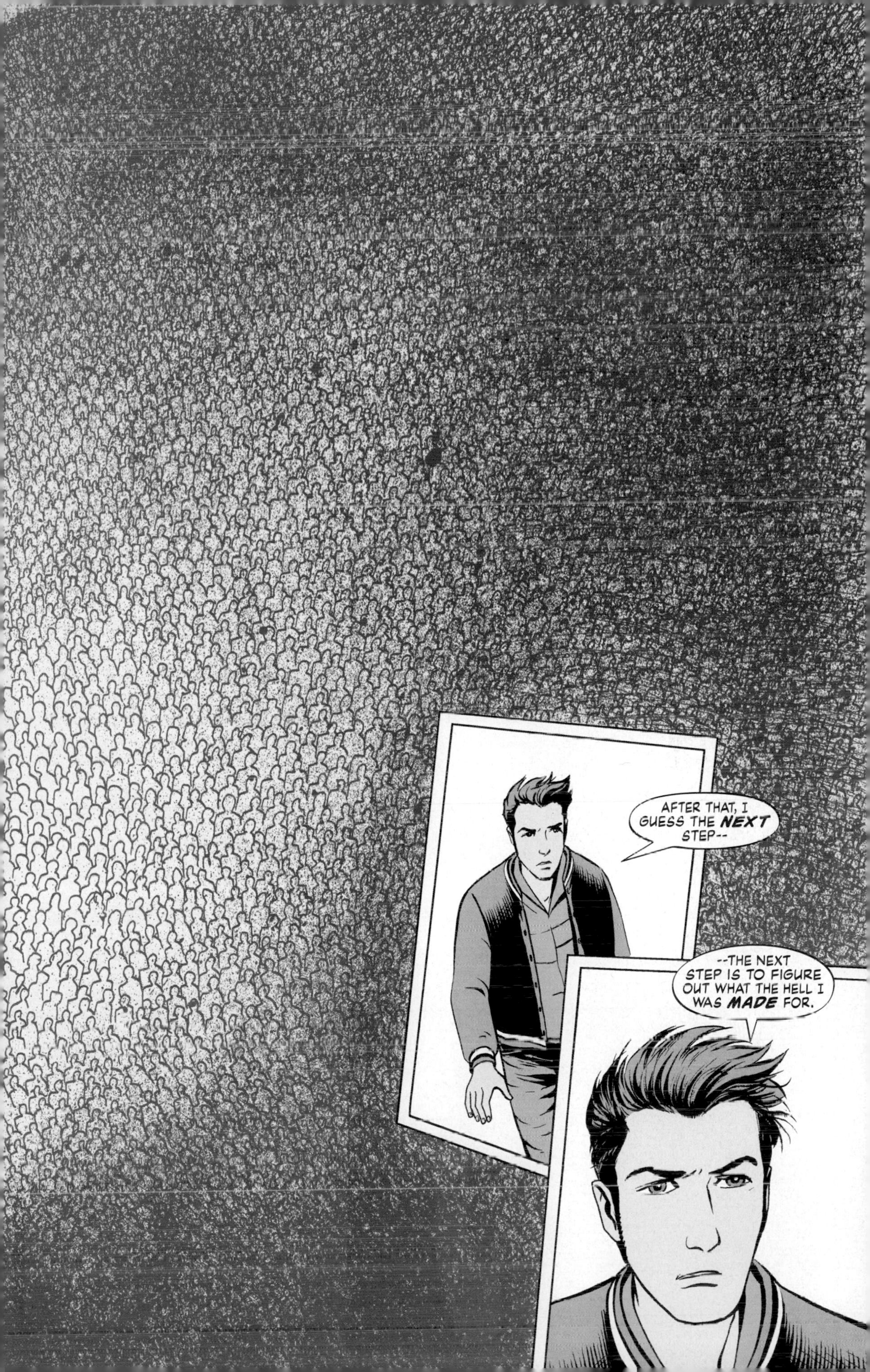

AFTER THAT, I GUESS THE NEXT STEP--
--THE NEXT STEP IS TO FIGURE OUT WHAT THE HELL I WAS MADE FOR.

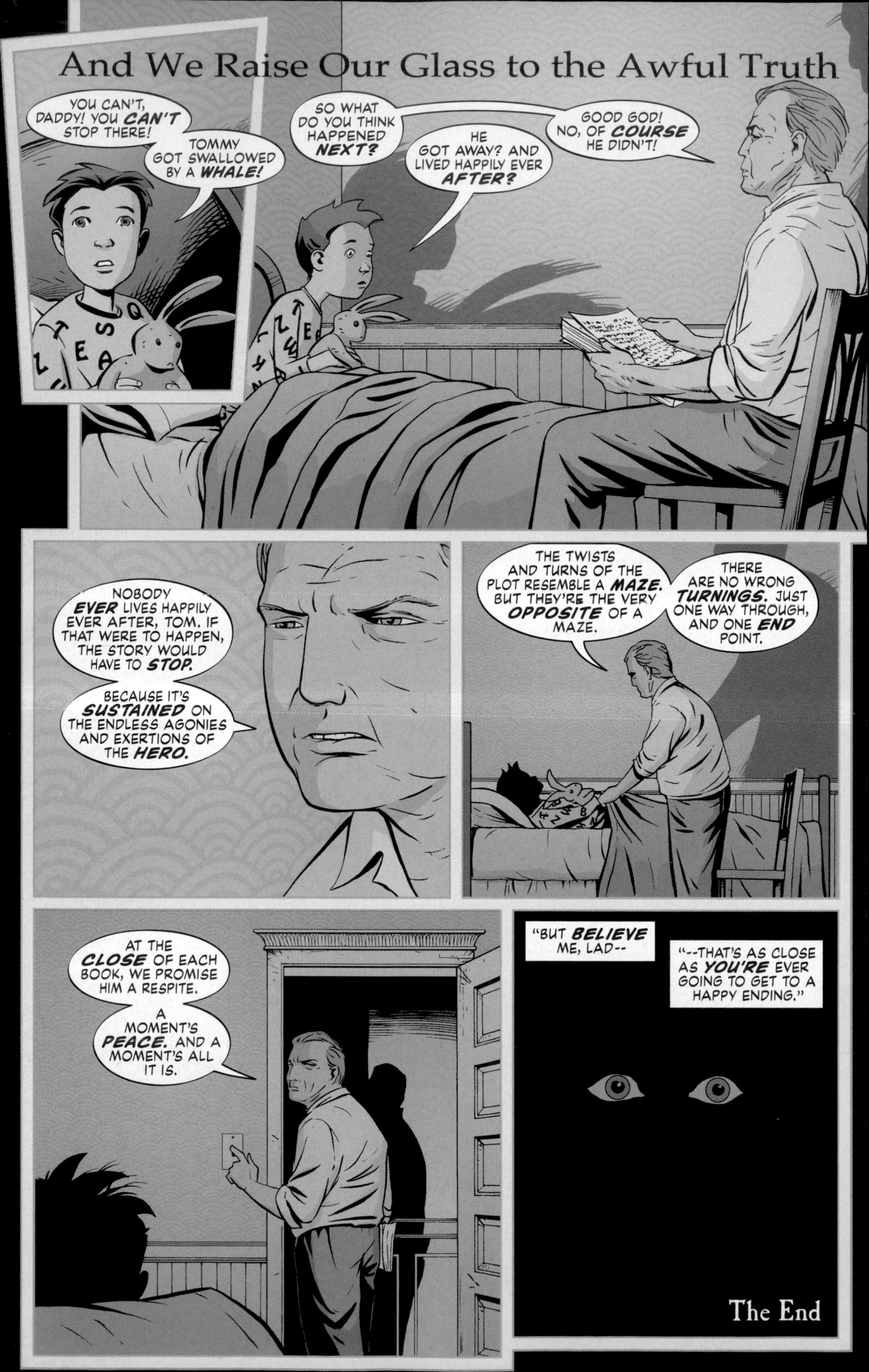

And We Raise Our Glass to the Awful Truth
YOU CAN'T, DADDY! YOU CAN'T STOP THERE!
TOMMY GOT SWALLOWED BY A WHALE!
SO WHAT DO YOU THINK HAPPENED NEXT?
HE GOT AWAY? AND LIVED HAPPILY EVER AFTER?
GOOD GOD! NO, OF COURSE HE DIDN'T!
NOBODY EVER LIVES HAPPILY EVER AFTER, TOM. IF THAT WERE TO HAPPEN, THE STORY WOULD HAVE TO STOP.
BECAUSE IT'S SUSTAINED ON THE ENDLESS AGONIES AND EXERTIONS OF THE HERO.
THE TWISTS AND TURNS OF THE PLOT RESEMBLE A MAZE. BUT THEY'RE THE VERY OPPOSITE OF A MAZE.
THERE ARE NO WRONG TURNINGS. JUST ONE WAY THROUGH, AND ONE END POINT.
AT THE CLOSE OF EACH BOOK, WE PROMISE HIM A RESPITE.
A MOMENT'S PEACE. AND A MOMENT'S ALL IT IS.
"BUT BELIEVE ME, LAD--
"--THAT'S AS CLOSE AS YOU'RE EVER GOING TO GET TO A HAPPY ENDING."
The End

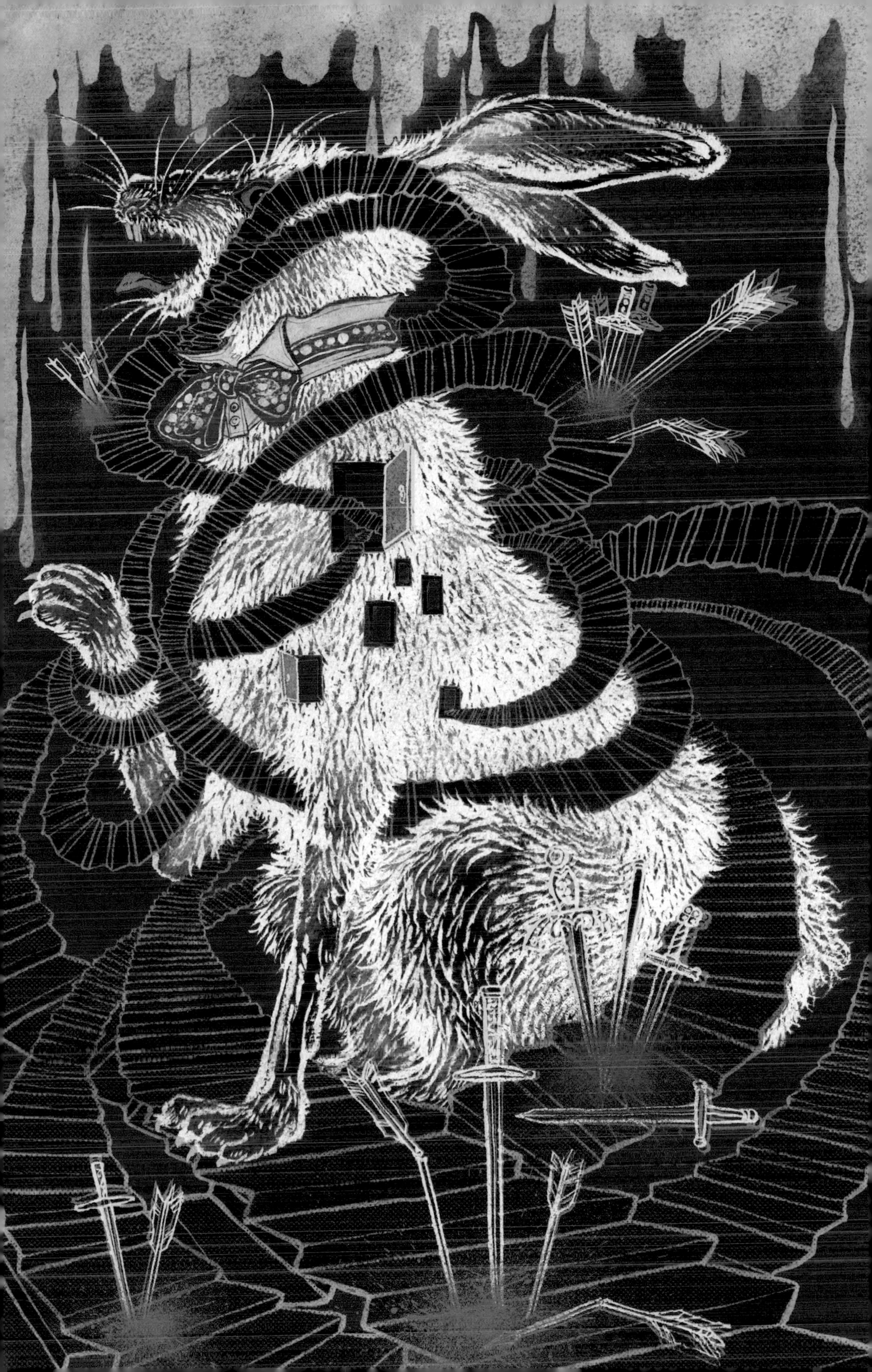

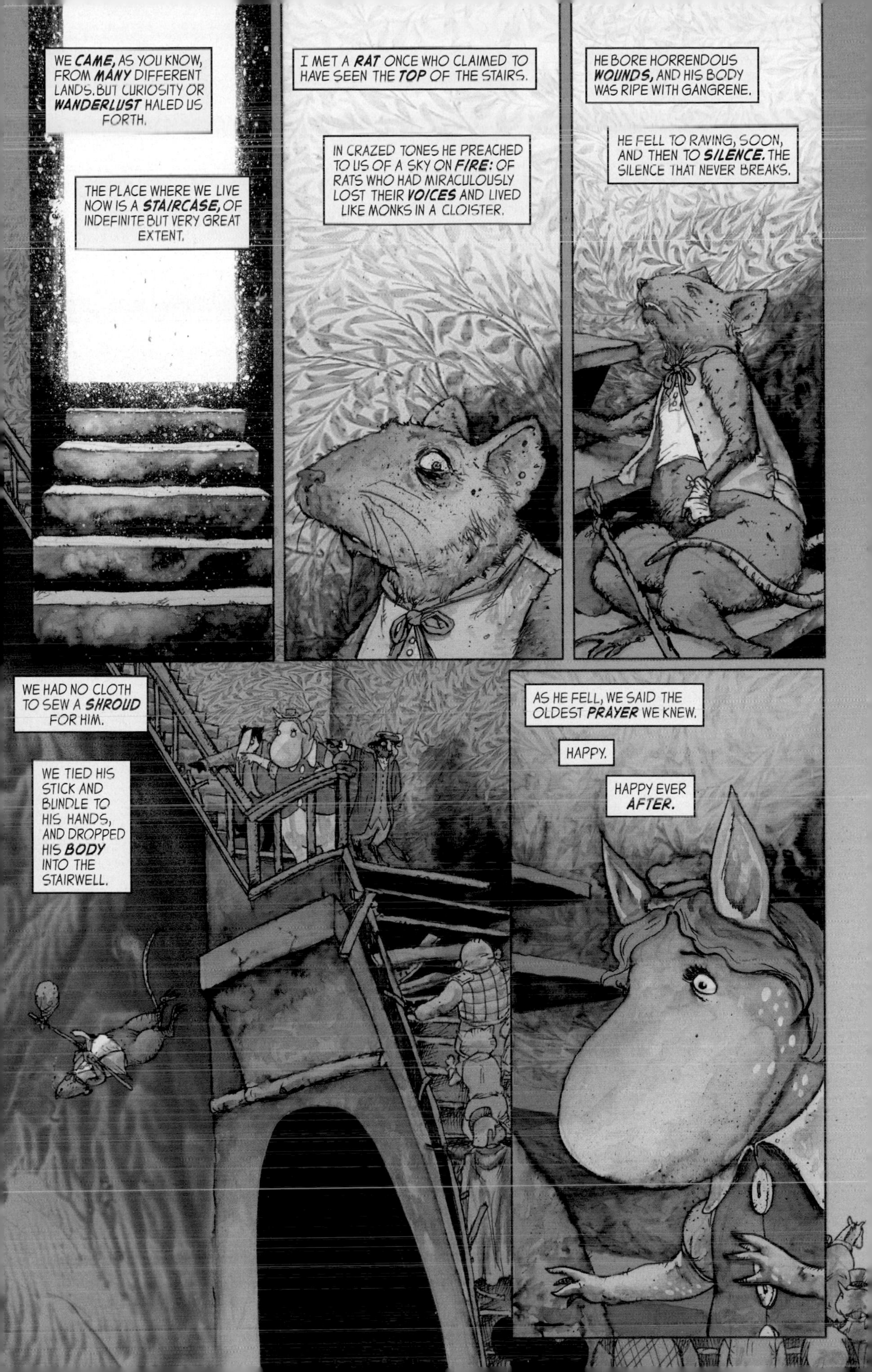
WE CAME, AS YOU KNOW, FROM MANY DIFFERENT LANDS. BUT CURIOSITY OR WANDERLUST HALED US FORTH.
THE PLACE WHERE WE LIVE NOW IS A STAIRCASE, OF INDEFINITE BUT VERY GREAT EXTENT.
I MET A RAT ONCE WHO CLAIMED TO HAVE SEEN THE TOP OF THE STAIRS.
IN CRAZED TONES HE PREACHED TO US OF A SKY ON FIRE: OF RATS WHO HAD MIRACULOUSLY LOST THEIR VOICES AND LIVED LIKE MONKS IN A CLOISTER.
HE BORE HORRENDOUS WOUNDS, AND HIS BODY WAS RIPE WITH GANGRENE.
HE FELL TO RAVING, SOON, AND THEN TO SILENCE. THE SILENCE THAT NEVER BREAKS.
WE HAD NO CLOTH TO SEW A SHROUD FOR HIM.
WE TIED HIS STICK AND BUNDLE TO HIS HANDS, AND DROPPED HIS BODY INTO THE STAIRWELL.
AS HE FELL, WE SAID THE OLDEST PRAYER WE KNEW.
HAPPY.
HAPPY EVER AFTER.

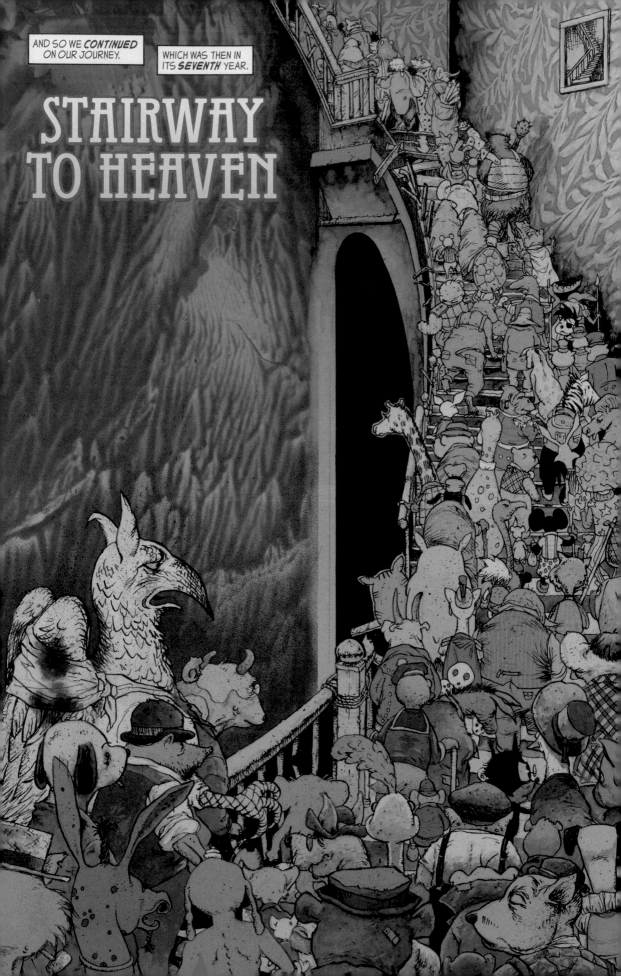

AND SO WE **CONTINUED** ON OUR JOURNEY.

WHICH WAS THEN IN ITS **SEVENTH** YEAR.

# STAIRWAY TO HEAVEN

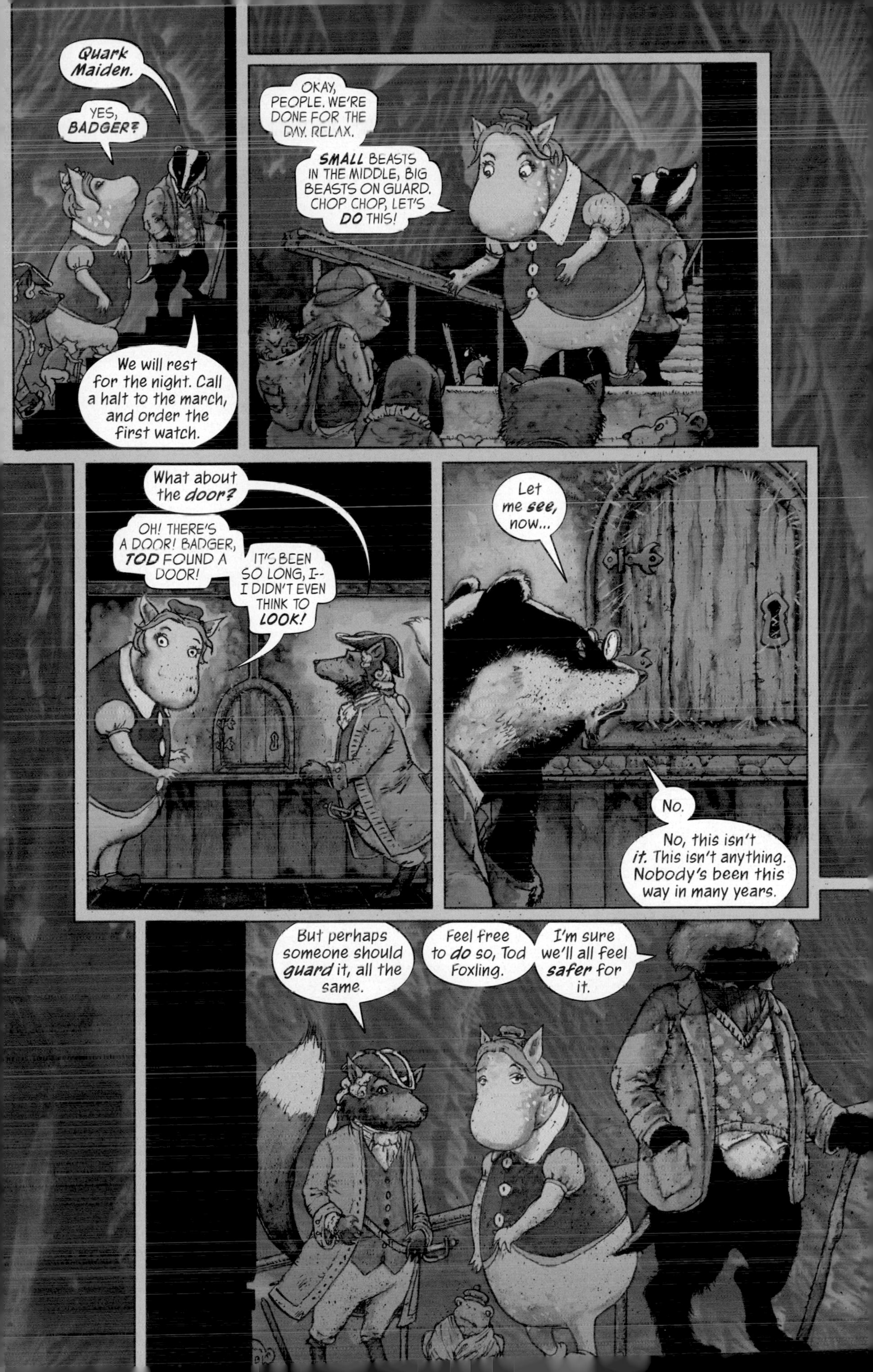

Quark Maiden.
YES, BADGER?
We will rest for the night. Call a halt to the march, and order the first watch.
OKAY, PEOPLE. WE'RE DONE FOR THE DAY. RELAX.
SMALL BEASTS IN THE MIDDLE, BIG BEASTS ON GUARD. CHOP CHOP, LET'S DO THIS!
What about the door?
OH! THERE'S A DOOR! BADGER, TOD FOUND A DOOR!
IT'S BEEN SO LONG, I-- I DIDN'T EVEN THINK TO LOOK!
Let me see, now...
No.
No, this isn't it. This isn't anything. Nobody's been this way in many years.
But perhaps someone should guard it, all the same.
Feel free to do so, Tod Foxling.
I'm sure we'll all feel safer for it.

BADGER WAS OUR **LEADER,** THEN. YOU WON'T REMEMBER HIM, OF COURSE. HE **DIED** BEFORE YOUR TIME.

OBEDIENT TO HIS WORD, WE SPREAD OUR **BLANKETS** AND SETTLED FOR THE NIGHT.

SOME DICED, AND SOME TOLD STORIES. THE **TURTLE-IN-A-TOPPER** SHARED OUT FOOD FROM HIS MAGIC HAT, BUT IT WAS **SAUSAGES** FOR THE THIRD NIGHT RUNNING.

MANY OF US WILL NOT BITE INTO A SAUSAGE FOR FEAR OF FINDING A CLOSE **RELATIVE.**

THEN THE VOICES **FADED,** ONE BY ONE, AND THE GREAT SILENCE OF THE STAIRWELL CLOSED IN ON US.

BUT IN THE SECOND **WATCH** OF THE NIGHT--

--THE SILENCE WAS **BROKEN.**

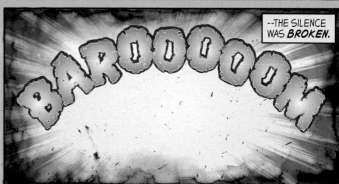

BAROOOOOM

ALL OF US HAVE HEARD THE THUNDER, AND SEEN THE SHINING WHITENESS.

IT CAME, FOR EACH OF US, IN THE MOMENTS WHEN WE FOUND THE **STAIRS** AND LOST THE LANDS WE WERE BORN IN.

SO I **KNEW.**

I KNEW THAT SOMEONE **NEW** WAS COMING.

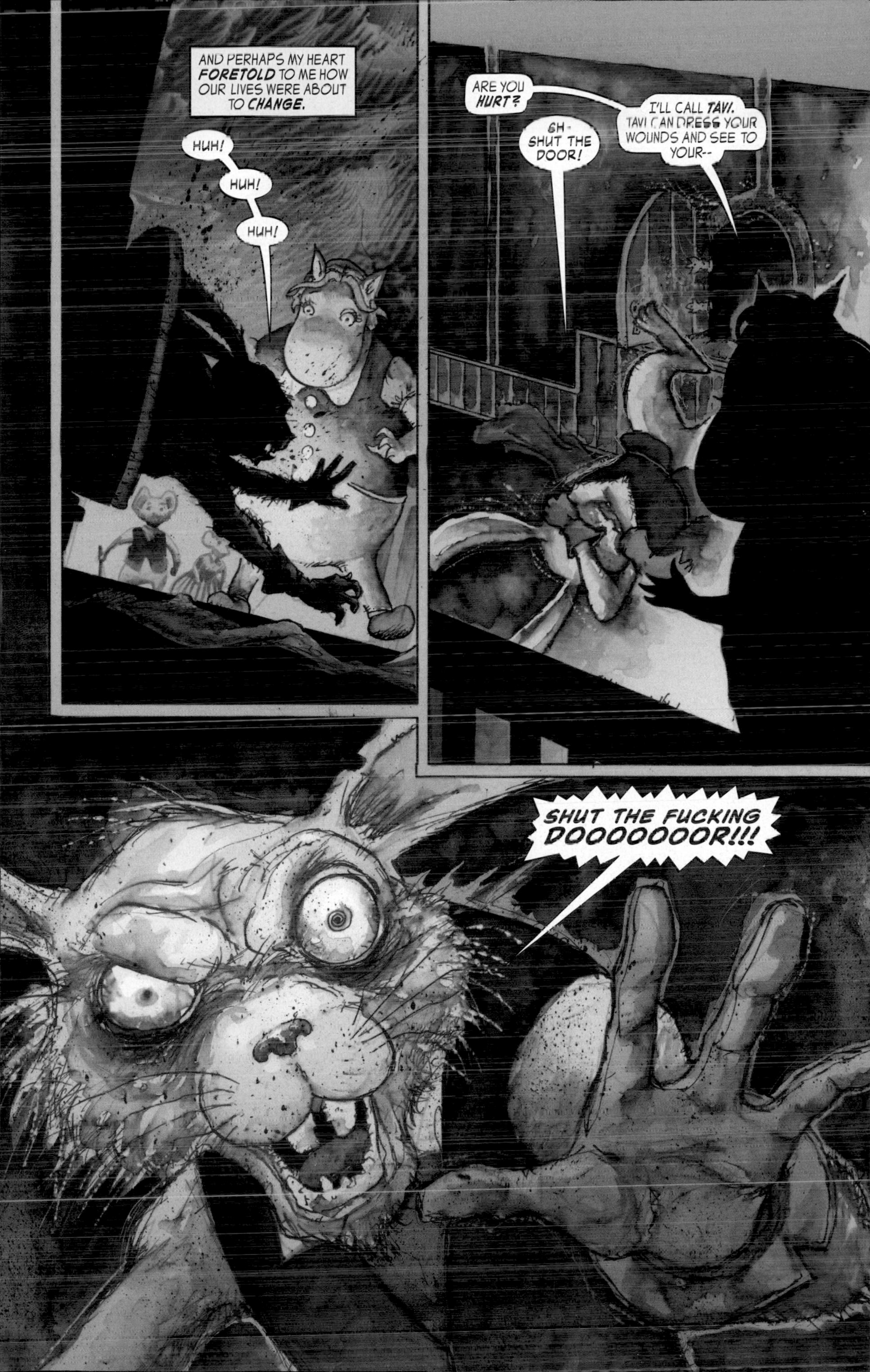
AND PERHAPS MY HEART FORETOLD TO ME HOW OUR LIVES WERE ABOUT TO CHANGE.
HUH!
HUH!
HUH!
ARE YOU HURT?
I'LL CALL TAVI. TAVI CAN DRESS YOUR WOUNDS AND SEE TO YOUR--
SH-SHUT THE DOOR!
SHUT THE FUCKING DOOOOOOOR!!!

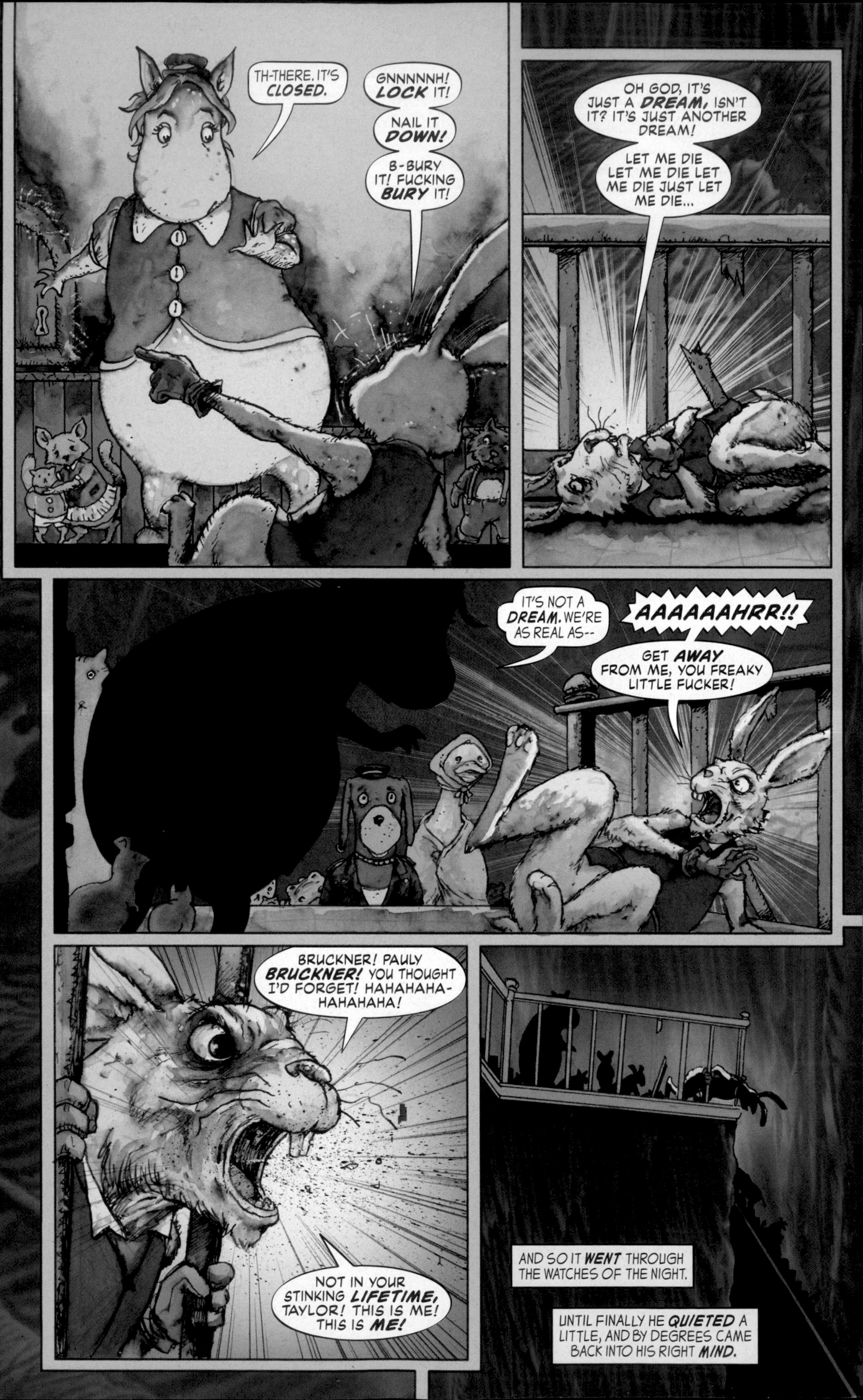
TH-THERE. IT'S CLOSED.
GNNNNNH! LOCK IT!
NAIL IT DOWN!
B-BURY IT! FUCKING BURY IT!
OH GOD, IT'S JUST A DREAM, ISN'T IT? IT'S JUST ANOTHER DREAM!
LET ME DIE LET ME DIE LET ME DIE JUST LET ME DIE...
IT'S NOT A DREAM. WE'RE AS REAL AS--
AAAAAAHRR!!
GET AWAY FROM ME, YOU FREAKY LITTLE FUCKER!
BRUCKNER! PAULY BRUCKNER! YOU THOUGHT I'D FORGET! HAHAHAHA-HAHAHAHA!
NOT IN YOUR STINKING LIFETIME, TAYLOR! THIS IS ME! THIS IS ME!
AND SO IT WENT THROUGH THE WATCHES OF THE NIGHT.
UNTIL FINALLY HE QUIETED A LITTLE, AND BY DEGREES CAME BACK INTO HIS RIGHT MIND.

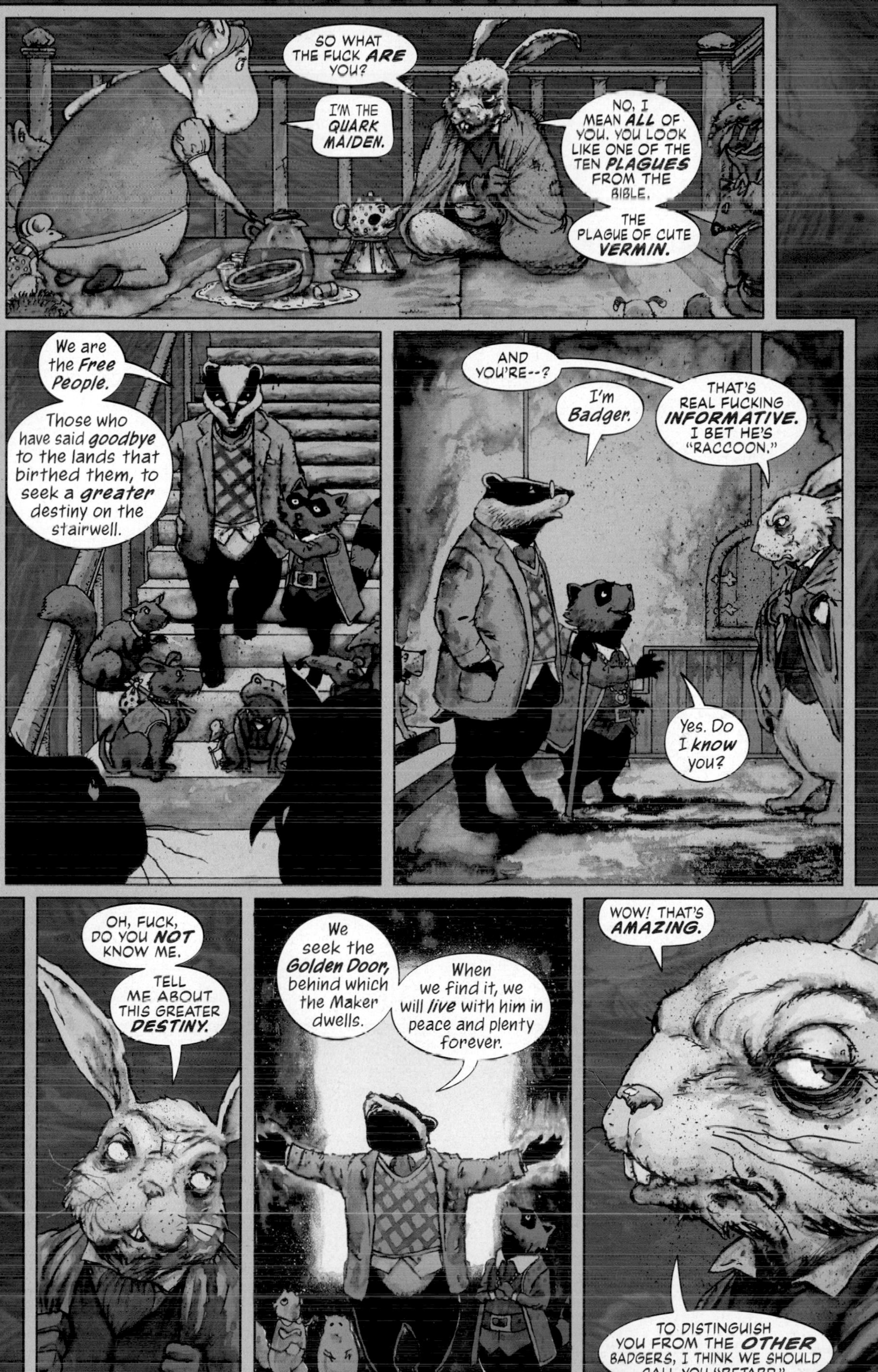
SO WHAT THE FUCK ARE YOU?
I'M THE QUARK MAIDEN.
NO, I MEAN ALL OF YOU. YOU LOOK LIKE ONE OF THE TEN PLAGUES FROM THE BIBLE.
THE PLAGUE OF CUTE VERMIN.
We are the Free People.
Those who have said goodbye to the lands that birthed them, to seek a greater destiny on the stairwell.
AND YOU'RE--?
I'm Badger.
THAT'S REAL FUCKING INFORMATIVE. I BET HE'S "RACCOON."
Yes. Do I know you?
OH, FUCK, DO YOU NOT KNOW ME.
TELL ME ABOUT THIS GREATER DESTINY.
We seek the Golden Door, behind which the Maker dwells.
When we find it, we will live with him in peace and plenty forever.
WOW! THAT'S AMAZING.
TO DISTINGUISH YOU FROM THE OTHER BADGERS, I THINK WE SHOULD CALL YOU "RETARD."

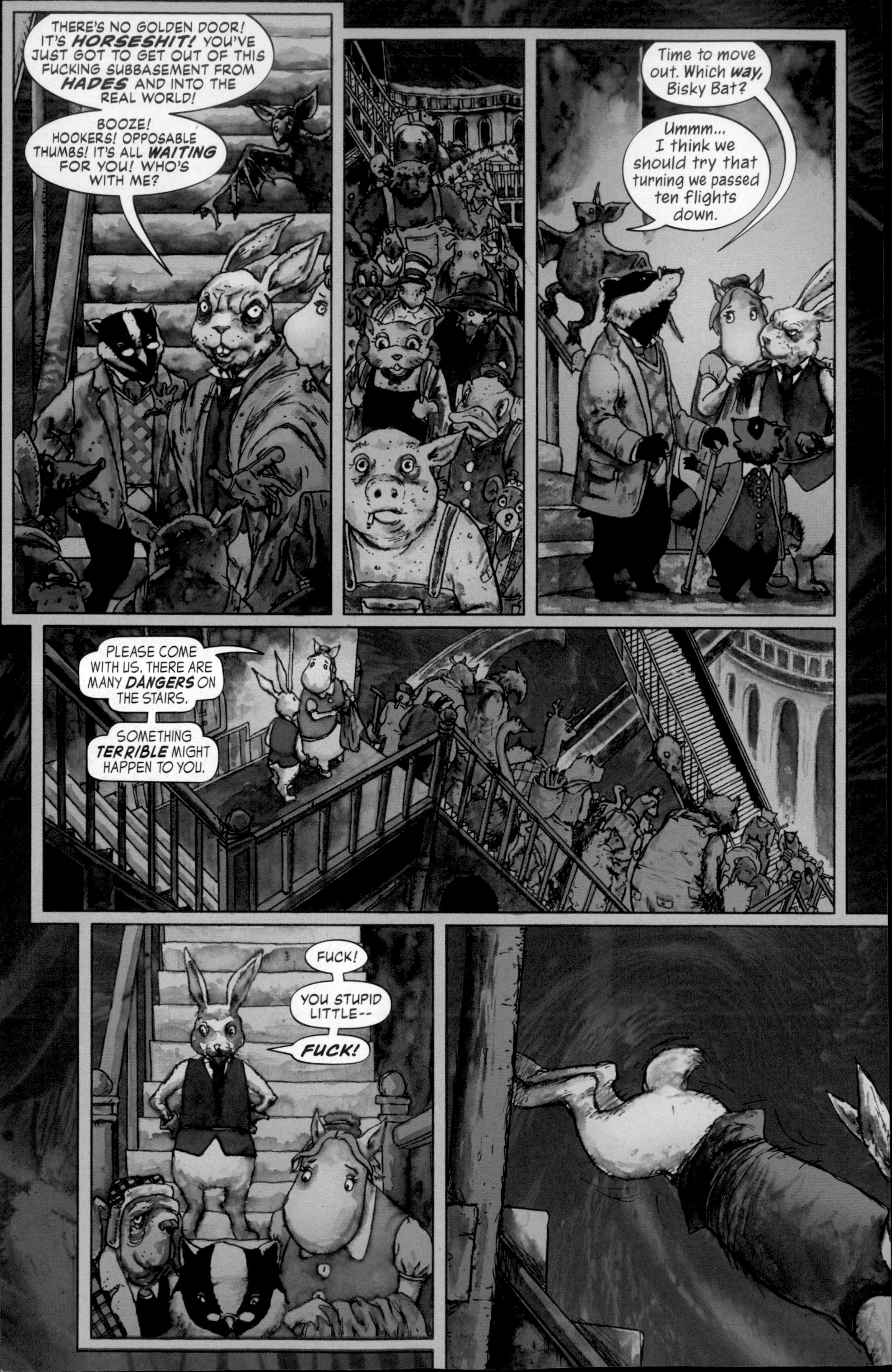
THERE'S NO GOLDEN DOOR! IT'S HORSESHIT! YOU'VE JUST GOT TO GET OUT OF THIS FUCKING SUBBASEMENT FROM HADES AND INTO THE REAL WORLD!
BOOZE! HOOKERS! OPPOSABLE THUMBS! IT'S ALL WAITING FOR YOU! WHO'S WITH ME?
Time to move out. Which way, Bisky Bat?
Ummm... I think we should try that turning we passed ten flights down.
PLEASE COME WITH US. THERE ARE MANY DANGERS ON THE STAIRS.
SOMETHING TERRIBLE MIGHT HAPPEN TO YOU.
FUCK!
YOU STUPID LITTLE--
FUCK!

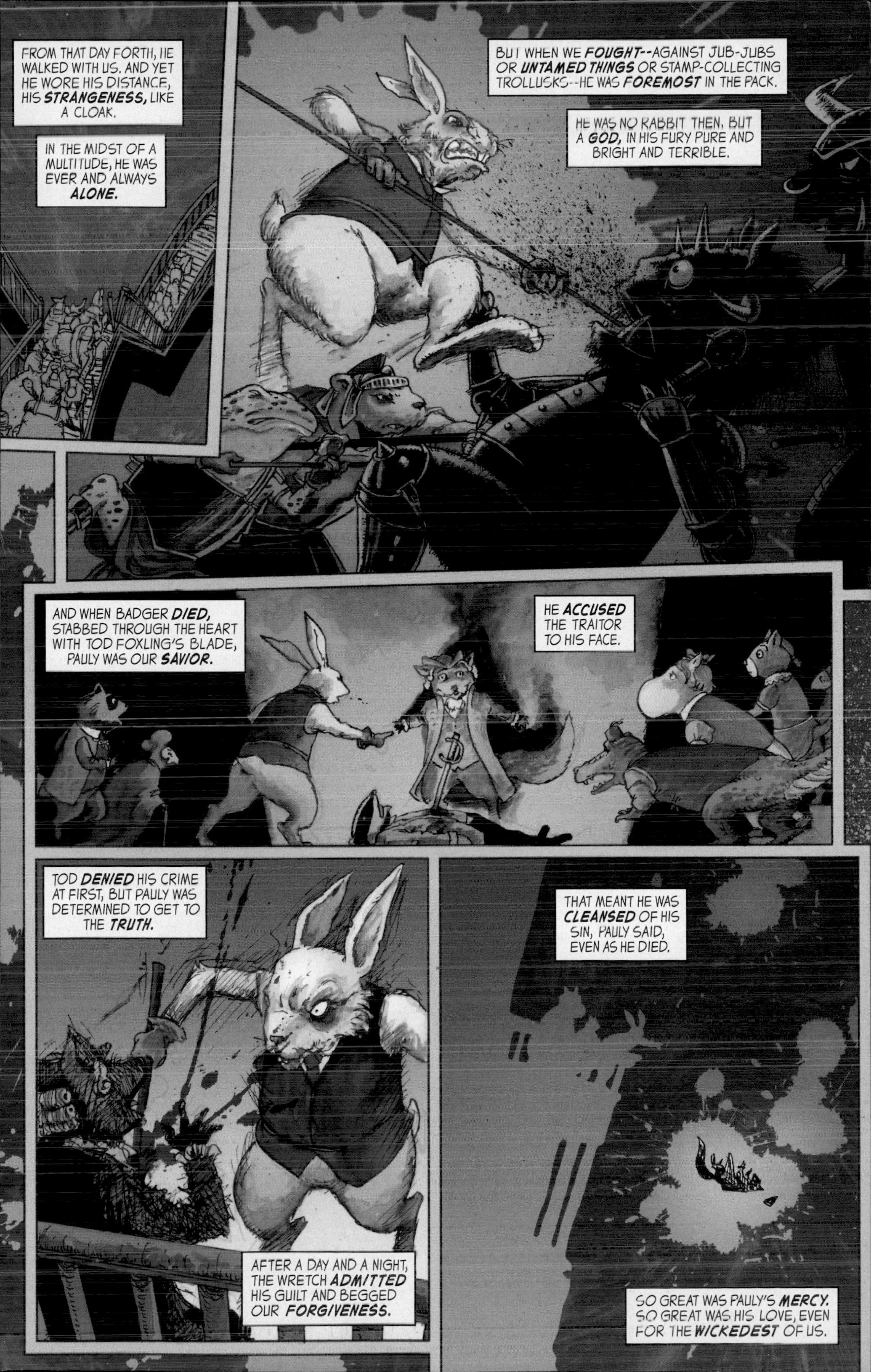
FROM THAT DAY FORTH, HE WALKED WITH US. AND YET HE WORE HIS DISTANCE, HIS STRANGENESS, LIKE A CLOAK.
IN THE MIDST OF A MULTITUDE, HE WAS EVER AND ALWAYS ALONE.
BUT WHEN WE FOUGHT--AGAINST JUB-JUBS OR UNTAMED THINGS OR STAMP-COLLECTING TROLLUSKS--HE WAS FOREMOST IN THE PACK.
HE WAS NO RABBIT THEN, BUT A GOD, IN HIS FURY PURE AND BRIGHT AND TERRIBLE.
AND WHEN BADGER DIED, STABBED THROUGH THE HEART WITH TOD FOXLING'S BLADE, PAULY WAS OUR SAVIOR.
HE ACCUSED THE TRAITOR TO HIS FACE.
TOD DENIED HIS CRIME AT FIRST, BUT PAULY WAS DETERMINED TO GET TO THE TRUTH.
AFTER A DAY AND A NIGHT, THE WRETCH ADMITTED HIS GUILT AND BEGGED OUR FORGIVENESS.
THAT MEANT HE WAS CLEANSED OF HIS SIN, PAULY SAID, EVEN AS HE DIED.
SO GREAT WAS PAULY'S MERCY. SO GREAT WAS HIS LOVE, EVEN FOR THE WICKEDEST OF US.

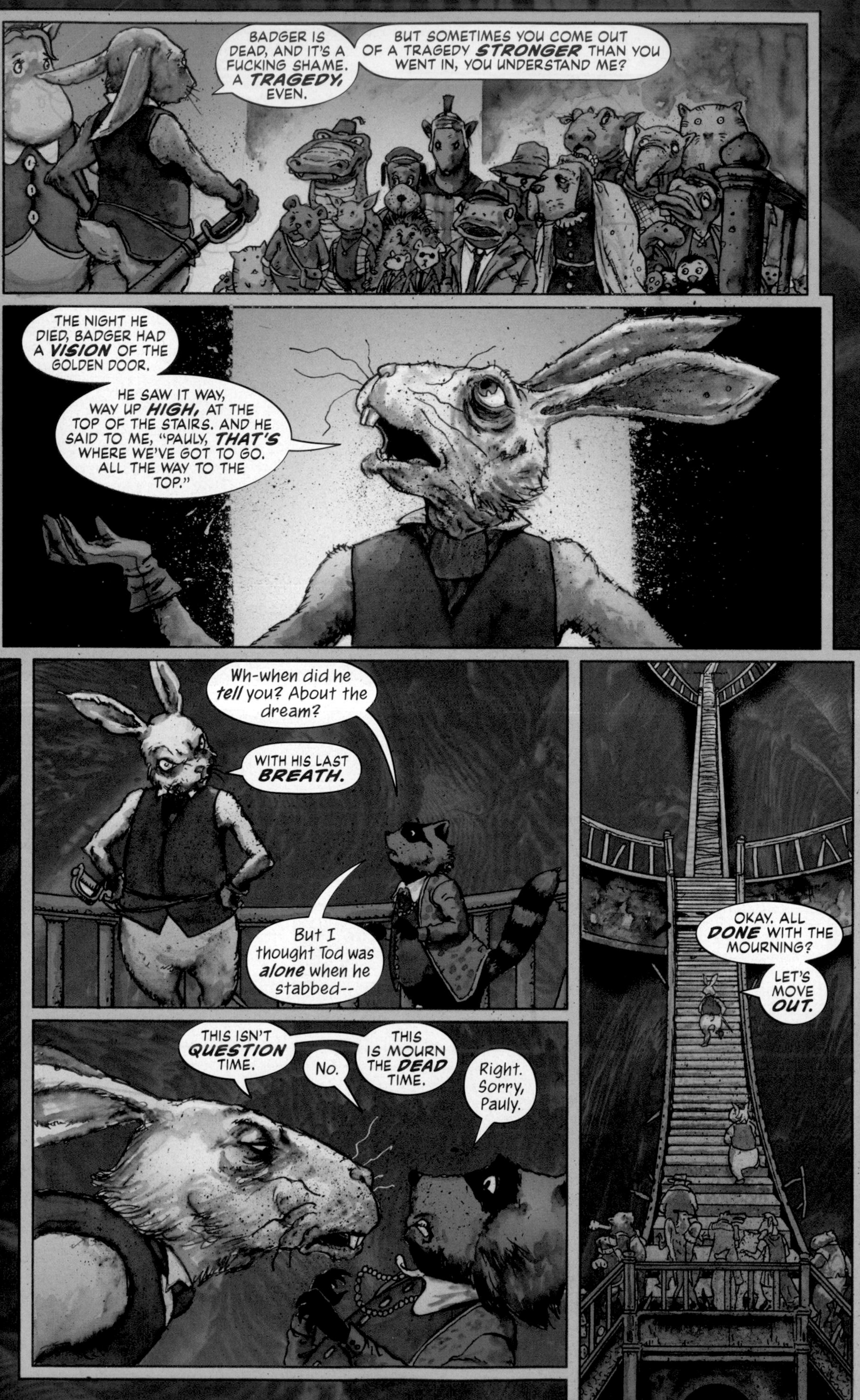
BADGER IS DEAD, AND IT'S A FUCKING SHAME. A **TRAGEDY,** EVEN.
BUT SOMETIMES YOU COME OUT OF A TRAGEDY **STRONGER** THAN YOU WENT IN, YOU UNDERSTAND ME?
THE NIGHT HE DIED, BADGER HAD A **VISION** OF THE GOLDEN DOOR.
HE SAW IT WAY, WAY UP **HIGH,** AT THE TOP OF THE STAIRS. AND HE SAID TO ME, "PAULY, **THAT'S** WHERE WE'VE GOT TO GO. ALL THE WAY TO THE TOP."
Wh-when did he *tell* you? About the dream?
WITH HIS LAST **BREATH.**
But I thought Tod was *alone* when he stabbed--
THIS ISN'T **QUESTION** TIME.
THIS IS MOURN THE **DEAD** TIME.
No.
Right. Sorry, Pauly.
OKAY. ALL **DONE** WITH THE MOURNING?
LET'S MOVE **OUT.**

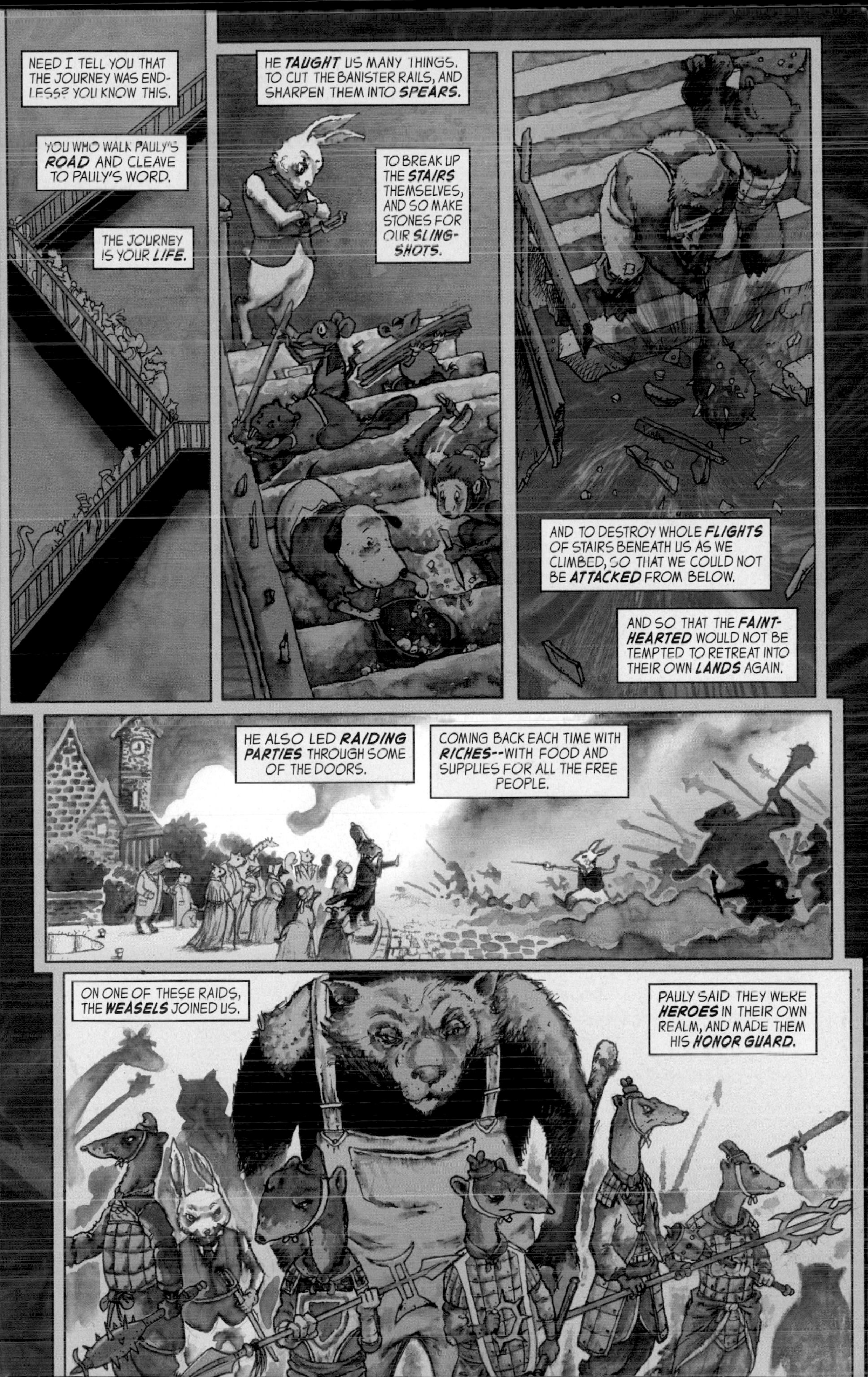
NEED I TELL YOU THAT THE JOURNEY WAS ENDLESS? YOU KNOW THIS.
YOU WHO WALK PAULY'S ROAD AND CLEAVE TO PAULY'S WORD.
THE JOURNEY IS YOUR LIFE.
HE TAUGHT US MANY THINGS. TO CUT THE BANISTER RAILS, AND SHARPEN THEM INTO SPEARS.
TO BREAK UP THE STAIRS THEMSELVES, AND SO MAKE STONES FOR OUR SLING-SHOTS.
AND TO DESTROY WHOLE FLIGHTS OF STAIRS BENEATH US AS WE CLIMBED, SO THAT WE COULD NOT BE ATTACKED FROM BELOW.
AND SO THAT THE FAINT-HEARTED WOULD NOT BE TEMPTED TO RETREAT INTO THEIR OWN LANDS AGAIN.
HE ALSO LED RAIDING PARTIES THROUGH SOME OF THE DOORS.
COMING BACK EACH TIME WITH RICHES--WITH FOOD AND SUPPLIES FOR ALL THE FREE PEOPLE.
ON ONE OF THESE RAIDS, THE WEASELS JOINED US.
PAULY SAID THEY WERE HEROES IN THEIR OWN REALM, AND MADE THEM HIS HONOR GUARD.

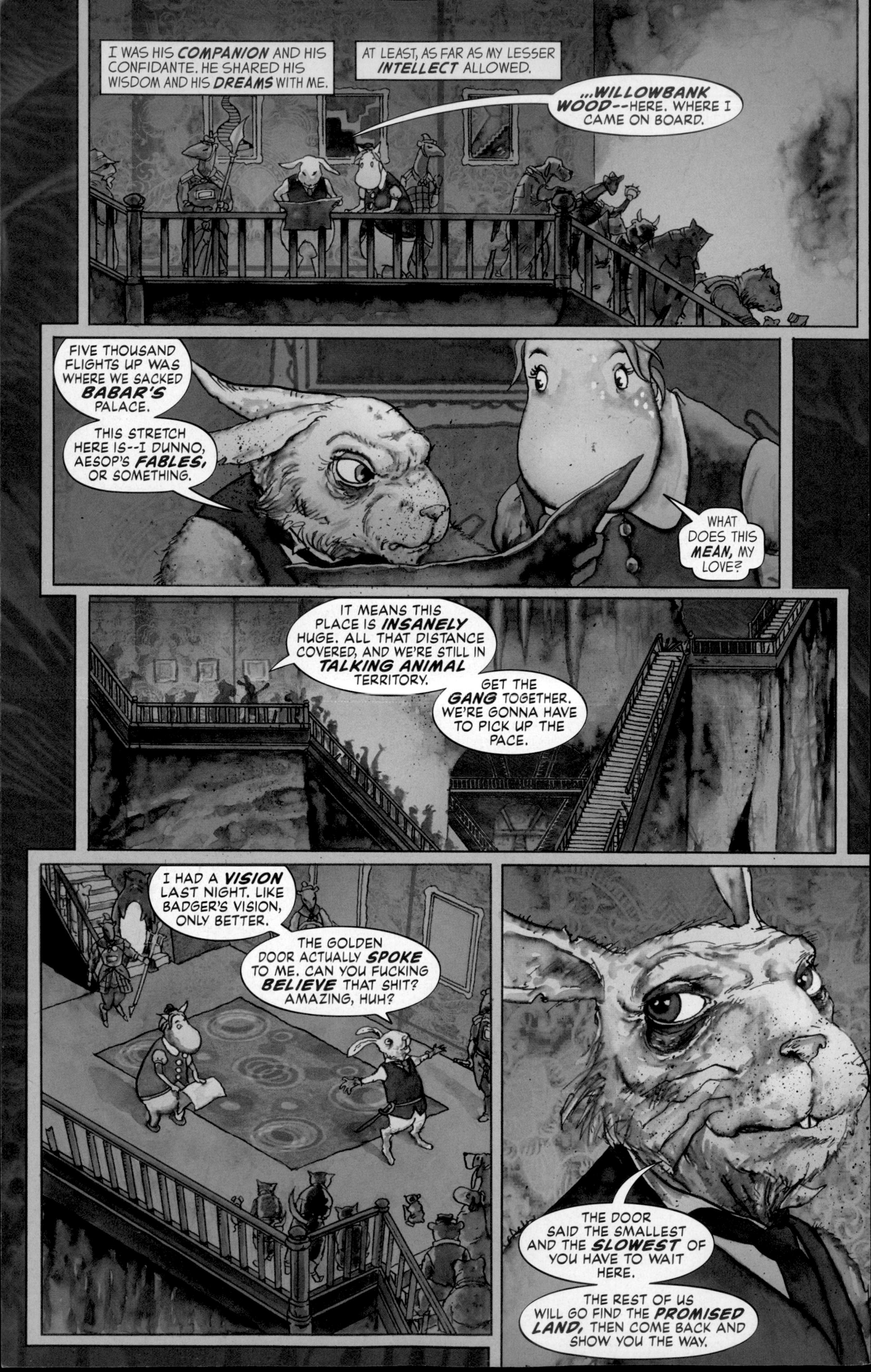

I WAS HIS COMPANION AND HIS CONFIDANTE. HE SHARED HIS WISDOM AND HIS DREAMS WITH ME.
AT LEAST, AS FAR AS MY LESSER INTELLECT ALLOWED.
...WILLOWBANK WOOD--HERE. WHERE I CAME ON BOARD.
FIVE THOUSAND FLIGHTS UP WAS WHERE WE SACKED BABAR'S PALACE.
THIS STRETCH HERE IS--I DUNNO, AESOP'S FABLES, OR SOMETHING.
WHAT DOES THIS MEAN, MY LOVE?
IT MEANS THIS PLACE IS INSANELY HUGE. ALL THAT DISTANCE COVERED, AND WE'RE STILL IN TALKING ANIMAL TERRITORY.
GET THE GANG TOGETHER. WE'RE GONNA HAVE TO PICK UP THE PACE.
I HAD A VISION LAST NIGHT. LIKE BADGER'S VISION, ONLY BETTER.
THE GOLDEN DOOR ACTUALLY SPOKE TO ME. CAN YOU FUCKING BELIEVE THAT SHIT? AMAZING, HUH?
THE DOOR SAID THE SMALLEST AND THE SLOWEST OF YOU HAVE TO WAIT HERE.
THE REST OF US WILL GO FIND THE PROMISED LAND, THEN COME BACK AND SHOW YOU THE WAY.

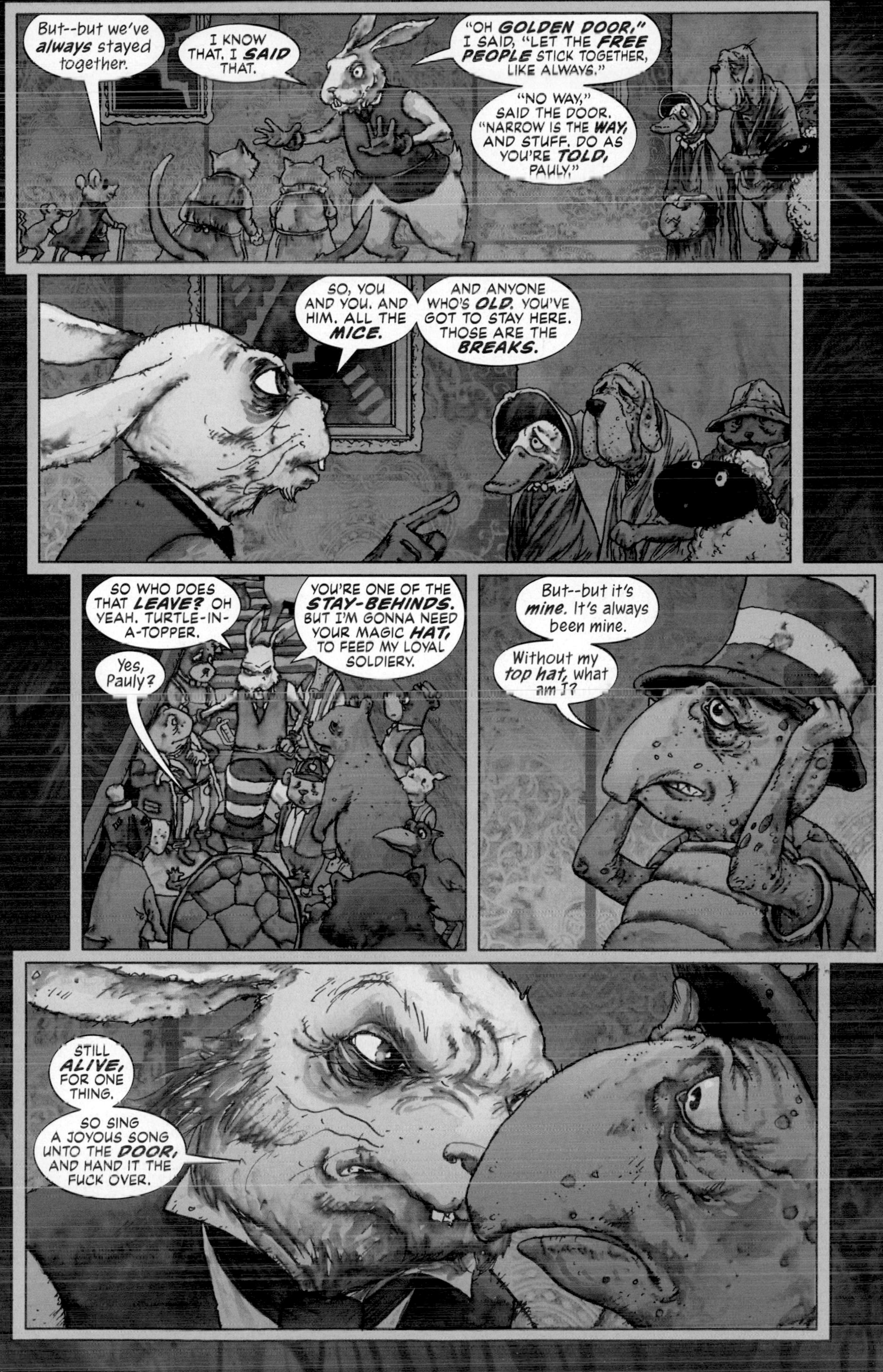
But--but we've *always* stayed together.
I KNOW THAT. I ***SAID*** THAT.
"OH ***GOLDEN DOOR,***" I SAID, "LET THE ***FREE PEOPLE*** STICK TOGETHER, LIKE ALWAYS."
"NO WAY," SAID THE DOOR. "NARROW IS THE ***WAY,*** AND STUFF. DO AS YOU'RE ***TOLD,*** PAULY."
SO, YOU AND YOU. AND HIM. ALL THE ***MICE.***
AND ANYONE WHO'S ***OLD.*** YOU'VE GOT TO STAY HERE. THOSE ARE THE ***BREAKS.***
SO WHO DOES THAT ***LEAVE?*** OH YEAH. TURTLE-IN-A-TOPPER.
Yes, Pauly?
YOU'RE ONE OF THE ***STAY-BEHINDS.*** BUT I'M GONNA NEED YOUR MAGIC ***HAT,*** TO FEED MY LOYAL SOLDIERY.
But--but it's ***mine.*** It's always been mine.
Without my *top hat,* what am I?
STILL ***ALIVE,*** FOR ONE THING.
SO SING A JOYOUS SONG UNTO THE ***DOOR,*** AND HAND IT THE FUCK OVER.

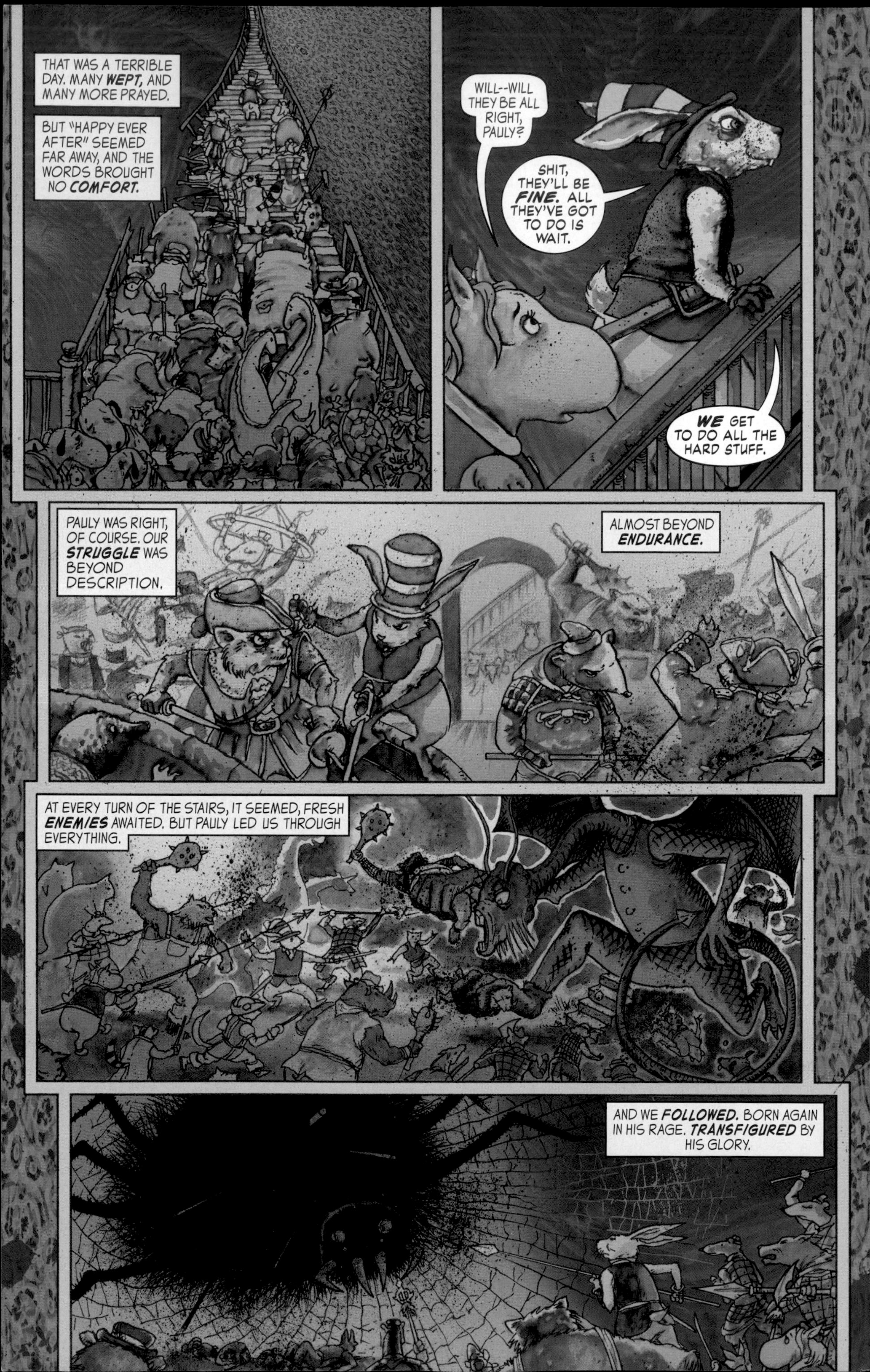

THAT WAS A TERRIBLE DAY. MANY WEPT, AND MANY MORE PRAYED.
BUT "HAPPY EVER AFTER" SEEMED FAR AWAY, AND THE WORDS BROUGHT NO COMFORT.
WILL--WILL THEY BE ALL RIGHT, PAULY?
SHIT, THEY'LL BE FINE. ALL THEY'VE GOT TO DO IS WAIT.
WE GET TO DO ALL THE HARD STUFF.
PAULY WAS RIGHT, OF COURSE. OUR STRUGGLE WAS BEYOND DESCRIPTION.
ALMOST BEYOND ENDURANCE.
AT EVERY TURN OF THE STAIRS, IT SEEMED, FRESH ENEMIES AWAITED. BUT PAULY LED US THROUGH EVERYTHING.
AND WE FOLLOWED. BORN AGAIN IN HIS RAGE. TRANSFIGURED BY HIS GLORY.

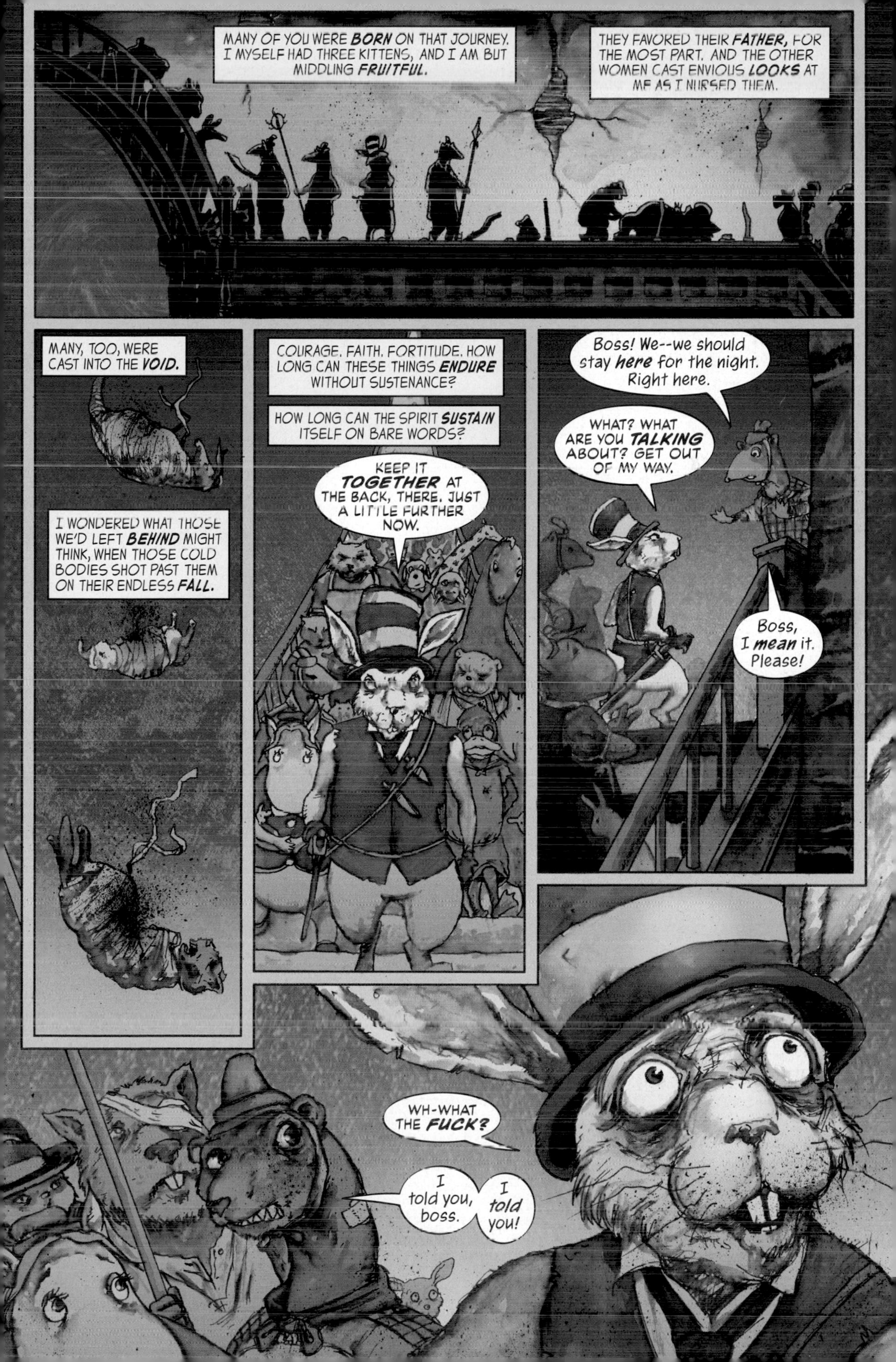

MANY OF YOU WERE BORN ON THAT JOURNEY. I MYSELF HAD THREE KITTENS, AND I AM BUT MIDDLING FRUITFUL.
THEY FAVORED THEIR FATHER, FOR THE MOST PART. AND THE OTHER WOMEN CAST ENVIOUS LOOKS AT ME AS I NURSED THEM.
MANY, TOO, WERE CAST INTO THE VOID.
I WONDERED WHAT THOSE WE'D LEFT BEHIND MIGHT THINK, WHEN THOSE COLD BODIES SHOT PAST THEM ON THEIR ENDLESS FALL.
COURAGE. FAITH. FORTITUDE. HOW LONG CAN THESE THINGS ENDURE WITHOUT SUSTENANCE?
HOW LONG CAN THE SPIRIT SUSTAIN ITSELF ON BARE WORDS?
KEEP IT TOGETHER AT THE BACK, THERE. JUST A LITTLE FURTHER NOW.
Boss! We--we should stay here for the night. Right here.
WHAT? WHAT ARE YOU TALKING ABOUT? GET OUT OF MY WAY.
Boss, I mean it. Please!
WH-WHAT THE FUCK?
I told you, boss.
I told you!

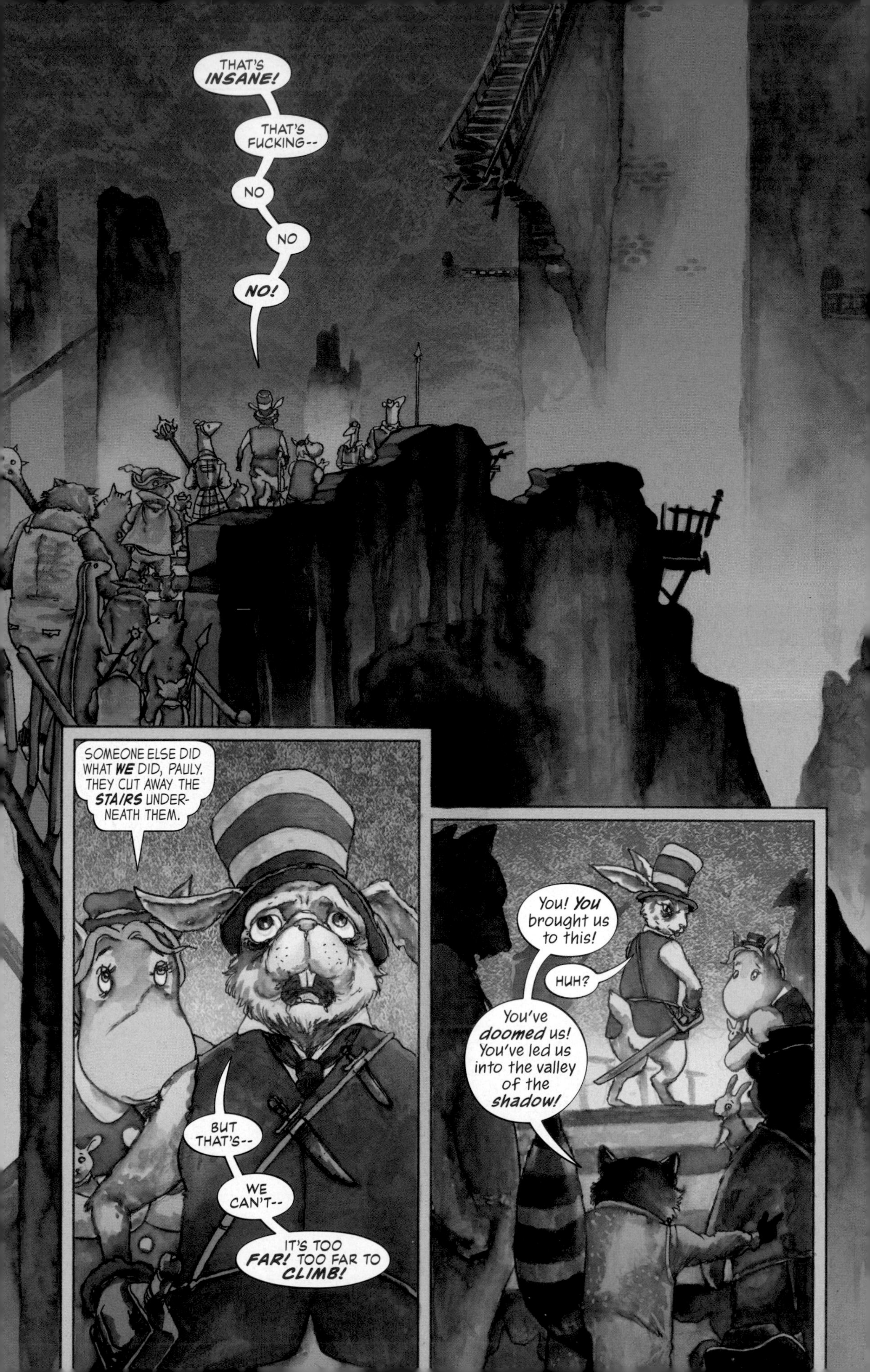
THAT'S **INSANE!**
THAT'S FUCKING--
NO
NO
**NO!**
SOMEONE ELSE DID WHAT **WE** DID, PAULY. THEY CUT AWAY THE **STAIRS** UNDERNEATH THEM.
BUT THAT'S--
WE CAN'T--
IT'S TOO **FAR!** TOO FAR TO **CLIMB!**
You! **You** brought us to this!
HUH?
You've **doomed** us! You've led us into the valley of the **shadow!**

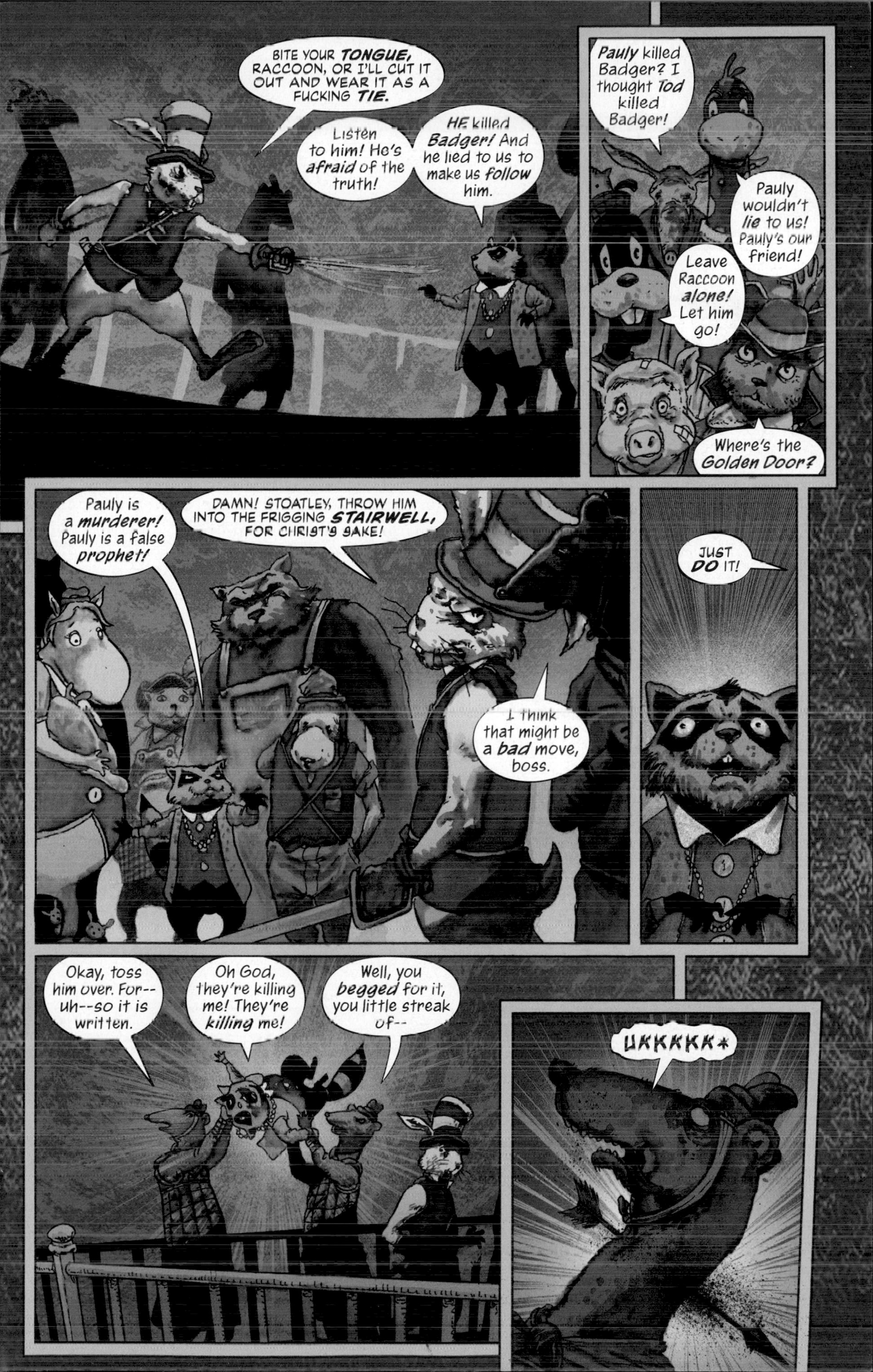
BITE YOUR TONGUE, RACCOON, OR I'LL CUT IT OUT AND WEAR IT AS A FUCKING TIE.
Listen to him! He's afraid of the truth!
HE killed Badger! And he lied to us to make us follow him.
Pauly killed Badger? I thought Tod killed Badger!
Pauly wouldn't lie to us! Pauly's our friend!
Leave Raccoon alone! Let him go!
Where's the Golden Door?
Pauly is a murderer! Pauly is a false prophet!
DAMN! STOATLEY, THROW HIM INTO THE FRIGGING STAIRWELL, FOR CHRIST'S SAKE!
I think that might be a bad move, boss.
JUST DO IT!
Okay, toss him over. For-- uh--so it is written.
Oh God, they're killing me! They're killing me!
Well, you begged for it, you little streak of--
UKKKKK*

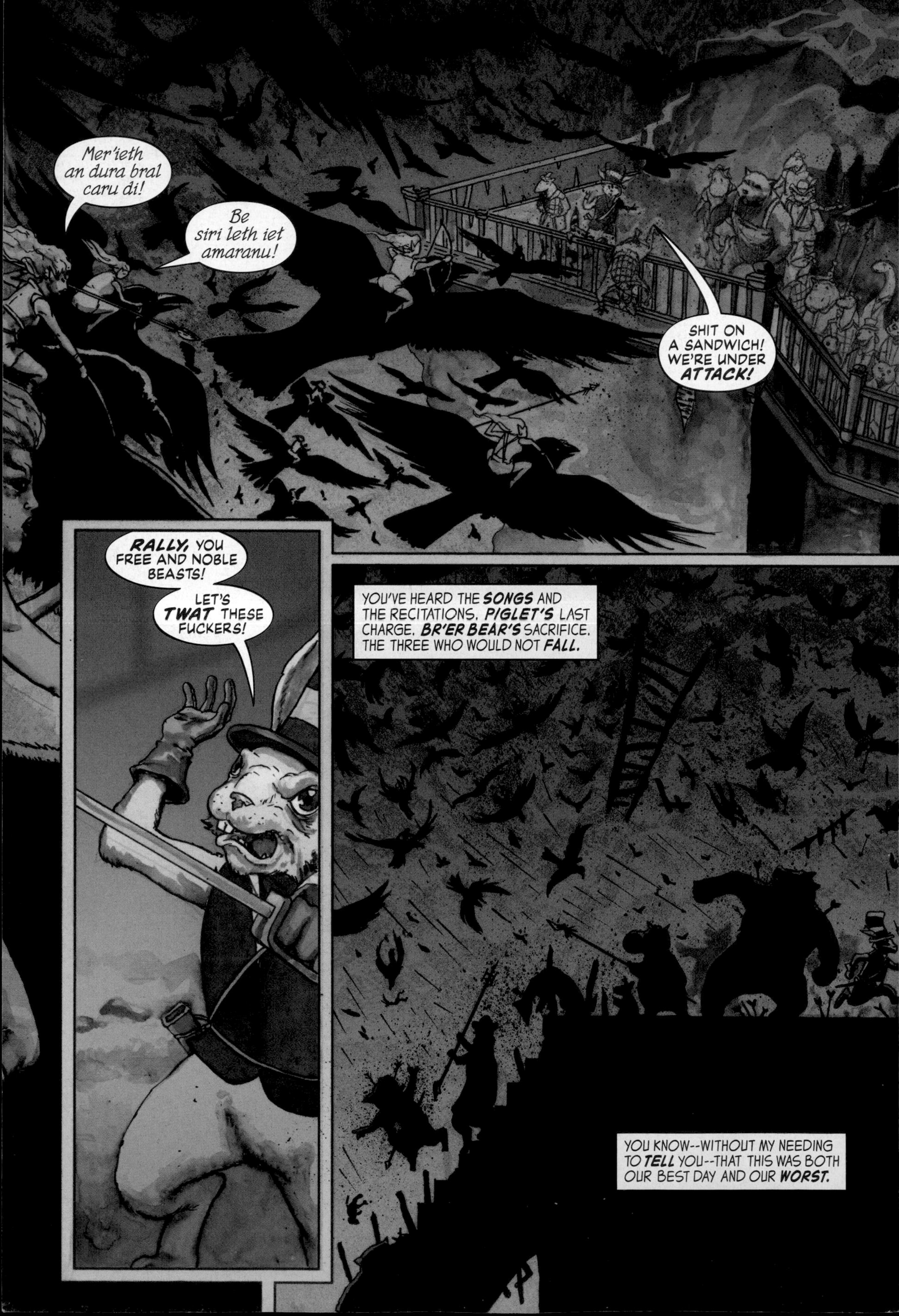
Mer'ieth an dura bral caru di!
Be siri leth iet amaranu!
SHIT ON A SANDWICH! WE'RE UNDER ATTACK!
RALLY, YOU FREE AND NOBLE BEASTS!
LET'S TWAT THESE FUCKERS!
YOU'VE HEARD THE SONGS AND THE RECITATIONS. PIGLET'S LAST CHARGE. BR'ER BEAR'S SACRIFICE. THE THREE WHO WOULD NOT FALL.
YOU KNOW--WITHOUT MY NEEDING TO TELL YOU--THAT THIS WAS BOTH OUR BEST DAY AND OUR WORST.

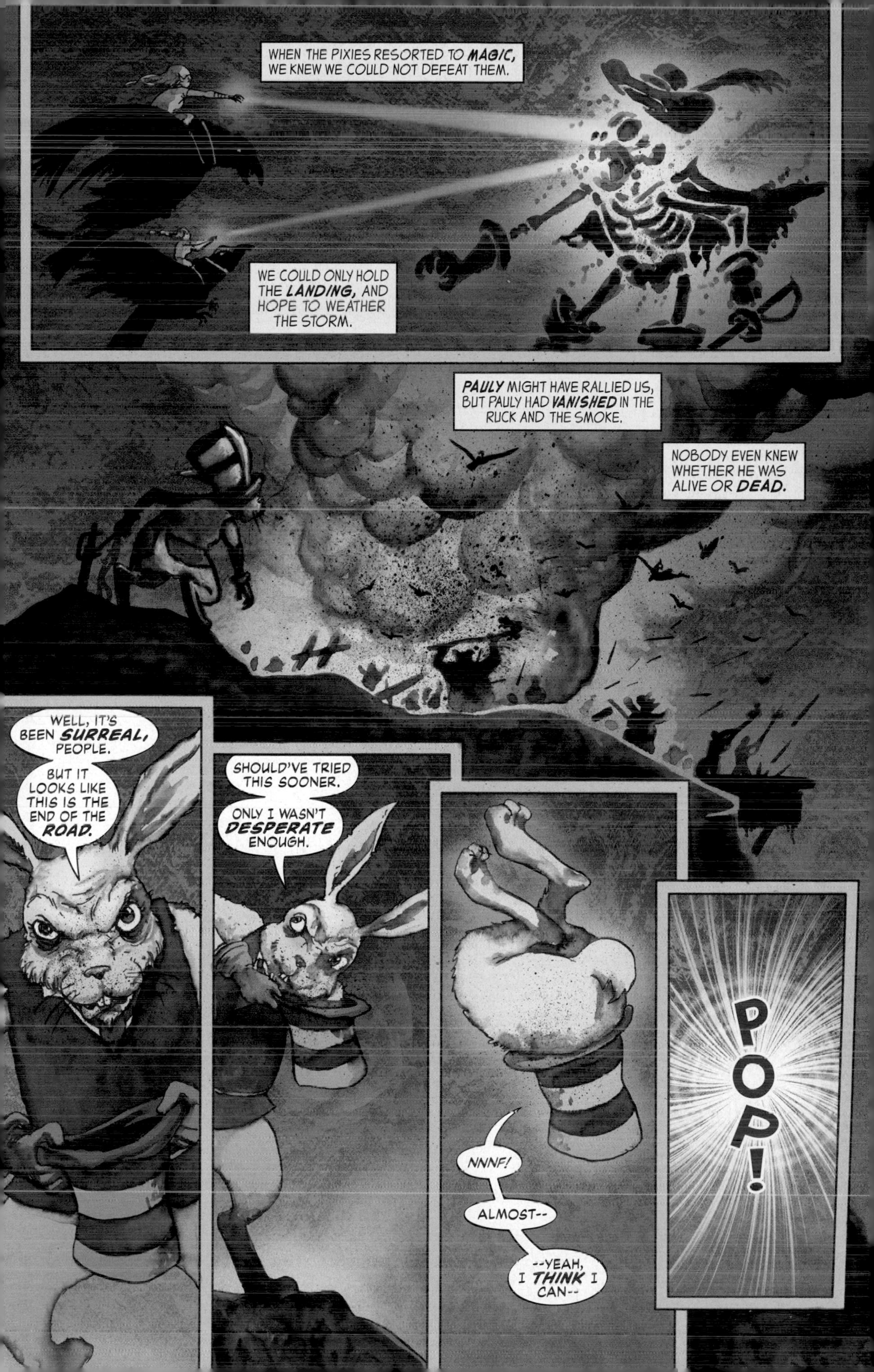
WHEN THE PIXIES RESORTED TO MAGIC, WE KNEW WE COULD NOT DEFEAT THEM.
WE COULD ONLY HOLD THE LANDING, AND HOPE TO WEATHER THE STORM.
PAULY MIGHT HAVE RALLIED US, BUT PAULY HAD VANISHED IN THE RUCK AND THE SMOKE.
NOBODY EVEN KNEW WHETHER HE WAS ALIVE OR DEAD.
WELL, IT'S BEEN SURREAL, PEOPLE.
BUT IT LOOKS LIKE THIS IS THE END OF THE ROAD.
SHOULD'VE TRIED THIS SOONER.
ONLY I WASN'T DESPERATE ENOUGH.
NNNF!
ALMOST--
--YEAH, I THINK I CAN--
POP!

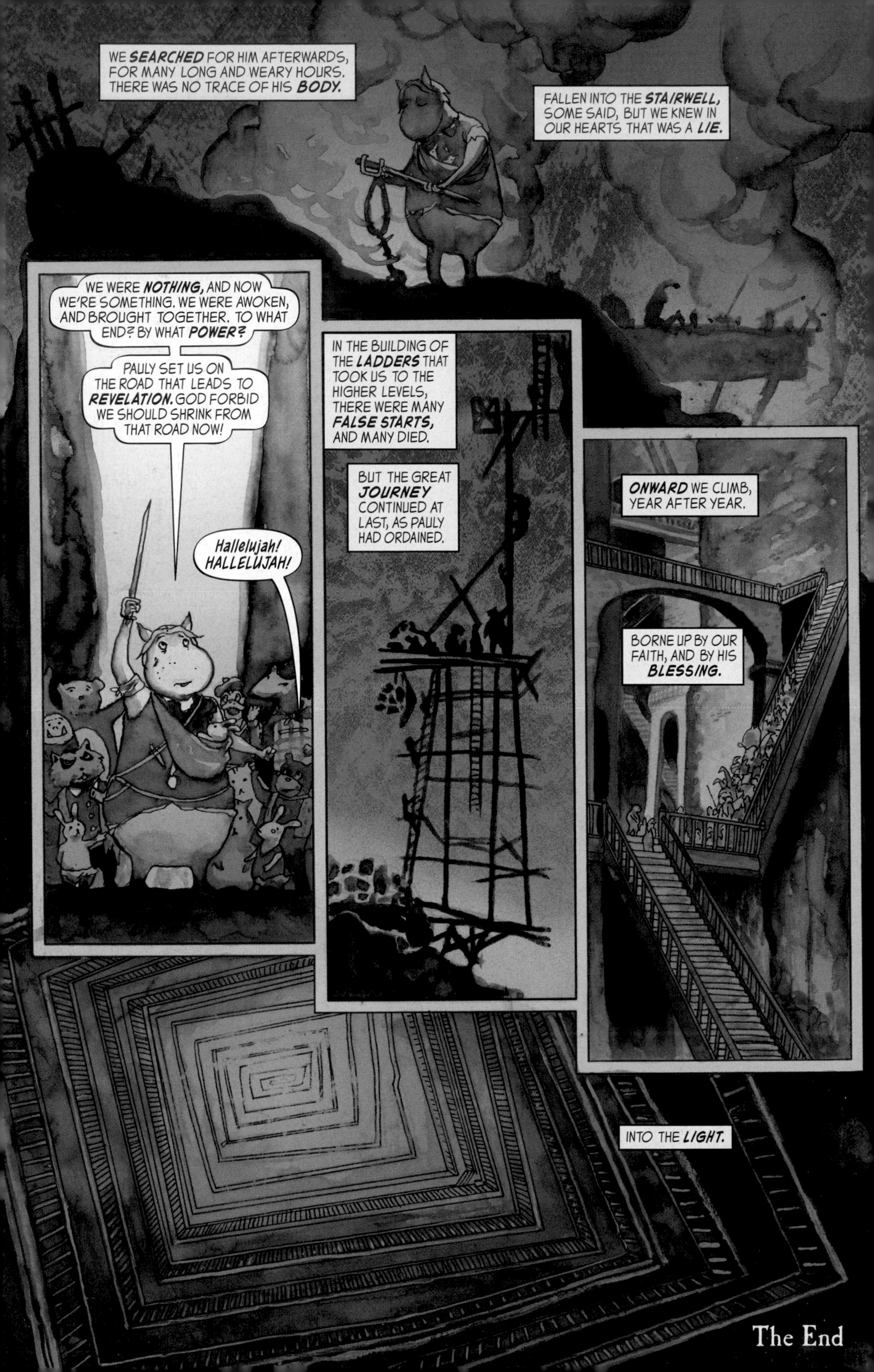
WE **SEARCHED** FOR HIM AFTERWARDS, FOR MANY LONG AND WEARY HOURS. THERE WAS NO TRACE OF HIS **BODY.**
FALLEN INTO THE **STAIRWELL,** SOME SAID, BUT WE KNEW IN OUR HEARTS THAT WAS A **LIE.**
WE WERE **NOTHING,** AND NOW WE'RE SOMETHING. WE WERE AWOKEN, AND BROUGHT TOGETHER. TO WHAT END? BY WHAT **POWER?**
PAULY SET US ON THE ROAD THAT LEADS TO **REVELATION.** GOD FORBID WE SHOULD SHRINK FROM THAT ROAD NOW!
Hallelujah! HALLELUJAH!
IN THE BUILDING OF THE **LADDERS** THAT TOOK US TO THE HIGHER LEVELS, THERE WERE MANY **FALSE STARTS,** AND MANY DIED.
BUT THE GREAT **JOURNEY** CONTINUED AT LAST, AS PAULY HAD ORDAINED.
**ONWARD** WE CLIMB, YEAR AFTER YEAR.
BORNE UP BY OUR FAITH, AND BY HIS **BLESSING.**
INTO THE **LIGHT.**

The End

> "FABLES is an excellent series in the tradition of SANDMAN, one that rewards careful attention and loyalty." – ENTERTAINMENT WEEKLY

# BILL WILLINGHAM

> "[A] wonderfully twisted concept... features fairy tale characters banished to the noirish world of present-day New York." – THE WASHINGTON POST

**WINNER OF EISNER AWARDS**

VOL. 1: LEGENDS IN EXILE
VOL. 2: ANIMAL FARM
VOL. 3: STORYBOOK LOVE
VOL. 4: MARCH OF THE WOODEN SOLDIERS
VOL. 5: THE MEAN SEASONS
VOL. 6: HOMELANDS
VOL. 7: ARABIAN NIGHTS (AND DAYS)
VOL. 8: WOLVES
VOL. 9: SONS OF EMPIRE
VOL. 10: THE GOOD PRINCE
VOL. 11: WAR AND PIECES
VOL. 12: THE DARK AGES
VOL. 13: THE GREAT FABLES CROSSOVER
1001 NIGHTS OF SNOWFALL

FABLES VOL. 3:
STORYBOOK LOVE

FABLES VOL. 6:
HOMELANDS

FABLES:
1001 NIGHTS OF SNOWFALL

GO TO
**VERTIGOBOOKS.COM**
FOR FREE SAMPLES OF THE FIRST ISSUES OF OUR GRAPHIC NOVELS

Suggested for Mature Readers

FROM THE PAGES OF
BILL WILLINGHAM'S FABLES

# JACK OF FABLES

*"It's got a little bit of everything that any sophisticated comics fan will enjoy."*
**– PUBLISHERS WEEKLY**

*"An unpredictable romp... it's a lot of fun."*
**–THE ONION**

*"Sharp, quick-paced, fun-to-read stuff that is sure to impress."*
**– METRO TORONTO**

*"This is fun."* **– BOOKLIST**

**VOL. 1: THE (NEARLY) GREAT ESCAPE**
**VOL. 2: JACK OF HEARTS**
**VOL. 3: THE BAD PRINCE**
**VOL. 4: AMERICANA**
**VOL. 5: TURNING PAGES**
**VOL. 6: THE BIG BOOK OF WAR**
**VOL. 7: THE NEW ADVENTURES OF JACK AND JACK**

NO ONE DESERVES HIS OWN COLLECTION MORE THAN
JACK OF FABLES
THE (NEARLY) GREAT ESCAPE
"Intriguing."
— The Onion
BILL Willingham
MATTHEW Sturges
TONY Akins
ANDREW Pepoy
VERTIGO

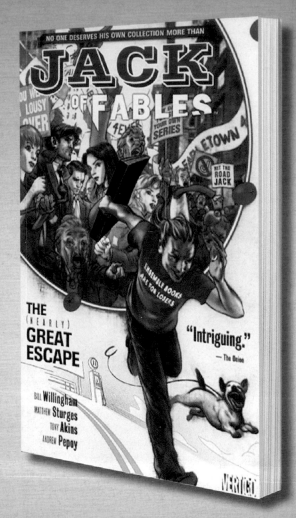

JACK OF FABLES VOL. 2:
JACK OF HEARTS

WILLINGHAM · STURGES · AKINS · LEIALOHA
GOOD LUCK COMES TO THOSE WHO
WELCOME
JACK OF FABLES
JACK of HEARTS
VERTIGO

JACK OF FABLES VOL. 3:
THE BAD PRINCE

JACK
The Bad Prince
WILLINGHAM
STURGES
AKINS
PEPOY
BRAUN
ROBINSON
VERTIGO

JACK OF FABLES VOL. 4:
AMERICANA

FOLKS JUST SEEM TO COTTON TO
JACK OF FABLES
AMERICANA
Bill WILLINGHAM
Matthew STURGES
Russ BRAUN
Tony AKINS
Andrew PEPOY
Steve LEIALOHA
VERTIGO

JACK OF FABLES VOL. 5:
TURNING PAGES

NOT EVEN SAM COLT COULD MAKE YOU EQUAL TO
JACK OF FABLES
Turning Pages
WILLINGHAM
STURGES
BRAUN
AKINS
MARZAN, JR.
PEPOY
VERTIGO

GO TO
**VERTIGOBOOKS.COM**
FOR FREE SAMPLES OF THE FIRST ISSUES OF OUR GRAPHIC NOVELS

Suggested for Mature Readers